AF608153

NEW DIRECTIONS IN SCANDINAVIAN STUDIES

TERJE LEIREN AND CHRISTINE INGEBRITSEN, SERIES EDITORS

NEW DIRECTIONS IN SCANDINAVIAN STUDIES

This series offers interdisciplinary approaches to the study of the Nordic region of Scandinavia and the Baltic States and their cultural connections in North America. By redefining the boundaries of Scandinavian studies to include the Baltic States and Scandinavian America, the series presents books that focus on the study of the culture, history, literature, and politics of the North.

Small States in International Relations edited by
Christine Ingebritsen, Iver B. Neumann, Sieglinde Gstohl, and Jessica Beyer

Danish Cookbooks: Domesticity and National Identity, 1616–1901
Carol Gold

Crime and Fantasy in Scandinavia: Fiction, Film, and Social Change
Andrew Nestingen

Selected Plays of Marcus Thrane translated and introduced by
Terje I. Leiren

Munch's Ibsen: A Painter's Visions of a Playwright
Joan Templeton

Knut Hamsun: The Dark Side of Literary Brilliance
Monika Žagar

Nordic Exposures: Scandinavian Identities
in Classical Hollywood Cinema
Arne Lunde

Icons of Danish Modernity: Georg Brandes and Asta Nielsen
Julie K. Allen

Danish Folktales, Legends, and Other Stories
Timothy R. Tangherlini

The Power of Song: Nonviolent National Culture
in the Baltic Singing Revolution
Guntis Šmidchens

Fascism and Modernist Literature in Norway
Dean Krouk

Christian Krohg's Naturalism
Øystein Sjåstad

Fascism and Modernist Literature in Norway

Dean Krouk

UNIVERSITY OF WASHINGTON PRESS
Seattle and London

THIS BOOK IS MADE POSSIBLE BY A COLLABORATIVE GRANT FROM THE ANDREW W. MELLON FOUNDATION.

Additional support was provided by the Office of the Vice Chancellor for Research and Graduate Education at the University of Wisconsin-Madison and the Department of Scandinavian Studies at the University of Washington.

21 20 19 18 17   5 4 3 2 1

University of Washington Press
www.washington.edu/uwpress

Cataloging-in-Publication Data available from the Library of Congress.

The paper used in this publication is acid-free and meets the minimum requirements of American National Standard for Information Sciences—Permanence of Paper for Printed Library Materials, ANSI Z39.48–1984.∞

CONTENTS

Acknowledgments vii

Introduction 3

1. Norwegian Modernism and Fascist Utopianism 9
2. Blind Forces of Life: Knut Hamsun's *Mysteries* 25
3. Wild Spring: Åsmund Sveen's Homoerotic Vitalism and Nazi Collaboration 47
4. Modernist Ragnarok: Rolf Jacobsen's Poetic and Political Anti-Nihilism 81
5. Unconscious Nazism: Sigurd Hoel's Psychoanalytic Antifascism 115

Conclusion 133

Notes 139

Bibliography 159

Index 171

ACKNOWLEDGMENTS

For their generous encouragement and assistance with this project, I owe debts of gratitude to colleagues, students, family members, and friends from Norway to California to the Upper Midwest. In its early stages, the project benefited tremendously from the constructive support and feedback of Mark Sandberg, Linda Rugg, Karin Sanders, Dorothy Hale, Amanda Doxtater, Laura Horak, and Anna Jörngården. For much of the long stretch of research and writing, Allen Young was an invaluable reader and source of encouragement. Other scholars, friends, and colleagues I wish to thank for their various forms of help and support at some stage of the project include Tone Selboe, Henning Howlid Wærp, Monika Žagar, Olivia Gunn, Ellen Rees, Peter Sjølyst-Jackson, Leif Høghaug and Hilde Nyeggen Martinsen, Claudia Berguson, Margaret O'Leary, Kari Lie Dorer, Christine Hærter Piñero, Sarah Wells, and Maria Vendetti. In addition, I would like to thank my colleagues in the Department of German, Nordic, and Slavic at the University of Wisconsin–Madison, as well as the editors and anonymous reviewers at the University of Washington Press, the Modern Language Initiative, and the New Directions in Scandinavian Studies Series.

Support for this research was provided by the University of Wisconsin–Madison Office of the Vice Chancellor for Research and Graduate Education with funding from the Wisconsin Alumni Research Foundation. The writing of this book was also conducted with generous support from the University of California–Berkeley, the American Scandinavian Foundation, St. Olaf College, the University of Oslo, the Norwegian Researchers and Teachers Association of North America (NORTANA), and the University of Wisconsin–Madison College of Letters and Sciences and Center for European

Studies. Earlier versions of small sections of this book, as well as related writings, have appeared in *Knut Hamsun: Transgression and Worlding* (Tapir Academic Press, 2011) and *"Der vårgras brydder": Nye lesninger av Åsmund Sveens diktning* (Oplandske Press, 2010).

My greatest gratitude is reserved for my parents, Marianne and Steven Krouk, whose devotion and support for educational pursuits from the earliest years were decisive for my academic and personal growth. The entire Krouk family is a continuous source of inspiration. I also wish to thank Jonathan Hart for his gracious support and encouragement over the years. My sister Leah, my niece Sofie, and my brother-in-law Courtney have all been wonderful presences in my life during the completion of this book, as has Nick Szczech—thank you all.

Fascism and Modernist Literature in Norway

Introduction

This book illuminates an underexplored area of twentieth-century European cultural history by examining the connections between fascism and Norwegian literature during the modernist period. It focuses on analyzing the writings—novels, poetry, essays—of several pro-fascist authors and one antifascist intellectual. Literary and cultural analysis of texts, films, and other media provides an enhanced understanding of the feelings and perceptions that drive political and ideological commitments. This is perhaps especially true in the case of fascism, which has often been understood as a "metapolitical phenomenon" that goes beyond ordinary party allegiances or typical categorical divisions of political thought.[1] While the specific forms and aesthetics taken by interwar fascism mostly belong to history, the affective and cultural dimensions of fascism are alive and well in the twenty-first century. The year 2016 gave the world stark reminders that the forces of ethnic and national belonging, racism, and misogyny continue to play a role in European and American politics, even after decades of neoliberal globalization and social progress. Contemporary parallels and resemblances to the 1930s need not pertain to the precise political forms on display but rather to the deep-seated nature of the affective narratives and myths. Racist and patriarchal narratives of unjust loss and proper belonging; myths of restored national greatness after liberal decline; political decisions motivated by inchoate anger, unresolved mourning, and smoldering resentment channeled into rage against minorities—all these metapolitical dimensions have been evident in the reactionary resurgence of our time.

Norwegian literature has had an extensive and complicated history of engagement with fascism, far-right nationalism, and Nazism. The final volume of Karl Ove Knausgård's autobiographical novel, *Min kamp* (*My Struggle*, 2009–11), devotes over four hundred pages to an essay titled "Navnet og tallet" (The Name and the Number). In a lengthy discussion of Hitler, Nazism, and the Holocaust, Knausgård takes the reader through a series of intense ethical, aesthetic, and philosophical reflections. Knausgård's interest in National Socialism in *Min kamp* is the tip of a literary-historical iceberg, which ultimately leads back to the interwar period and the five-year Nazi occupation of Norway during World War II. This larger context includes the Norwegian authors examined in this book, three of whom sympathized with fascism and Nazism in Norway: the Nobel Prize–winning novelist Knut Hamsun and the modernist poets Rolf Jacobsen and Åsmund Sveen. The fourth author, the cultural-radical novelist Sigurd Hoel, was persistently opposed to all forms of fascism. These four authors represent varying aspects of the modernist literary imagination in Norway, which includes disparate aesthetic and ideological features such as anti-realism, vitalism, anti-nihilism, and cultural radicalism, as I will explore in this book.

Beyond these four, there were numerous other literary or cultural figures in Norway who stridently opposed fascism, as well as a small but vocal minority that supported the ideology and the Nazi occupation. One important cultural collaborator during the war was the author and critic Finn Halvorsen, who was responsible for official theater productions during the occupation.[2] Cultural life in occupied Norway was subject to strict censorship and control—radios were banned, publishing houses and newspapers were eventually Nazified. During the postwar legal purge known as *landssvikoppgjøret*, around 46,000 Norwegians were sentenced for treason. A total of sixteen Norwegian authors were sentenced for treason after the occupation ended.[3] Active and overt commitment to the fascist utopian promise of national rebirth was never anything close to a majority position in a young nation marked by strong adherence to democratic norms and, increasingly in the 1930s, the dominance of the social-democratic Arbeiderpartiet (Labour Party).

In addition to Sigurd Hoel, prominent literary figures on the side of opposition and resistance included the leftist, non-modernist poets Arnulf Øverland and Nordahl Grieg, who are justly remembered in Norway for their anti-Nazi publications and activities. Øverland's

1936 poem "Du må ikke sove" (You must not sleep) remains one of the interwar period's signature political poems, while his 1945 collection *Vi overlever alt* (*We Will Survive*) includes clandestine resistance poetry as well as inspiring texts he wrote as a prisoner in the concentration camps Grini (in Bærum, Norway) and Sachsenhausen.[4] Similarly, Grieg's posthumous poetry collection *Friheten*, from 1945, contains much of his popular antifascist poetry. Grieg died in 1943 while serving as a war correspondent in an Allied aircraft raid over Berlin. Another literary voice of the resistance was the novelist and journalist Johan Borgen, who mocked the Nazi regime during the war under the pseudonym "Mumle Gåsegg" in the newspaper *Dagbladet*. Borgen was also imprisoned in Grini, and eventually he fled to Sweden later in the occupation. From a conservative political position, the neo-realist Catholic novelist Sigrid Undset was an early critic of Hitler and an outspoken voice of opposition from exile in Brooklyn during the Nazi occupation.[5]

In the postwar decades, Norwegian writers interpreted Nazism and related ideological problems in retrospective fictions. Some of these probed the psychology of treason and betrayal, such as Hoel's *Møte ved milepelen* (*Meeting at the Milestone*, 1947), which I will discuss in the fifth chapter. Novels by Jens Bjørneboe addressed the medical experiments that took place in the Nazi camps (in *Før hanen galer*, 1952) and the problem of evil committed in the name of ideologies, in the trilogy *Bestialitetens historie* (The History of Bestiality, 1966–73).[6] The ongoing concern with the Nazi occupation in Norwegian culture includes fiction and film of recent decades, often centered on representations of war memories and stories of resistance and collaboration.

In addition, memory and study of the Holocaust now has an established institutional location in Oslo. Since 2005, the Center for Studies of Holocaust and Religious Minorities has been located in Villa Grande, the house where the fascist party leader and nominal head of government Vidkun Quisling resided during the Nazi occupation. The center's website calls its choice of location a "symbolic act of reappropriation" and explains, "Once a house of shame it is now filled with activities in strong contrast to its former role."[7] The opening of the center was one of the results of a national commission in the 1990s that led to restitution for Norwegian victims and survivors of the Holocaust. This process was a sign of the ways in which Scandinavian memory of World War II and the Holocaust has been changing in recent decades. For a long time, the "master narrative" of the Norwegian nation in resistance to the Nazi occupation hardly mentioned the Norwegian Jews—a silence in both collective memory and historiography.[8] Although World War II has played a prominent role in Norwegian national memory and shaped Norwegian identity in the postwar era, addressing the exclusion of the Jews and Norway's role in the Holocaust has been difficult.[9] The historians Bjarte Bruland and Mats Tangestuen connect this difficulty to the fact that nationalist memories of occupation and resistance, with clearly polarized good and evil actors—patriotic resistance heroes against Nazis and collaborators—were for a long time central to the representation of the war period.[10]

Another indication that official memory and historiography of this period have given way to greater nuance and greater recognition of the fate of Norwegian Jews came on International Holocaust Remembrance Day in 2012, when Prime Minister Jens Stoltenberg officially apologized for the Norwegian role in the Nazi genocide. He invoked the fate of the young diarist Ruth Maier, who was arrested and deported from Oslo harbor with over five hundred other Jews in November 1942.[11] Maier was an intimate friend of the important modernist poet Gunvor Hofmo, who preserved her diaries after the war.[12] She was killed at Auschwitz. Stoltenberg said in his speech:

> What about the crimes against Ruth Maier and the other Jews? The murders were unquestionably carried out by the Nazis. But it was Norwegians who carried out the arrests. It was Norwegians who drove the trucks. And it happened in Norway. In the course of the war, 772 Norwegian Jews and Jewish refugees were arrested and deported. Only 34 survived. Without relieving the Nazis of their responsibility, it is time for us to acknowledge that Norwegian policemen and other Norwegians took part in the arrest and deportation of Jews. Today I feel it is fitting to express our deepest apologies that this could happen on Norwegian soil.[13]

In taking responsibility and apologizing for the actions of a small number of Norwegians, Stoltenberg emphasized the equal worth and equal rights of Jews and other minorities in Norway. His promise to counteract the views of contemporary extremists with "humanity and equality" echoed the speech he gave less than six months earlier, two days after the terrorist massacre by a far-right extremist on July 22, 2011, shook the country to its core.

The first chapter of this book will develop the intellectual-historical context needed to understand the complex relationship of literary modernism to fascism. Initial snapshots of each author in 1933, the year Hitler came to power, will introduce the cast of characters and provide glimpses of the issues covered in later chapters. Following that, I explain literary modernism as a countercultural and critical discourse within modernity. Drawing on interdisciplinary studies of fascist ideology and culture, I explore the reasons that fascist movements were able to exert a utopian and regenerative appeal for some writers and intellectuals in the interwar period.

The second chapter focuses on Knut Hamsun (1859–1952), who looms large over any discussion of the politics of literature in modern Norway. With a focus on the novel *Mysterier* (*Mysteries*, 1892) and related polemical texts, this chapter discusses features of Hamsun's early modernist fiction in relation to the historical emergence of fascist ideology. We see how *Mysteries* overturns the aesthetic and ideological program of the progressive and critical-realist "Modern Breakthrough," the preceding period in Scandinavian literature. In my reading, the fragmented form of Hamsun's novel subverts the typical logic of realist narrative, replacing rationality and clarification with indeterminacy and violent epiphany. Hamsun's fascism has sometimes been treated as an end-of-career anomaly, but this book argues that it was a contingent continuation of the adversarial cultural-critical project that began in the 1890s with his modernist rebellion.

The third chapter turns to the seemingly paradoxical case of the gay vitalist poet Åsmund Sveen (1910–63). I present Sveen's poetic eroticism in its cultural-historical context, arguing that his vitalistic and mystical view of sexuality intersected in unexpected and challenging ways with his embrace of fascism. Vitalism, an important concept of early twentieth-century aesthetics in Scandinavia, played a role in both Sveen's fabrication of a spiritual eroticism that included same-sex desire and his fascist utopianism. In addition to seeing National Socialism as an anti-rationalist form of idealism destined to save "white" Europe, Sveen misrecognized the movement as compatible with his own open and modern eroticism. This chapter includes readings of poetry from throughout Sveen's literary career, both before and after his treasonous collaboration almost completely derailed it.

The fourth chapter investigates the poetry and politics of Rolf Jacobsen (1907–94). Although he is Norway's major modernist poet, Jacobsen's wartime Nazism has often been ignored or dismissed as irrelevant. Against the received view, this book explains Jacobsen's support for National Socialism as something more than a regrettable, but meaningless, hiatus between his interwar modernism and his postwar return as an ecologically minded and newly Catholic poet. This chapter argues that an underlying concern with modernity's culture of nihilism—the lack of a foundation for beliefs and actions, the lack of direction and commitment—lay at the center of both his poetry and his political engagements on the left and the right.

The book's fifth chapter turns away from the pro-Nazi writers and examines the response to fascism found in the work of the seminal interwar novelist and critic Sigurd Hoel (1890–1960). Hoel used the nonconformist psychoanalyst Wilhelm Reich's interwar theories of mass psychology and sexual repression to come to grips with the authoritarian mentality motivating fascism and Nazism. Through readings of little-known and untranslated essays, this chapter explains how Hoel extended his urgent critical analysis of Nazism into a more fundamental self-critique that addressed all patriarchal forms of authority. Following that, a brief conclusion returns to the issue of fascist utopianism and retraces its main connections to the modernist literary imagination in Norway, in the light of the textual analyses offered in each chapter.

CHAPTER 1

Norwegian Modernism and Fascist Utopianism

Some snapshots of the interwar period can help introduce the four Norwegian modernist writers whose relations to fascism, both for and against, were crucial to their literary and political itineraries and legacies. In 1933, Adolf Hitler was appointed chancellor in Germany in January, and Vidkun Quisling formed the fascist Nasjonal Samling party in Norway in May. In October of the same year, seventy-four-year-old Knut Hamsun, having already cycled through many triumphs, fiascos, and comebacks in his long, erratic career, published the third novel in a popular neo-realist trilogy about a charismatic and charlatanical vagabond named August. Earlier that year, in a letter to his publisher Harald Grieg, a Jewish friend who would later be sent to a concentration camp (and released), Hamsun voiced his private praise for fascism: "Mussolini skulle jeg nok hat lyst til å nedlægge min høie beundring og dype ærbødighet for—Gud nåde os for en kar midt i vår forvirrede tid!" (I would like to express my great admiration and deep respect for Mussolini—my God, what a guy in this confused age!).[1]

The Nobel laureate's first public defense of Nazism would come the following year, in 1934, as part of a feud with literature professor Johan Fredrik Paasche in the newspaper *Aftenposten.* Paasche advised the public to think twice about any sympathies they might have for the Norwegian fascist party and to take a lesson from the current climate of political repression in Germany. (Concentration camps for political dissenters were already in full swing at this time.) Hamsun responded that such repression was the necessary price to pay for the "ethical transformation" of an entire society. He mocked Paasche for wanting to return to the pre-Nazi Germany of the Weimar Republic, "when the communists, the Jews, and [Heinrich] Brüning ruled in this Nordic country."[2] At many points in the next decade, the elderly Hamsun would loudly proclaim his approval for his Germanic brethren in the new Reich, whose conquest over England he saw as a necessity of nature. Hamsun even sent his Nobel Prize to Joseph Goebbels in 1943, considering it a gift to a great idealist.[3] Was this really the same author who had revolutionized the European novel forty years earlier, anticipating and shaping the direction of modernist prose with works such as *Sult* (Hunger) and *Mysterier*?

Rolf Jacobsen was in his mid-twenties in 1933, the year he published *Jord og jern* (Earth and Iron), a collection still considered the pioneering work of poetic modernism in Norway. In the early 1930s, Jacobsen was involved with the communist organization Mot Dag (Toward Day), as well as other culturally and politically leftist groups. In the fall of 1934, he traveled to Berlin with a friend who was entering a pro forma marriage to a German Jewish woman to help her escape the regime. Like many other artists and writers in the interwar decades, Jacobsen was captivated by Berlin as a metropolitan cultural and industrial center. He rushed around the city's streets and subways, visited cinemas that showed Nazi propaganda films, and witnessed the spectacle of uniformed men marching on Unter den Linden. One day, Jacobsen glimpsed Hitler emerging from a car; at another point he caught sight of Goebbels high on a platform above the crowds.[4] After this taste of Hitler's Reich—which did not convert him to National Socialism—Jacobsen returned to Norway.

The following year, Jacobsen published a pessimistic and alienated collection of urban poetry called *Vrimmel* (Swarm, 1935). He remained engaged in leftist political activity and was to all appearances anti-capitalist, antifascist, and pacifistic for the rest of the decade. Then, in an abrupt political about-face, Jacobsen joined Nasjonal Samling and became the editor of a fascist newspaper during the war. This move might be seen as expedient and opportunistic, but it was in fact based in a genuine desire for political redemption. During the occupation, Jacobsen signed his name to many incriminating editorials, including one that said that the war was only as unpleasant as the capitalist society created by the Jews.[5] After serving a sentence for treason and struggling for many postwar years, Jacobsen was eventually rehabilitated as one of Scandinavia's most acclaimed and widely translated writers, known especially for his ecological awareness. Many readers today have no knowledge of his service to the National Socialist press and propaganda machine in Norway.

Åsmund Sveen was in his early twenties when Hitler came to power, yet he had already published an acclaimed work of expressionistic and homoerotic poetry, *Andletet* (The Face, 1932), and he was completing a second collection for publication that year. Sveen, like Jacobsen, gave no indication of any serious support for Hitler's Germany until later in the decade. He identified as a pacifist and wrote as a critic for the leftist *Dagbladet* while developing a peculiar brand of vitalist mysticism in his poetry. He too visited Nazi Germany in 1934, a few months before Jacobsen's visit, as a sort of literary ambassador at the Deutsch-Nordisches Schriftstellerhaus in the Baltic seaside resort of Travemünde. Although Sveen insisted at the time that he was no National Socialist, he also wrote that he was beginning to understand "the new mentality" and to acquire greater insight into what the young Nazi men really thought.[6]

After returning from Germany in the fall of 1934, Sveen submitted the manuscript of an experimental novel about homosexual life, *Vinduet og vaaren* (The Window and the Spring). Unfortunately, the consultant at his publisher, none other than Sigurd Hoel, deemed the novel too decadent, worse than "the most artificial 1890s romanticism."[7] It has never been published and the manuscript is lost. During the war, Sveen defended his support for National Socialism as support for a "new idealistic movement that seeks spiritual truth and arises from an elementary religiosity."[8] Although Sveen published additional collections of poetry before and after the war, with many bizarre and fascinating modernist texts, he was never rehabilitated in the eyes of the postwar public, and his work has only recently gathered new attention in Norway.

Sigurd Hoel was already a respected novelist and critic in his early forties by 1933, the year he published *Veien til verdens ende* (The Road to the End of the World), a classic depiction of a boy's rural childhood in late nineteenth-century Norway. Although it may sound like an apolitical novel, *Veien til verdens ende* partakes in Hoel's broader cultural-radical critique of the deforming influence of repressive patriarchy. This was the critical lens through which Hoel, aided by Wilhelm Reich's radical interwar revision of psychoanalysis, diagnosed and attacked the cancer of Nazism. In 1933, Hoel was still married to one of Norway's first female psychoanalysts, Nic Waal, who trained under Reich in Berlin and even accompanied the Austrian analyst to Oslo. In the course of the 1930s and into the postwar period, Hoel continued to develop his psychoanalytic antifascism and to explore his own society's problems with authority, sexuality, and aggression in essays and novels such as *Fjorten dager før frostnettene* (*A Fortnight Before the Frost*, 1936) and the occupation novel *Møte ved milepelen* (*Meeting at the Milestone*, 1947).

Hoel belonged to the generation of Scandinavian writers for whom the impact of Knut Hamsun's novels is difficult to overestimate; he wrote incisive essays on Hamsun repeatedly throughout his career. Furthermore, his work as a literary critic and consultant at the publishing house Gyldendal brought him into contact with the poetry of Sveen and Jacobsen in the 1930s. Although Hoel knew their work, reviewed it, and even influenced it as an editorial consultant, he defined his intellectual life in utter opposition to what they later embraced as a movement of utopian rebirth. Both Hoel and Nic Waal participated in the Norwegian resistance movement (albeit separately, since they divorced in 1936). Waal has been honored by Yad Vashem, the World Holocaust Remembrance Center in Israel, for planning the rescue of fourteen Jewish children from a home in Oslo after the Nazis ordered the deportation of all Jews late in 1942.

Hoel was pressured into fleeing to Sweden in the fall of 1943. Earlier that year, a propaganda volume about Norwegian fascist writers called *Nasjonalsosialister i norsk diktning* (National Socialists in Norwegian Literature) was published. The book was based on a lecture series broadcast on Norwegian radio in the winter of 1942–43. To herald this publication, the newspaper then edited by Jacobsen, *Glåmdalen*, printed the book's cover, a photographic collage of the faces of the writers discussed in the lectures.[9] Among others, one can see here the faces of Hamsun, Sveen, and Jacobsen.

As Peter Sjølyst-Jackson has written in relation to Hamsun, Nazism is a stain that doesn't come out in the wash.[10] It becomes an unavoidable mark on a localized part of the biography but also something more pervasive—a stain that colors the whole body of (textual) material, seeping into the fibers of the fabric like an insoluble pigment. This pigment may be distorting to some degree, pressuring us to view the literature in relation to political contexts that might not always be relevant. The greater risk, however, is the assumption that the stain can simply be ignored. In the case of Hamsun, the various apologetic critical maneuvers that have been utilized to cleanse his literature of any alleged association to fascism—as though this were required to make it "safe" for aesthetic appreciation—seem finally to have run their course in critical and popular discussions. This book views Hamsun as both a modernist novelist (if only earlier in his career, before his neo-realist phase) and a fascist (if only later in his career, when fascism had coalesced as a political identity). Although Hamsun was not officially a member of Nasjonal Samling, this is merely a technicality. He published a series of pro-Nazi articles during the war, including an infamous obituary for Hitler, and the longstanding similarities of his writings to the developing ideological discourses of European fascism are well documented.[11] The question that matters in this book is the relationship between these two sides of Hamsun. Similarly, Sveen and Jacobsen's status as Nazi sympathizers has already been thoroughly documented at the biographical level. My aim is to pose further questions for the analysis of their literary modernism in light of these facts.[12]

The Norwegian critic and literary historian Øystein Rottem once characterized the debate about Hamsun's literature in legal terms, as a trial with prosecutors, defenders, and judges.[13] Writing in a twenty-first-century North American context, at a historical and cultural remove from their collaborations, my approach can be guided less by the need to condemn, to put on trial, or to apologize and protect. Instead, their political commitments reach us across the decades as *facts* about the literary history of modernism in Norway. Distance in time and place gives us the freedom to argue and contextualize more clearly, and to pose questions for analysis that would not have been possible with closer proximity. How can we understand the appeal of fascism to the modernist literary imagination in Norway? What sort of role did fascism play in the interwar and wartime literary developments in Norway? How can the many historical and cultural studies of modernism and fascism in Europe help us understand these Norwegian cases?

A SPECTRUM OF MODERNIST-FASCIST INTERFACES

Just as scholars now recognize that European literary modernism existed in various modes and drew upon disparate philosophical, aesthetic, and sociopolitical groundings, so should we recognize the variety of modernist-fascist interfaces. Even in the small country of Norway, with its often disregarded but prolific literary culture, modernism exhibits not one but several historical engagements with fascism. The interaction of modernism and fascism in Norway is characterized by instances of coalescence, embrace, and collaboration, but also by cases of resistance, interrogation, and diagnosis. The name "Knut Hamsun" directs us toward the first set of terms, while the antifascist Sigurd Hoel leads us toward the latter. Rolf Jacobsen and Åsmund Sveen are notable for having been both for and against fascism at different times. Given these differences, we can work loosely with the idea of a spectrum of modernist-fascist interfaces in Norway, which stretches from Hamsun's long-term coalescence with Nazism on one end, through the short-term, but genuine, commitments of Jacobsen and Sveen, and on to Hoel's enduring antifascism on the other end.

It has become standard in studies of fascism, aesthetics, and literature to stress that there is no discrete artistic or literary style inherent to fascist or National Socialist ideology.[14] Scholars readily acknowledge the heterogeneity of European fascist aesthetics in the interwar period and question any notion of an autonomous fascist aesthetic.[15] Fascist cultural and literary production is part of European modernity, and it should not be separated off into a separate compartment, into what Jobst Welge calls a "monstrous, perversely fascinating corner of aberration."[16] The absence of a single style is especially conspicuous when we examine individual figures with some sort of fascist inclination or sympathy, such as the painter Emil Nolde or the poet Ezra Pound, as opposed to state-sponsored artistic or cultural projects, such as Leni Riefenstahl's *Triumph of the Will* or the 1932 Italian Exhibition of the Fascist Revolution.[17] Since this book is about four individual Norwegian modernist writers, one of whom was an antifascist (Sigurd Hoel), we should expect little consistency in terms of literary aesthetics or styles. Although they all are connected to distinctive strands of the modernist literary imagination in Norway, they do not comprise a separate stylistic category called "fascist modernism." Their cases are distinct to a degree that merits individual attention to the intellectual, biographical, and literary specifics. However, at a general level, each writer was modernist in the sense that they were intimately involved in the complex, crisis-driven reorganization of literary representation and form that arose in response to modernity's vast social, technological, and cultural changes. In fact, Knut Hamsun and Rolf Jacobsen can without controversy be called the central figures of Norwegian literary modernism, in the novel and poetry, respectively.

There are many different ways to delimit Norwegian or Scandinavian literary modernism historically; this book takes a long view that stretches roughly from the 1880s to the 1960s. Dating the period in this way allows us to recognize successive waves of modernist activity across genres, from the era of Henrik Ibsen to post–World War II poetic modernism, when influential core models of modernist poetry such as Ezra Pound and T. S. Eliot were received in the Nordic countries by figures like Paal Brekke. Scholars of Scandinavian modernism such as Toril Moi and Leonardo Lisi have focused on the late nineteenth century as an initial phase of peak significance, presenting modernism as continuous with realism and naturalism, rather than defined by a break from them.[18] These views give pride of place to the towering figure of Henrik Ibsen, who is linked to the critical Brandesian program of the Modern Breakthrough period (ca. 1870–90).[19]

Of course there are alternatives to such a periodization. With a focus on prose narrative rather than drama, Knut Hamsun would be the clear agent of a modernist break with realism, starting around 1890.[20] In poetry, it has become standard to view Norway's 1890s neoromanticism as a sort of overture or first wave of modernism, with the key figure being Sigbjørn Obstfelder. There then follows something of a lag until the 1930s, when Rolf Jacobsen's early poetry appears on the scene, along with the work of figures such as the poet Claus Gill and the prose modernist Cora Sandel.[21] Jacobsen's interwar modernism, although late by international standards, is sometimes portrayed as a predecessor of the "real" arrival of poetic modernism in postwar Norway, around the time of the historiographically fetishized Tungetaledebatten (the belated postwar debate between proponents and opponents of modernist form in poetry).[22] The key point is that a capacious concept of modernism as a period better accounts for the variety of literary and aesthetic developments across genres, without giving too much weight to a single potential emphasis, such as the adoption of free verse in poetry or the extensive use of interior narration and free indirect discourse in prose.

One reason that the interface of fascism and modernism is so multifaceted is that both terms are burdened by contradictory significance and tend to vary by national context and disciplinary definition. Taken as a whole, European fascism was a notoriously eclectic political ideology that drew on diverse currents of fin-de-siècle intellectual life and came to power after the catastrophic collapse of bourgeois values and economies in World War I. No longer considered an outbreak of abnormal irrationality in an otherwise securely enlightened and civilized West, fascism as studied today appears more deeply intertwined with European modernity.[23] Fascism is famously contradictory—it has been interpreted as modern and anti-modern, rational and irrational, futuristic and nostalgic, populist and elitist. These contradictions are partly a result of differing interpretative positions, but they are also based in the phenomenon itself. Fascism presents a twisted hybrid of modern techno-futurism and nostalgic ruralism; instrumental rationality at its most effective and atavistic, mythic unreason; the rigidly lockstep organization of the new racial collective and the supposed liberation of the vital energies and dynamism of youth. What is further unsettling about National Socialism in particular was its ability to appeal in many different ways, "in various keys," to gather support for its "vast project for social, political, and racial renewal."[24] Nazism has always been difficult to fathom not only because it frustrates notions of social, political, and economic classification but also because it had ineffably traumatic results—in Peter Fritzsche's words, "the Holocaust destroyed expectations about how the world worked."[25]

Likewise, modernism's unsettling challenge takes many forms, not all of which bear an immediate resemblance to Anglo-American high modernism. The spatial image of modernism as a towering monolith, or even as a tree with different branches, has been replaced by a multidirectional image of "burrows" or "rhizomes."[26] Rather than an imposing unit, literary modernism designates an upheaval in multiple directions, a multifarious shattering of consensus about the official narratives and models of modernity. It is a stylistically and ideologically eclectic concept that has come to designate nothing less than several generations' worth of literary responses to the multiple transformations of late nineteenth- and early twentieth-century culture and society. Modernism touches on gender, class, consumerism and mass culture, secularization, war, technology, and epistemology, to name just a few important contact points. Even when restricted to European literature, this enormously heterogeneous concept can name starkly opposed stylistic variations, from primitivism to futurism, from intense subjectivism to extreme impersonality.

It is best to imagine modernist literature not just as a series of textual events but as the transgressive, contestatory, and, as Michael Levenson writes, "self-consciously post-traditional activity" of an oppositional culture within modernity.[27] Levenson describes it as "an ill-defined collection of acts and responses—representation and abstraction, engagement and abstention, fascination and detachment, contemplation and critique—that has offered *not one value but a region of commitments*."[28] Despite its ideological and aesthetic plurality, the concept retains its value and helpfulness. In this book, I view Norwegian literary modernism in terms of the crisis of values and the accompanying senses of inner and outer chaos, loss of traditional meaning, amplification of uncertainty and doubt, and cultural disembedding that are standardly associated with the process of modernization.[29] When we speak of literary modernism, then, we refer to a transgressive and shocking, but also anxious and unsettled, response to the vertiginous changes and disruptions of the modern.

Modernism was not only unsettled but *unsettling*: formally difficult, ethically troubling, and politically challenging. Scholars now take for granted modernism's disruptive or subversive relation to the world of bourgeois modernity, including the latter's complacent conformism, rationalist and materialist assumptions, and leading political and economic framework of liberalism. As we know from examples in Anglo-American and European literature, the modernist or avant-garde critique of bourgeois modernity does not always land in a progressive or leftist political stance: think of Ezra Pound, Ernst Jünger, Gottfried Benn, or Wyndham Lewis. European aesthetic modernisms exist in the void left by the evacuation of liberal humanist certainties about democracy, progress, autonomous subjectivity, and liberty. The political and ethical commitments of a literature that emerges from this void are bound to be as diverse as they are unreassuring from the perspective of traditional liberal humanism or contemporary progressivism. The politics of literary modernism should thus not be taken to refer to a single set of values but instead seen as a post-traditional or post-bourgeois scattering into what Levenson calls "a region of commitments." Among these commitments is fascist utopianism.

THE MYTH OF FASCIST UTOPIAN REGENERATION

The historian Roger Griffin has developed a heuristic concept of generic fascist ideology that includes National Socialism in Norway and Germany, as well as Italian Fascism and other smaller, unsuccessful movements. This concept has become associated with interdisciplinary scholarship loosely belonging to the "new consensus" in fascist studies.[30] The latter term is Griffin's creation, and it has attracted criticism from other scholars who deny that there is any such agreement.[31] However, the "new consensus" model provides the best way to understand fascism's relationship to the literature, art, and culture of early twentieth-century Europe. Even critics have recognized its achievement in illuminating the nature of fascist ideology and cultural production in a range of contexts.[32]

Following pioneering work by historians such as George L. Mosse and Zeev Sternhell, Griffin argues that fascism was a utopian and revolutionary reaction to the anomie, rootlessness, and disembedding effects of modern social and economic developments. He defines fascism as a form of modern revolutionary politics that aims to renew and cleanse the culture of a particular national or ethnic community. Fascism is "palingenetic" in that it relies on "a core myth that a period of perceived decadence and degeneracy is imminently or eventually to give way to one of rebirth and rejuvenation in a post-liberal new order."[33] Such myths of regeneration can be found in many ideologies, including communism, but in fascism they support "projects of national, social, racial or cultural cleansing" that are "designed to bring about collective redemption, a new national community, a new society, a new man."[34]

In the interwar period, the attempt to fabricate a "new man" was shared by both fascism and communism, as well as other political and artistic programs. Whereas the communist "new man" was a project of social and political reeducation, in Nazism, a regime based on racial policy, the new human type was imagined as a project of biological regeneration.[35] In *Life and Death in the Third Reich*, Peter Fritzsche describes how the biopolitical goal of "racial grooming" was essential to the National Socialist fabrication of a new man and a nationalist collective. Hitler declared in 1933 that the new German regime would have to develop a new kind of person, relying on modern biological techniques of racial hygiene and instilling a visual regime that taught Germans how to perceive desirable racialized bodies.[36] While not obsessed with racial purification in this manner, Italian Fascism also aimed to craft a "new man" that was vigorous, violent, and liberated from the past, even as an idealized vision of Roman civilization served as a model for a regenerated, decisively modern nation.[37] The new Italian created by fascism was supposed to save Europe from a doubly decadent state of liberal-individualist hedonism and communist materialism.[38]

While fascism has sometimes been perceived as reactionary and anti-modern (not to mention anti-modernist), contemporary historians describe it as a revolutionary ideology desiring to establish an alternative modernity, one based on a mythical vision of nationalist regeneration. This rebirth would constitute a break with the modern society fascists perceived as spiritually empty, degenerate, and lingering on the verge of an apocalyptic collapse. In the typical fascist imagination of such a utopian break, a new order would emerge from the ruins of the collapse. Rolf Jacobsen furnishes an example in a wartime editorial, which refers to this collapse and rebirth as "Ragnarok."[39] This use of Ragnarok, the final battle and twilight of the gods in Norse mythology, displays how fascists often found informing narratives of destruction and regeneration in their own national-cultural past.

Against the social and economic individualism of liberalism, fascism located well-being in the national or racial collective, considered as an organic entity that was as much spiritual as material. Obviously, its nationalist and anti-materialist focus put fascism fiercely at odds with socialism and communism, even though it shared with them a critique of capitalism and laissez-faire economic policy. But fascism's aversion to capitalism was based on a revolt against the standardization and rationalism of bourgeois culture and industrial society; it offered a Romantic form of anti-capitalism rather than one based in Marxist theory.[40] The universal exchangeability of capital and the globalizing effects of capitalism threatened to dissolve particular national values and ethnic communities, which fascism in turn glorified.

Some historians trace the emergence of fascist ideology to the leftist revolt against the positivism and mechanistic materialism of much late nineteenth-century thought. Zeev Sternhell influentially locates the origins of fascism in fin-de-siècle France as a combination of organic nationalism and anti-materialist revisionary socialism that stood against the rationalist culture of the Enlightenment heritage.[41] Revolting against rationalism and materialism, fascism positioned itself as a secular and idealistic surrogate for traditional spirituality. As a political and cultural ideology with a secular basis, fascism was not a religion; it aimed to transform society in historical time through human agency.[42] However, fascism was idealistic in its rejection of rationalism and materialism, which we will see was a major factor in its appeal to Hamsun and Sveen. Even more explicitly, Jacobsen understood his Nazi commitment in hindsight as a surrogate for his lost Christian faith. In an important sense, fascism could only occur in a post-Christian context. Stanley Payne argues that it aspired to remake "non-rationalist myth structures" for modern individuals who had lost a traditional belief system.[43] As did many modernist writers, fascism looked to the instinctive, the mythic, and the irrational to construct post-traditional forms of spirituality or enchantment.

Sternhell, in his description of the origins of fascism as an "alternative political culture" in fin-de-siècle France, points to the writer Maurice Barrès's emphasis on the "cult of deep and mysterious forces." Barrès favored "impulses which determine human behavior and which constitute the reality and truth of things as well as their beauty."[44] According to this way of thinking, the irrational has both a greater claim to truth and a greater aesthetic appeal than do the intellectual and the rational. The extra feature that tilts this garden-variety romantic anti-intellectualism into something specifically fascist is that rationalism is supposed to belong to the "deracinated" and to blunt the collective forces of national activity.[45] To overcome such degeneration and rootlessness, the national and racial spirit would need to be reborn after a total break with the present. Barrès is an interesting figure in relation to Hamsun, because his ideas bring together both the early Hamsun's irrationalist obsession with mysterious forces and the later Hamsun's frequent concern with deracination.

Fascists often aligned the perceived destruction of culture and spirit in modernity with Jews, capitalists, or Americanism. In various national versions of fascism, this configuration of rationalist liberal culture as spiritual death and sterility was often opposed to an authentic local culture whose values the fascists co-opted and elevated.[46] A Norwegian example of this is the propaganda anthology of Norwegian literary history Åsmund Sveen edited during the war. This work was based on the idea of an authentic national tradition that would provide values opposed to the degenerate anti-culture of modernity. It was called *Norsk ånd og vilje* (Norwegian Spirit and Will), and it included an ideologically warped version of the national literary tradition that began with Old Norse-Icelandic Eddic poetry, included the nineteenth-century greats Bjørnstjerne Bjørnson and Henrik Ibsen, and ended with speeches by Vidkun Quisling. The Norwegian scholar Eivind Tjønneland has argued that Sveen utilized selective citations from Norwegian literature to inspire nationalist sentiment and identification in a time when the ability to feel Norwegian was perceived to be threatened by the international influence of the English, the Jews, and the Bolsheviks.[47]

Norway did not have a mainstream fascist presence in culture and politics in the interwar period; the National Socialist movement was politically embodied in a peripheral party, the Nasjonal Samling, which remained very small until the Nazi invasion of Norway in 1940. The ideology of the Norwegian fascist party is often seen as national-romantic, anti-urban, and nostalgic for a simpler or more authentic dream of peasant society.[48] There was a division in Norwegian fascism between those who favored the specifically Norwegian and those who looked to a broader idea of the Germanic. While the former focused on seemingly innocuous things like folk costumes, "family values," camping, and closeness to nature, the latter promoted a biological racism that favored Germanic unity against corrupting forces such as cultureless Americans, jazz, Jews, Bolsheviks, and democracy.[49] Although anti-Semitism became a key feature of Norwegian fascism only after 1933, the ideology was always based on a view of Nordic racial superiority.[50] Quisling idealized the Viking period and claimed that Norway would lead the modern self-assertion of the Nordic race, whose purity and health were threatened.[51] This fascist appropriation of the Viking past for the purposes of utopian palingenetic myth is quite visible in much of the party's visual propaganda and iconography.

Years before Nazi Germany invaded Norway (on April 9, 1940), Hamsun had praised a popular book by the Danish doctor Konrad Simonsen. This 1917 work, *Den moderne mennesketype* (The Modern Human Type), argued that material progress and comforts in modern Europe had been gained at the expense of soul and intuition; the modern type was rootless, mechanical, and empty.[52] As Monika Žagar explains, the book argued that "the mixing of the healthy, noble Germanic race with other races, deemed inferior, has brought about . . . the gradual process of de-Germanization (*Afgermanisering*)."[53] Hamsun's fear of racial mixing and racial decline, though not exclusive to fascist ideology at his time, provided a crucial impulse in his turn to National Socialism.[54] The same attitudes were also motivations for Åsmund Sveen and Rolf Jacobsen, as we will see.

In Nazism, the threatening forces of liberalism, finance capitalism, and Bolshevism (incongruous as these are) were all condensed in the figure of the Jew. Political and economic fears, as well as fears of social fragmentation, were projected onto the racial enemy. As Fritzsche shows in *Life and Death in the Third Reich*, Nazism's revolution was more "biological" than that of Italian Fascism. The National

Socialist mental or spiritual revolution was inseparable from its project of biologically engineering a new racial collective and breeding a "new German person" through modern techniques of racial hygiene and health.[55] This project necessitated the exclusion of the racially undesirable—the continent's Jews, among others—to accomplish the "objective of creating new men and new women who would acknowledge one another as racial comrades."[56] In Nazism, as opposed to Norwegian and Italian fascism before World War II, national reinvigoration was to be accomplished through "radical surgery and biological cleansing," which required a pitiless rejection of conventional morality and an adherence to the purifying potential of new biomedical techniques.[57] The Nazi murder of Europe's Jews resulted from the regime's central project of protecting the nation's racial and political health from alleged forces of disintegration.

While Hamsun, Sveen, and Jacobsen did not express ultraviolent forms of anti-Semitism, they did share these concerns for the purity of "Germanic" Europe. These authors most likely did not realize that their visions of rebirth and redemption would entail the merciless elimination of Europe's Jews and the other victims of the Nazi genocide. Yet anti-Semitism unmistakably constituted a major part of the regimes and parties they decided to support in Norway and Germany. The persecution of the Jews in Norway was happening for all to see during the years when they gave their names, their labor as writers and intellectuals, and their symbolic capital to the occupying regime. Arguments that they were not motivated by racism or anti-Semitism often appear rather strained.[58] In hindsight, their commitment to National Socialism as a means of overcoming the spiritual and cultural crisis of European modernity seems remarkably naïve at best.

The Norwegian scholar Arild Linneberg has written, "The image of fascist art as *Blut und Boden* fiction needs to be nuanced. Model: Marinetti and Italian Futurism. The fascists had their own avant-garde, and Hamsun was its leader. Another Norwegian example: the modernist poet Åsmund Sveen."[59] Linneberg's readiness to consider fascist aesthetics in relation to the avant-garde and modernism reflects an awareness that has become more widespread in recent decades. To understand fascism and modernism in this way, we need to avoid what Andrew Hewitt once called "the critical conflation of political and aesthetic 'progressiveness.'"[60] These intersecting histories may be upsetting to those who imagine the arts or poetry to be inherently worthy of ethical or political approval, but such views generally rely on an insipid notion of literature and culture.[61]

Studies of the relationship between modernism and fascism have shown two potential emphases. First, there is the fascism of modernism: the fascist inclinations or sympathies of individual modernist literary or artistic figures such as Ezra Pound, Gottfried Benn, Wyndham Lewis, or Filippo Marinetti.[62] Second, there is the modernism of fascism, meaning the way fascist regimes incorporated or co-opted modernist aesthetic principles, whether this was due to a canny use of propaganda or to inner similarities of aesthetic and social vision. In this case, the predominant focus has been on Fascist Italy and Italian Futurism. To a greater degree than Nazism, Italian Fascism is recognized for its modernist art, design, and architecture. There was no artistic movement as closely associated to Nazism as Futurism was to the Fascist regime in Italy.[63] Griffin has tried to amend this picture by arguing that Nazism's relationship to aesthetic modernism—despite the famous "Degenerate Art" exhibit—was not as wholly negative as usually presumed, and that there was a space and function for aesthetic modernism within Nazi culture.[64]

Both approaches to the topic benefit when they understand modernism and fascism as separate but at times converging reactions to shared sociohistorical preconditions. In *Avant-garde Fascism*, Mark Antliff observes that "many of the paradigms that spawned the development of modernist aesthetics were also integral to the emergence of fascism," and this shared reaction to the cultural environment acted as "a stimulus for alliances between modernists and anti-Enlightenment ideologues throughout the nineteenth and twentieth centuries."[65] Similarly, Griffin identifies their common features in the search for transcendence and regeneration, "whether confined to a personal quest for ephemeral moments of enlightenment or expanded to take the form of a cultural, social, or political movement for the renewal of the nation or the whole of Western civilization."[66] In the context of France, as David Carroll has shown, literary fascists turned to the strong classical tradition in their national culture to construct a more authentic, alternative modernity that would at the same time enable "a profound continuity with the authentic past . . . the (re)birth of a 'new man' paradoxically modeled after a radical notion of an original, poetic . . . 'classical man.'"[67] Although the ideological pattern here—anti-liberal revolution based on continuity with an authentic national past combined with a future vision of the new man—is generically fascist, there is also a telling aesthetic contrast with Norwegian fascism. Without a strong aesthetic tradition of classicism, fascism in Norway could not look back to such a precedent to shape its vision of nationalist palingenesis. Instead, the Norwegian fascists drew on native forms of romanticism, Norse mythology, and folk culture, or on broader visions of the Germanic. This contrast illustrates an important point about the aesthetic heterogeneity of the various European fascisms: as opposed to French neoclassicism, the Norwegian case shows the use of primitivism and vitalism as the aesthetic paradigms of a fascist modernity.

The decisions Hamsun, Sveen, and Jacobsen made to support the myth of fascist utopian regeneration were not simply unfortunate biographical events. These decisions were intimately connected to the patterns of response to modernity laid out in their cultural-critical form of literary modernism. In their literature, these authors locate the value of existence outside of the instrumental rationality, reductionist exchange value, and technological nihilism that characterize bourgeois modernity. They aspired to overcome this paradigm, in art through literary explorations of aesthetic, erotic, or existential depth, or in politics through a fantasy of fascist renewal. As I argue in the following chapters, fascism furnished these authors with a distorted vision of redemption, a radical cure for liberal modernity's sociopolitical and existential chaos, and the seduction of utopian regeneration in a purified new order. The case of the antifascist cultural radical Sigurd Hoel, the subject of the final chapter, shows that this vision was not shared by all Norwegian modernists of the period.

CHAPTER 2

Blind Forces of Life

Knut Hamsun's Mysteries

The architecturally bold Hamsunsenteret (Hamsun Center) in Hamarøy, Northern Norway, was designed by Steven Holl and opened in 2009. Its multimedia displays educate the public about the Nobel Prize–winning novelist and Nazi sympathizer Knut Hamsun, who has been the most persistently debated Nordic literary figure since World War II. Hamsun's large body of work spans many decades of artistic and political change in Europe, beginning with his fin-de-siècle anti-realist lectures and the psychological novels that are now considered modernist texts: *Sult* (1890), *Mysterier* (1892), and *Pan* (1894). In addition to being Norway's major modernist novelist, Hamsun has also been called Norway's major fascist intellectual.[1] In 1936, he exclaimed that he would give ten votes if possible to Vidkun Quisling, the leader of the tiny Norwegian fascist party Nasjonal Samling. There was no other Scandinavian figure of a comparable stature who gave his support so fully to European fascism, including both Italian Fascism and Nazism, in addition to the smaller Norwegian version. But Hamsun was more than simply the literary Quisling; he had admirers of many political stripes and nationalities in the early twentieth century. The question of the relationship between his modernist literature and his fascist politics remains complex.

Part of this complexity has to do with the length and range of Hamsun's literary career. The anti-realist Hamsun of the 1890s went on to become a neo-realist novelist around World War I, winning the Nobel Prize in 1920 more for *Markens grøde* (*The Growth of the Soil*) than for his earlier psychological modernism.[2] Later, in a move that appalled the small country that lauded him as a national symbol, Hamsun published pro-Nazi newspaper articles during the eight weeks of Norwegian resistance to the German invasion. One of these notorious articles, published in May 1940 in *Fritt folk*, the journal of Nasjonal Samling, exhorted Norwegians to put down their weapons and let the Germans rule. Such articles led to Hamsun's postwar trial for treason, his time under psychiatric observation, and eventually his final literary work, a disturbingly poignant record of the immediate postwar years called *Paa gjengrodde stier* (*On Overgrown Paths*, 1948).[3]

In the case of such a long career, understanding the production and reception of Hamsun's literature involves attention to multiple and shifting contexts: from the particularities of the Scandinavian Modern Breakthrough in the late nineteenth century to the Nazi celebration of Hamsun as a genius from the racially idealized North. We should bear in mind that Hamsun's cultural identification with Germany predated the rise of Nazism. As a defiant outsider seeking freedom from constrictive form in both aesthetic and social-political spheres, the early Hamsun identified lastingly with what he saw as the more youthful and authentic nation of Germany, where his early success reinforced a mutual admiration. Through the lens of his cultural-critical pessimism, Hamsun imagined Great Britain as a natural archenemy: an imperialistic, arrogant, conservative power maintaining a status quo of desiccating rationalism and weary, degenerate civilization. In 1910, Hamsun wrote that "the Anglo-Saxon has derailed *life*," a term that for him meant everything of value threatened by bourgeois modernity.[4] In defense of "life," Hamsun backed Germany's fascist revitalization project, greeting National Socialism as a force that would lead Europe "into a new age and a new world" and create the conditions for pan-Germanic cultural and racial regeneration.[5] Hamsun shared with Norwegian fascists such as Quisling and the race-hygienist Jon Alfred Mjøen the belief in a need for pure ethnic reassertion in modernity.[6]

The novelist's collaboration with the Nazis during the occupation of Norway has been analyzed in depth for many years. Key biographical studies from this century include the two-volume biography by Ingar Sletten Kolloen (2003–4), translated as *Dreamer and Dissenter*, the literary biography *Solgudens fall* by Jørgen Haugan (2006), and *Knut Hamsun: Reisen til Hitler* by Tore Rem (2014), which is organized around Hamsun's complicated meeting with Hitler in 1943.

Critical studies by Monika Žagar and Peter Sjølyst-Jackson have offered analyses of Hamsun's essays and novels in connection to issues of modernism and migration, discourses of decline and regeneration, and race and gender politics. Sjølyst-Jackson points out that the question "Was Hamsun a Nazi?" usually ends up provoking "the blinded compulsions of condemnation and apologia."[7] Much postwar critical commentary on Hamsun's literature has tended toward either ideological unveiling or aesthetic apology. The former tends to condemn Hamsun's literary work in political or moral terms by aligning it with Nazism, while the latter aims to protect the literature for apolitical appreciation. Each position has obvious problems. Suspicious ideology-critical readings have often been accused of interpretive reductionism or lack of attention to the formal features of Hamsun's texts.[8] Apologetic attempts to explain away the issue of Hamsun's political engagements or make them seem irrelevant to his literary achievements often appear deliberately ignorant of contextual pressures.[9]

In recent decades this polarization between critique and apology has somewhat lost its hold, perhaps because historical distance from World War II makes Hamsun approachable in ways less guided by a need either to condemn or to protect. Atle Kittang, the author of an influential study of Hamsun's modernism, diagnosed postwar apologetic avoidance maneuvers and reductive ideological readings alike as "defense mechanisms" that transform Hamsun from an object of ambivalence into an object of simple love or hate. In this way, suggests Kittang, interpretive myths were formed, such as the one that splits Hamsun into a bad philosopher or politician but a great writer.[10] On the other hand, Kittang's own reading of Hamsun's "novels of disillusionment" has been criticized as a form of apology that obscures ideological elements of Hamsun's literature.[11]

Despite the wealth of scholarship that confronts Hamsun's politics directly, Hamsun the modernist and Hamsun the fascist continue to occupy separate compartments. At the same time, the significance of the case of Hamsun for modernist studies remains underexplored. Hamsun's centrality to the emergence of the modernist novel in Europe has still not been recognized in the English-speaking world, while the question of how to situate him with regard to the issue of "fascist modernism" calls for further exploration.

The reason that this chapter takes the 1890s novel *Mysterier* as its focal point is that Hamsun's early modernism is often understood as irrelevant or even opposed to his later fascism. Discussions of the latter have often been remarkably narrow, confining the issue to a stock image of Nazism circa 1940, even though both European fascism and Hamsun's coalescence with it were longer and more nuanced. Against the grain of this compartmentalization, my reading of *Mysterier* and related documents reveals how Hamsun's novelistic modernism involves more than the creation of new prose forms to narrate unconscious psychological life, superseding realism and naturalism. It also has a cultural-critical and ideological significance; his famous subversion of the Scandinavian Modern Breakthrough realism and liberalism is at once aesthetic and political—but of course not simply fascist avant la lettre.

No individual Hamsun novel, viewed in isolation, can justly be called fascist literature, not even *Markens grøde*, which has sometimes been read through categories of fascist aesthetics. The Norwegian critic Jon Langdal concedes this even while chastising the "ahistorical and melancholy" literary establishment for what he regards as a scandalous choice to protect the myth of Hamsun as a mystery or enigma, rather than to analyze his connections to fascist cultural and ideological discourses.[12] *Markens grøde*, an idealistic novel about modern humanity's need to embed itself again in nature, is certainly more complicated than a reductive "Blut-und-Boden" reading would suggest. Unlike most German fascist literature, it was received enthusiastically by diverse political groups, leading to Hamsun's Nobel Prize in 1920.[13] Thomas Mann wrote that no author had ever been more deserving of the prize, and Hamsun sent the prize medal to another admirer, Joseph Goebbels, in 1943. In the Nazi reading, *Markens grøde* offered an ideology of healthy, vitalistic nature as a cure for a sick, degenerate modern culture.

Although it would seem that the Nazis might have more trouble fitting Hamsun's neurotic modernist texts into their aesthetic-ideological framework, they tended to ignore the split between the early and the later Hamsun that has become a fixture of stylistic and ideological periodization in scholarship.[14] The Nazis did not perceive Hamsun's 1890s novels through the lens of our current "modernist" label, nor did they approach them with ideological or aesthetic suspicion. Copies of *Pan* as well as *Segen der Erde* (the German title of *Markens grøde*) were even distributed to Nazi soldiers on the Eastern Front. Joseph Goebbels in particular was enamored of Hamsun as a novelist; no other author is named more frequently in his diaries, which contain extravagant praise for Hamsun's greatness and wisdom.[15] Nazi propaganda portrayed Hamsun as a Nordic alternative to "the Jewish" in both spirit and physical appearance; he was understood as an essentially "Germanic" author.[16] Even *Sult* was open to an optimistic and triumphalist reading in the Nazis' hands, rather than being read as an epitome of modernist disillusionment, urban alienation, and psycho-narration.[17] Despite this appropriation by the Nazis, it would be mistaken to claim that *Sult* or *Mysterier* somehow exemplifies National Socialist literature, even if we were somehow to expand that category to include works that weren't written in German between 1933 and 1945.[18] While obvious enough, this observation should not be a conclusion. There are other, less anachronistic ways to understand the relevance of Hamsun's early modernist moment to his later fascism.

Øystein Rottem, borrowing a phrase from Hamsun's essay on August Strindberg, views the term "reactionary radical" as central to an understanding of Hamsun's early period.[19] This perspective arises through the narrative form and thematic structure of *Mysterier*, a convoluted and hallucinatory "anti-novel" from 1892, which has been a key text in discussions of Hamsun's literary modernism.[20] *Mysterier* carnivalizes and overturns the aesthetic and ideological program of the Modern Breakthrough, the preceding period of progressive liberalism, realism, and naturalism in Scandinavian literature. The fragmented form of *Mysterier* subverts the logic of realist narrative, replacing ratiocination and clarification with indeterminacy and epiphany. The antihero of *Mysterier*, Johan Nagel, bitterly and self-consciously opposes the rationalist Doctor in the small town he has entered as a stranger.

The reactionary-radical discourse in which Hamsun's prose modernism emerges shows how his fascist sympathies developed from sociopolitical values and viewpoints traceable to the 1890s. To recognize this is not to argue that Hamsun's modernism was fascist (or "proto-fascist") according to a predetermined teleology. Elsewhere, I have criticized what can be called the "backshadowing" approach to Hamsun—a retrospective and teleological reading of the connection between literature and fascism, which gives explanatory weight to the end of Hamsun's story.[21] Instead, I argue for an approach that emphasizes the contingency of Hamsun's gradual coalescence with fascism, which was, after all, a nascent phenomenon during much of his authorship. But what has too often been neglected in debates about Hamsun's literature and politics is that fascist ideology in Europe emerged in parallel to Hamsun's early work, as a modern (and even modernist) ideology drawing on strands of the intellectual revolts against materialism, positivism, bourgeois society, and liberal democracy at the fin de siècle. Viewing Hamsun's narrative of coalescence with fascism non-teleologically, without deterministic hindsight constructions, involves attention to both the reactionary-radical content and the anti-realist form of his early modernism.

REACTIONARY RADICALISM AND PSYCHOLOGICAL LITERATURE

In the thirteenth chapter of *Mysterier*, the antihero Johan Nagel hosts a drinking party for the men of the small Norwegian town where he has recently arrived unexpectedly, only to amuse and baffle the townspeople with his inscrutable behavior, stories, and opinions. Before the carousing starts, Doctor Stenersen, who is by now familiar with Nagel's shenanigans, says to him, "Jeg for min part blir ikke forskrekket over nogen ting fra Dem" (I won't be astounded by anything coming from you). Nagel replies with comical understatement, "Jeg er stundom litt slem til å motsi . . . og iaften er jeg særlig opsat derpå" (Occasionally I have an inclination to contradict, and this evening I'm particularly bent on doing so).[22] By the end of the evening, Nagel has denounced Tolstoy, altruism, Ibsen, and reigning conceptions of scientific and social progress, many of which formed a basis for the Modern Breakthrough period of critical realism and naturalism. Carousing and drunkenness ensue, the Doctor's pince-nez is crushed, and only a mood of intoxicated disintegration prevails, as it is with the novel as a whole.

Commentators have understood *Mysterier* in terms of early Hamsun's infatuation with the unknowable depths of the individual human psyche, often aligning it with later psychological novels in the Anglo-American modernist canon, or with the works of Dostoyevsky.[23] Johan Nagel is an eccentric outsider who disrupts the ordinary life of a small town. Part dandy, part nature-mystic, he possesses the flair of counternormative subversion but also the torment of role-consciousness and self-contempt. Nagel can also be seen as a pantheistic mystic seeking authenticity in harmony with nature, outside of an alienating modern civilization and social life. The novel presents the natural landscape as the site of mystical disintegration of the normal boundaries of the self, a place for the "oceanic feeling" Freud located in religious experience or other kinds of de-individualizing moments.

In the course of *Mysterier*, Nagel enters several unusual and unstable relationships with the townspeople, such as his pathologically humble alter-ego Minutten and his beloved femme fatale Dagny. My reading of the novel focuses on the relationship between Nagel and Doctor Stenersen, the freethinking liberal rationalist, who can be connected to Hamsun's anti-positivist figuration of the Doctor in the lecture "Psykologisk Literatur." Doctor Stenersen functions in the character design of *Mysterier* as the primary representative of what Nagel and Hamsun consider the nihilistic falsity and dogmatic power of bourgeois and scientific rationality.[24]

By spotlighting this antagonism between Nagel and Doctor Stenersen and linking it to the early Hamsun's anti-realism, I argue that *Mysterier* carnivalizes the liberalism and rationalism of the Doctor figure and the Modern Breakthrough. Going against the grain of Hamsun's own well-known attack on character typology, I describe Nagel as an instance of the character type Michael André Bernstein has called the "abject hero."[25] Through this carnivalizing dialogue, the novel advances ideological positions that are also found in Hamsun's contemporary statements, which I will examine first in the article "Lidt om Strindberg" (A Bit About Strindberg) and then in the lecture "Psykologisk Literatur."

The early Hamsun's combination of reactionary and radical elements is a crucial feature of the cultural criticism underlying his literary modernism. Hamsun's cultural pessimism and preference for the primitive or uncivilized, and also his interest in the unconscious mind, were adapted from the nineteenth-century writers who were his biggest influences: Dostoyevsky, Schopenhauer, Strindberg, and Nietzsche. Of these, Strindberg was the one Hamsun actually wrote about and probably the one he read the most. For the early Hamsun, Strindberg represented a reactionary *and* anarchistic challenge to late Victorian bourgeois culture, with its social conformism, its idolization of scientific progress and rationality, and its degenerate over-civilization.

Hamsun first described Strindberg as "reactionary and radical" in 1888 during a lecture series in Minnesota.[26] In the 1894 article "Lidt om Strindberg," Hamsun begins by praising the multiplicity and idiosyncrasy of Strindberg's interests. He admires "Nervøsiteten,

Ustadigheten i denne Bevægelse" (the nerves, the unsteadiness in this movement) and praises the attitude of "jublende Raseri" (joyous Rage) with which Strindberg approaches all sorts of artistic, scientific, and religious problems.[27] In all of Strindberg's various objects of interest, the constant has been a roving dissatisfaction with all that exists, and "Lyst til at slaa altsammen ned og . . . Kræfter til at forsøge det" (desire to knock down everything and . . . the power to attempt it).[28] This spirit of anarchistic individualism leads to no movement or school, writes Hamsun; it only awakens the admiration of a few inconsistency-loving individual followers.

Hamsun's essay identifies three stages in Strindberg's development, from a devout pietist to an aesthetic idealist to a "reaktionære Rebel" (reactionary rebel). An early pietistic upbringing marked Strindberg's entire intellectual life with "den religiøse Fanatismes Hektik" (the fever of religious fanaticism).[29] After he lost his religious faith, he turned to what Hamsun calls a "Dyrkelsen af den rene Harmoni" (worship of pure harmony), or aesthetic idealism as surrogate religiosity. This was a failure that eventually caused the reactionary rebel to awaken in Strindberg, along with a harsh rejection of beauty and art as useless idols. In the newly anti-aesthetic phase, Strindberg was attracted to positivist science—what Hamsun calls "Tidens totale Magt, den moderne Gud" (the total power of our times, the modern God)—but Strindberg eventually found this just as useless as art.[30]

Hamsun admiringly summarizes Strindberg's view of scientific research as criminally useless. Economic and social resources are diverted to scholarly research—in his sarcastic examples, nailing insects and naming stars, or discovering a comma in an old manuscript—while people are starving. Science is a vampire, and in view of the supposed improvements it has brought modern society, Hamsun asks whether it wouldn't be better to have kept one's good sight than to have invented optical lenses. In other words, he views modern technology and scientific research as insufficient compensations for a decadent loss of natural health and vigor. Beyond doubting whether the great inventions of modern science and industry have improved life, Hamsun derides modern progress as the destruction of individual and social health. Agreeing with Strindberg's cultural-critical observations, Hamsun demonizes both science and literature as criminal luxuries that symptomatize "et galt Udviklingsspor" (a mad path of development) to the modern condition of *overkultur.*[31]

The phrase "reactionary radical" is used in Hamsun's article as a label for the ideological position that opposes modernity's progress narratives and the hegemony of positivist science in bourgeois culture, in favor of an imaginary return to nature and wild animality. He exclaims, "Har Udviklingen ført Menneskeheden ind i Elendighed, skal man paa Stand gøre Tilbagetoget ind i det Uudviklede!" (If development has led humanity into misery, then one must instantly retreat into the undeveloped!).[32] Strindberg possesses "Kulturfiendtlighed i Blodet" (animosity toward culture in his blood); he is "en vild Vekst" (a wild growth) whose roots are searching for soil, who calls himself "et Dyr, der længter mod Skogen" (an animal, longing for the forest).[33] In comments like these, Hamsun's own counter-Enlightenment position appears more clearly: "Mennesket har efter Strindbergs Aar efter Aar gentagne Lære udviklet sig bort fra Naturen og derved løsgjort sig fra det første Grundvilkaar for en organisk Tilværelse" (In the doctrine Strindberg has repeated year after year, humans have developed away from Nature and in so doing have severed themselves from the only basic condition of an organic existence).[34] Strindberg desires to become a wild creature again, and Hamsun embraces this position as "tyk, veritabel Reaktion" (thick, veritable reaction)—the only real cure for modernity's degenerate individuals.[35] This is also, unsurprisingly, a return to patriarchy; by embracing the reactionary and turning back to nature, "vilde man ogsaa kunne rette paa dette kvindelige Herskervæsen, der sammen med al Unatur forøvrigt gør Livet til en Absurditet" (one could also correct the dominance of the feminine, which along with all else that is unnatural makes life an absurdity).[36]

Seduced by pseudo-progress, *kulturmenneske* (civilized man) has lost the joy and health of animal immediacy and has failed to see that human consciousness is inevitably pain.[37] Hamsun's appropriation of Strindberg's reactionary-radical critique of *overkultur* includes a Schopenhauerian recognition of consciousness as misery: "Alle Folk har opfundet Bedøvningsmidler, forat slukke sin Bevidsthed; Asien sover, men Europa drikker Morfin. Ti med Bevidsthed opstaar Smærte" (All peoples have invented anesthetics, in order to extinguish consciousness; Asia sleeps, while Europe drinks morphine. For with consciousness arises pain).[38] Strindberg is extreme enough, writes Hamsun, "at foretrække (ialfald teoretisk) det vilde, ubevidste, dyriske Liv fremfor det nuværende" (to prefer [at least theoretically] wild, unconscious, animal life over the modern sort).[39] The tragic-pessimistic insight into the inevitable pain of consciousness motivates Hamsun's elevation of *unconscious* life as a way backward/forward from modern, degenerate *overkultur* toward a more vital and primitive condition. Here we see how a key term in Hamsun's turn to the psychological novel—*det ubevidste* (the unconscious)—is closely tied to his reactionary-radical critique of modernity.[40]

The Strindberg article displays Hamsun's reactionary radicalism as a neo-romantic and anarchistic revolt against liberal modernity's pseudo-progress and against the God-like power of positivism in bourgeois culture. In *Mysterier*, many of Nagel's speeches and actions form a brutal defense of the mysteriousness of nature and the human psyche—of what he calls "livets blinde kræfter" (the blind forces of life)—against the Doctor's rationalizing and disenchanting modernity. In the lecture "Psykologisk Literatur," from 1891, but first published in 1960, Hamsun explicitly states that the Doctor in his fiction represents the contemporary epistemological and social attitudes that he finds so limited. Here, he associates doctors not only with positivism but also with public power and dogma.

> Derfor har jeg gærne med en Doktor i min Digtning, som skal repræsentere Videnskaben, og Doktorerne, disse Folk, der som Stand betragtet er næst Teologerne de mest dogmatiske Menneske i Samfundet, Doktorerne staar der Respekt af. Doktorerne i vor Literatur er kloge Hjærner og humane Hjærter, de har Viden om alt muligt, de er liberale om en Hals og er aldeles fortræffelige Fritænkere. Bedre Repræsentanter for Videnskaben end slige Doktorer, kan en Literatur aldrig faa.[41]
>
> (That's why I like to include a doctor in my fiction, who is supposed to represent science, and doctors, these people who are as a profession the most dogmatic members of society other than theologians—there's respect for doctors. The doctors in our literature are wise minds and humane hearts, they have knowledge about everything; they're liberal to a fault and wholly excellent freethinkers. A literature could hardly have better representatives for science.)

Although Hamsun blames Scandinavian literary realism for portraying doctors too respectfully, this need not be taken as an accurate view of Modern Breakthrough literature, least of all in the drama of Ibsen. Nonetheless, in this lecture, as in "Fra det Ubevidste Sjæleliv" (From the Unconscious Life of the Mind), Hamsun rebels against socially critical realism in favor of a psychologically subtler and deeper subjectivist alternative. His figure of the doctor unites progressive politics with the literary and scientific positions that appear narrow and demoralizing from an irrationalist or neo-romantic point of view. Accordingly, Doctor Stenersen in *Mysterier* represents everything targeted by Hamsun's reactionary-radical revolt against the Modern Breakthrough.

As a contemporary statement of Hamsun's novelistic aims, "Psykologisk Literatur" continues to cast light on *Mysterier.* Hamsun rejects realist characterization in favor of a view into the inner "electricity" and "nervousness" of the modern individual.[42] The tempo of modern life, he claims, has made us more nervous and complicated than people in Shakespeare's time; yet the typological and shallow character psychology of our literature has not kept pace. Here, Hamsun again shows his similarity to Strindberg, echoing the latter's attack on nineteenth-century dramatic characterization in the preface to *Miss Julie.* Both Hamsun and Strindberg were relying on a broader cultural discourse that linked nervous exhaustion and the modern metropolis, and they display a positive appraisal of "nervousness" whose history in modernist aesthetics goes back at least to Baudelaire.[43]

Hamsun's rather scandalous criticism of Shakespeare's character psychology is a typically attention-grabbing and iconoclastic gesture. His repeated point is that "det modne, nervøse, forfinede Menneske er bleven et overmaade indviklet Væv af Sammensætninger . . . et Væsen, som ikke paa nogen Maade kan gaa op i en Sum eller udtrykkes i en eller to særskilte Egenskabsbetegnelser" (the mature, nervous, refined person has become an extremely intricate web of contradictions . . . a being who can in no way be summed up or expressed in one or two distinct character descriptions).[44] As a response to the intricate electricity of the modern soul, Hamsun calls for a literature that focuses primarily on hidden interiority. This anti-typological character psychology emerges in a confrontational differentiation from realism that is also somewhat infantile: "Jeg vil udstyre mine Mennesker som jeg føler Dem, og ikke som Positivismen byder og befaler" (I will make up my characters as I feel them, not as positivism commands and orders).[45] Rejecting the alliance of literature with shallow positivistic science—"Tidens eneste totale Magt" (the only total power of our time)—Hamsun claims that science cannot explain the singular and unpredictable psychological phenomena that are most worthy of attention.[46]

The lecture's plea for a superior "moderne Sjælemaleri" (modern soul-painting) rejects literary realism for its inability to capture the unseen life of the mind.[47] The anti-positivism of "Psykologisk

Literatur" relegates visible facts to the superficial minds of merchants and capitalists or, as he suggests at one point, the mercantile aspect of our being ("mit merchantile Væsen").[48] Hamsun revolts against the doctrinaire superficiality of the positivist era, whose rationalism is condensed in the observing eye of the Doctor, and he defends the "Omraader i vort Væsen, som levnes uberørte af et Faktum" (areas of our being that are left untouched by a fact).[49] In doing so, he reveals his fixation on what Robert Musil later called "the non-ratioid"—"the area of the dominance of the exceptions over the rule" and the region where "facts do not submit, laws are sieves, events do not repeat themselves but are infinitely variable and individual."[50] Hamsun's modernist narrative form is greatly influenced by this frantic obsession with the non-ratioid. His hostility to the Doctor's rationalist vision disrupts his narrative structures in an innovative departure from novelistic realism. In these ways, Hamsun is a major figure in the aesthetic reorientation of modernist narrative toward interiority and subjectivity.

Mysterier has been compellingly read as an "anti-novel" that subverts the logical and generic expectations of realist fiction.[51] While the novel's first several chapters suggest a murder plot, it ends with many gaps, and any initial detective story is displaced by something much more hallucinatory and vague. Martin Humpál argues that the gaps in *Mysterier* function as indeterminacies, what the phenomenological critic Roman Ingarden called *Unbestimmtheitsstellen* (sites of indeterminacy).[52] In most realist fiction, such indeterminacies exist only temporarily; the inexplicable exists only to be explained in an unambiguous account of events as the narrative reaches closure. In Hamsun's novel, indeterminacies remain unresolvable and unknowable, which constitutes a conscious and radical rejection of a major narrative code of nineteenth-century realism.[53]

As an example, consider what the reader faces in the tiny final chapter of *Mysterier*. Dagny and Martha, Nagel's two love interests, are walking home from a party together a year after the stranger's arrival. Dagny says to Martha, "Jeg går og tænker på alt det som blev talt om Nagel iaften. Det var meget som var nyt for mig" (I've been thinking of all the things that were said about Nagel this evening . . . much of it was new to me).[54] Before the reader can even pause to wonder what this new information might be, the next mystery appears. Dagny continues, "Nagel sa til mig allerede ifjor sommer at Minutten vilde komme til å ende galt. Jeg forstår ikke hvorledes han alt hadde set det da. Han sa det længe, længe før du fortalte mig hvad Minutten hadde gjort mot dig" (Nagel told me last summer that Miniman would come to a bad end. I can't figure out how he'd seen it already then. He said it long, long before you told me what Miniman had done to you).[55] These lines strongly suggest a sexual assault, although the novel doesn't include any direct account of what Nagel said to Dagny, or what Miniman did to Martha. Readers may draw their own conclusions; my point is that the final pages of the novel introduce new structured absences of information, rather than accounting for indeterminacies. This would probably have been very strange to readers in 1892, although we can now recognize it as a modernist narrative strategy.

Such plot indeterminacies in *Mysterier* function to disparage realist models of clarification and to promote Nagel's nervous powers of intuition—in this case, his nonempirical conviction that Miniman had an evil nature of some sort.[56] Nagel can be seen as a neo-romantic Sherlock Holmes; he renounces science and empirical fact for an alternative way of knowing that is the privilege of the mystical mind.[57] In the nineteenth century, detective narratives operated according to the era's trust in instrumental reason and the gradual explanatory progress of science.[58] Hamsun's *Mysterier* rejects such a belief in the explicability of human behavior by frustrating the reader's expectations of ratiocinative narrative. Hamsun's inversion of the realist novel becomes especially startling in the visionary and epiphanic eighth chapter of *Mysterier*, called "White Nights" ("Lyse Nætter").

FOREST EPIPHANY AND NARRATIVE DISINTEGRATION

In *Downcast Eyes*, Martin Jay notes "the tendency of the visionary tradition to posit a higher sight of the seer, who is able to discern a truth denied to normal vision. Here the so-called third eye of the soul is invoked to compensate for the imperfections of the two physical eyes. Often physical blindness is given sacred significance."[59] Hamsun's anti-rationalist use of blindness is a secular continuation of this tendency among visionaries. In one of the many eerily beautiful incidents of fantasy, dream, or hallucination in *Mysterier*, Nagel recounts a luminous and violent fairy tale to his love interest Dagny as they walk through the forest on a long Norwegian summer night. This story-within-a-novel alternates between light and dark and contains many motifs of vision and loss of sight.

The chapter begins during the white night of a Nordic summer. After a quick glimpse of the town as "et underlig, grenet kjæmpeinsekt, et fabeldyr som hadde kastet sig flat på buken og strakt armer og horn og føletråder ut i alle retninger" (a weird, splayed giant insect, a fabulous creature that had thrown itself flat on its belly, extending arms and horns and feelers in all directions), the narrative turns to Nagel smoking a cigar and walking with Dagny in a mood of calm satisfaction.[60] Nagel recounts a fairy-tale experience that occurred eight years earlier, in 1883, somewhere outside Norway. He says he was reading by lamplight during a pitch-black night. Suddenly he feels someone's breath and hears a voice whispering for him to come. Out of nowhere appears "en liten blek mand med rødt skæg og et tørt, stivt hår" (a pale little man with a red beard and dry, stiff, bristly hair).[61] Nagel follows the little man out into the darkness but loses track of him and decides to wander alone into the forest, where dewy branches and leaves start to touch his face. Tired and wet from the dew, he lights another cigar and wanders aimlessly, now with the little man somewhere nearby, breathing on him constantly. A tower clock strikes midnight, and Nagel sees the little man in front of him, with two front teeth missing, glowing brilliantly: "han lyste av et forunderlig lys som syntes å være bak ham, å stråle ut fra hans ryg og gjøre ham gjennemsigtig" (he shone with a strange light that seemed to be behind him, radiating from his back and making him transparent).[62] The sight astonishes Nagel and he involuntarily turns away, only to look back and find that the man has disappeared.

The fairy tale continues as Nagel approaches an octagonal tower, in the first vault of which he meets the little man again, who stares at him laughing, with eyes full of the many horrible things he has seen. Nagel turns to see a young woman enter, with red hair and black eyes. Taking a wildly glowing lantern from the little man, she walks toward Nagel and asks him to forgive her father, who is sick and mad. She leads him up into a second vault, where they can still hear "den vanskapte gale" (the deformed madman).[63] The second vault is utterly dark. Nagel locates the bed and takes off his clothes as requested by the young woman, who then says goodnight and leaves, despite his protests.

At this point in Nagel's tale, Dagny blushes, her breasts heave, her nostrils quiver; she asks if the maiden left. After a seductive pause, Nagel continues, saying that his story now becomes "en rosenrød erindring" (a rose-colored reminiscence).[64] Strange shifts of light and darkness continue, as Nagel tells Dagny to imagine a white night, yet immediately adds, "Jeg var alene, mørket omkring mig var tungt og tykt som fløiel" (I was alone; the darkness around me was thick and heavy, like velvet).[65] All of a sudden the vault fills up with a rustle of noise. He waits expectantly until he experiences something that he says still intoxicates him with "en sælsom, overnaturlig nydelse" (a mysterious, supernatural pleasure): "en strøm av bitte små blændende væsener bryter pludselig ned til mig; de er aldeles hvite, det er engler, myriader av småengler, som strømmer ned fra oven som en skrå mur av lys" (a stream of tiny little dazzling creatures suddenly descends upon me; they are perfectly white, angels, myriads of little angels streaming down from on high like an oblique wall of light).[66] Waves of tiny singing angels fill the vault, all of them naked and white; some of them sit on Nagel's hand, and he notices that they are blind. He captures more and more handfuls of angels, noticing that all of them are blind; "hele tårnet var fuldt av blinde engler som sang" (the whole tower was full of blind angels singing).[67] When the city clock strikes one again, the angels stop singing and fly away in a stream of light, the last ones turning back to look at Nagel, even though they are blind. Darkness ensues. Nagel later discovers that the young woman with red hair is also blind. When he returns to the forest after this magical night to look for her, he finds her crushed and dead outside the tower, with the mad father pacing around wailing, with a horrifying gaze that sends Nagel running back to the town.

This incident is one of the most evocative in the novel, and its resistance to simple decoding is part of its enthralling effect on both Dagny and the reader. What I find important here is the convergence of erotic and spiritual epiphany in the forest, a natural landscape that functions throughout the novel as an alternative to the town's social space of rationality and conformist superficiality. While the Doctor is strongly associated with the town and the faults of the modern era in his scientific approach to all phenomena, the anti-ocularcentric imagery and opacity of this dark tale defy his worldview. Like the angels, the young woman is blind; they are denizens of a mysterious, nonvisual realm of fantasy that is resistant to the Doctor's disenchanting explanations. The intoxications of the fairy tale are thus part of Hamsun's poetics of the irrational, which concerns not only the inconsistent and murky psyche but also the unfathomable forest landscape. This forest is a subjective, even narcissistic, dream of a landscape, containing all the torments and terrors of Nagel's mind, but it is also the volatile dream of an alternative to the "total power" of the positivist doctor.

In *Forests: The Shadow of Civilization*, Robert Pogue Harrison writes that "forests represent an outlying realm of opacity which has allowed [Western] civilization to estrange itself, enchant itself, terrify itself, ironize itself, in short to project into the forest's shadows its secret and innermost anxieties."[68] The Hamsunian forest, as Steinar Gimnes explains, is romantic rather than rationalistic; it is opposed to the disenchanting Enlightenment "forest ideology," which stripped the forest of all symbolism, reducing it to a material and utilitarian object.[69] The terror and enchantment of Nagel's story of the blind girl in the tower are palpable enough. The tale's opacity to the positivist eye is also inscribed in its very symbolic texture, with its emphasis on distortions of and alternatives to normal vision. The forest itself is what Harrison calls "an obstacle to visibility . . . an obstacle to human knowledge and science."[70] In terms of Hamsun's narrative structure, "White Nights" ruptures the prosaic world of the novel—the social life depicted in *Mysterier* and the nineteenth-century genre itself—with a moment of sacred terror and awe.

IN THE MIND OF THE ABJECT HERO

While "White Nights" shows Nagel as a storyteller within the world of the novel, another main context of his speech is dialogic. Nagel's role in the town's conversation structure also reveals his reactionary-radical subversion of modern culture. I view Nagel as an instance of the "abject hero," a character type that Michael André Bernstein has described in *Bitter Carnival.* Bernstein traces the development of the abject hero from its origins in the figure of the fool or slave in classical Saturnalian dialogue, through its emergence in Diderot's *Le Neveu de Rameau*, and into the nineteenth and twentieth centuries in two writers with whom Hamsun has much in common: Dostoyevsky and Celine. Saturnalian dialogue involves "a master and his slave, a monarch and his fool, a philosopher and a madman," and by convention it contains a reversal in which the fool appears wiser than the powerful figure who upholds the reigning norms or cherished truths of the day.[71] The wise fool, or licensed fool, is the conventional agent of Saturnalian reversal, pitted against a king or another powerful and influential figure. In general, notes Bernstein, this figure functions as "a promising vehicle for a satiric challenge to an era's dominant values."[72] The momentary collapse of hierarchy in the Saturnalian dialogue is a form of the Bakhtinian carnivalesque, a liberating destabilization of normally functioning distinctions.

The abject hero is a version of the fool embittered by resentment and tormented by self-consciousness about the prescripted role he is playing in the dialogic confrontation. Like the fool or charlatan in the Saturnalian dialogue, the abject hero carnivalizes the dominant norms and values of the era, its official wisdom, but he is tormented by his awareness of performing a role provided by a conventional model. Crucially, Bernstein's conception of abjection relies on a context of dialogue, and it is "always governed by the mapping of prior literary and cultural models." Abjection arises "in conversation with another, with a voice, whether internal or external, whose oppressive confidence arises through its articulation of the normative values of society as a whole."[73] Nagel's mind, as the reader experiences its texture through the novel's free indirect discourse and extended thought quotations, contains these other voices of normative wisdom—those of Modern Breakthrough liberalism.

In the novel's first extended thought quotation, Nagel imagines himself lecturing an audience of "gentleman and ladies." Here readers witness the abject hero in dialogue with the internalized voice of his opponent—the freethinking liberal that Doctor Stenersen eventually comes to embody. In Nagel's imagination (or memory) the voice of a bluestocking takes offense at his disparaging remarks about the enlightened and progressive "great men" of the nineteenth century (the ones whose wisdom and worldviews Hamsun attacked as superficial in his own speeches). Nagel responds, "Min frue, du storeste Gud hvor det lyder halvdannet, tarvelig åndelig dannet, det De der sa. Undskyld forresten at jeg taler så direkte; men hvis De var en mand og ikke en kvinde så vilde jeg gjøre min salighets ed på at de var venstremand" (Great God, madam, how half-educated what you said just now sounds to me, how intellectually shabby. I'm sorry to speak so plainly, but if you were a man instead of a woman, I would say you were a liberal).[74] Nagel's response continues, first with the typically Hamsunian statement of his trust in "mit blods subjektive logik" (my blood's subjective logic) and then with the claim that to educate the powerful, "de utvalgte og overlegne, herremenneskene, de store, Kaifas, Pilatus og keiseren" (the chosen few, the masters of life, the great ones, Caiaphas, Pilate, and the emperor), is more important than democratic progress or social improvement.[75] The most important thing for Nagel is a victory of "åndelig grundværdi" (fundamental spiritual value) and of "den høie mand, de høie mænd, herrerne, verdensåndene tilhest" (the superior man, the superior men, the masters, universal spirits on horseback).[76] The diatribe ends with Nagel's opinion that there is something greater than "creating exchange value." In a frequently quoted passage, Nagel exclaims internally: "*mit* blods røst sier at *den* er størst som har tilført tilværelsen mest grundværdi, mest positiv profit. Den store terrorist er størst" (the voice of *my* blood says that *he* is the greatest who has contributed most fundamental value, most positive profit, to human existence. The greatest one is the great terrorist).[77] Here we see a notion of "positive profit" opposed to the quantitative exchange value of capitalist modernity. Nagel's call for the great terrorist expresses a desire for an alternative to the disparaged "great men" of the Victorian era, such as Gladstone or Tolstoy. It would certainly be possible to argue that this passage reveals Hamsun's proto-fascist cultivation of the authoritarian leader. However, instead of taking this moment alone as a foreshadowing instance of the author's eventual politics, I would like to observe the dialogic situation within the novel itself.

As abject hero, Nagel is in dialogue with the voice of progressive liberal culture, the freethinking doctor. Nagel's abjection entails a feeling of oppression or demoralization by a representative of social normativity and bourgeois reasonableness. In keeping with the role-consciousness of the abject hero, Nagel is also frequently aware of his performance as a licensed fool in the court of Doctor Stenersen. A scene that exemplifies both Nagel's demoralization and his role-consciousness is the Doctor's party with the townspeople in chapter 7. Here, Nagel initially refuses to explain an offhand comment that Gladstone, a prominent British Liberal of the day, was a bigot. When the Doctor's wife says it would be amusing to hear him explain, Nagel responds, "If it will amuse you all, that's quite another matter," and the narrator comments: "Vilde han ved denne bemærkning gjøre en liten jeip til sig selv og sin rolle? Han fortrak munden litt" (Did he intend, by this remark, to sneer at himself and the part he was playing? His lips curled slightly).[78] This mocking smile signals resentment for having to perform to the applause of the "kjøtæterne" (carnivores), as Nagel later refers to his liberal audience with contempt.[79]

Nagel's subsequent explanation of his comment about Gladstone could be taken right out of *Notes from Underground*, a key text of abject heroism. It even contains the same example of the irrational will to deny that two plus two equals four. Nagel's denial of this fact is not literal but is part of an effort to resist "denne rettens professionist" (this professional of rightness).[80] His *blood* responds to this man, whose "moral er av sundeste og varigste slag, han arbeider for kristendommen, for humanismen og for civilisation" (morality is of the healthiest and most enduring kind . . . working for humanism and civilization), with a feeling of vague injury and of being trivialized.[81] Doctor Stenersen, frustrated by Nagel's apparently foolish underground discourse, shouts, "Jeg har Gud strafe mig aldrig hørt maken til nonsense! . . . Oprører det Dem at Gladstone altid har ret?" (I'll be damned, but I never heard such nonsense in my whole life! Does it offend you that Gladstone is always right?)[82] In response, Nagel smiles a smile of "sagtmodighet eller . . . affectation" ("meekness or affectation")—the narrator cannot tell. Then he says, "Det oprører mig ikke, det demoraliserer mig heller" (It does not offend me, rather it demoralizes me).[83]

Nagel's sneer at his own performance and his affectation in response to the Doctor reveal yet another feature of the abject hero: an obsessive theatricality.[84] Hamsun in *Mysterier* is preoccupied with theatricality and falsity, both voluntary and involuntary. Consider, for example, Nagel's captivating violin performance at the bazaar, which he afterward passes off as false and inauthentic, or the darkly comic scene of Nagel's unwittingly histrionic pseudo-suicide. Nagel is obsessively aware of potential falsity in social interaction, although he tries to persuade himself that he is adept at exploiting this potential. His awareness of deception is also present in introspection, in his internal masking and the groundlessness of his psyche and motivations. Although Nagel fantasizes immersion in nature as a liberation from the theatricality that accompanies self-consciousness and self-representation, and he even tries to convince Martha to marry him by depicting such an Edenic paradise, he is tortured by the recognition that this dream is also a sham.

Rather than providing a stable foundation that would rescue the volatile self, nature itself is theatricalized in *Mysteries*. In one of the novel's final thought quotations, Nagel fancies that he experiences mystical knowledge of "den uendelige sammenhæng i tingene" (the infinite interconnectedness of all things), a vision "tilbunds i alt" (to the bottom of everything).[85] However, this illumination is immediately undercut by his recognition that everything is a farce, "alt hvad jeg ser og hører og fornemmer er bedrag, ja selve himlens blå er ozon, gift, snikgift" (everything I see and hear and perceive is a fraud, even the blue of the sky is ozone, poison, insidious poison).[86] Nagel's train of thought moves with startling haste from a mystical recognition of the ground of all things to the realization that this ground itself is a mask or curtain to be pulled away. Nature then appears to him as the ultimate deceptive facade. The only option left after this radical skepticism is an aestheticist delight in falsity, as Nagel dreams of a quiet journey in his sailboat of aromatic wood through this "blå, bedragersk ozon" (fraudulent blue ozone).[87] In this voluntary preference for fantasy or the fictional, Øystein Rottem identifies a Nietzschean moment of aesthetic redemption or justification of inauthentic existence: "opp mot tilværelsens løgnaktighet og bedrag setter nemlig Nagel bevisst sine egne 'løgner': fiksjonens falskmyntneri, kunstens illusjoner" (against the falsity and deception of existence, Nagel consciously sets up his own "lies": the false currency of fiction, the illusions of art).[88]

HAMSUN AND THE QUESTION OF FASCIST MODERNISM

As an abject hero, Nagel gives voice to Hamsun's modernist antirationalism: the worship of the chosen few, the preference for the inexplicable and dark forces of nature, the subjective logic or whisper of the blood, the irrelevance of a truth/lie distinction, and the preference for "fundamental value" above quantitative exchange value. In his dialogue with the representatives of bourgeois modernity, Nagel subverts the utilitarian and progressive social goals of nineteenth-century liberalism. Nagel has much in common with many other figures of modernist literature who reject what Lionel Trilling, in "The Fate of Pleasure," called the "specious goods of pleasure" in bourgeois society, with its shallow consolations and deluded unawareness of the psychological self-laceration that, in Hamsun, is the distinction of a superior individual.[89] In opposition to the superficial and false culture, Nagel offers the sensuous and primitive brutality of Dionysian suffering. Yet he too is fraudulent—a "charlatan" and liar from the first moment the reader meets him.

The rhetoric of Saturnalian reversal in *Mysterier* pressures the reader to identify at least intellectually with the abject hero, the figure of subversion and depth, rather than with his opponent, the shallow voice of prosaic rationality. Bernstein observes a general tendency in the Saturnalian confrontation: "we find ourselves expected to have an identificatory sympathy with whichever voice claims to embody anarchy and rebellion, the voice that strives to topple normative or prudential reasoning."[90] But despite this pressure, our knowledge of the reactionary-radical politics of Hamsun's fiction limits our sympathy. Even in the narrative outcome of Hamsun's novel, the Saturnalian reversal is not a solution to the crisis it enacts in bourgeois culture. The protest ends with the abject hero's intoxicated and suicidal disintegration in the grip of the very "blind forces of nature" whose power he extolled. The Norwegian townspeople are left to contemplate the strange combination of therapy and terror produced by his destabilizing transgressions.

Hamsun's carnivalization of Modern Breakthrough realism in *Mysterier* rigidifies over the following decades into a reactionary-radical position that coalesces with fascism, the only major political ideology to emerge out of Europe's fin-de-siècle crisis of culture. Hamsun's ideological itinerary takes him to a position of fundamental agreement with National Socialist views of society and politics, modernity, democracy, and race.[91] As I have argued here, *Mysterier* is quite revealing for understanding the author's later politics. To recognize this connection does not entail any historical claim of inevitability or aesthetic claim that Hamsun's modernist works express some supposedly fascist or Nazi style. While *Mysterier* is not simply "fascist modernism," we can nonetheless discern the important connections between Hamsun's literary modernism and his fascism.

Hamsun's reactionary-radical breakthrough is the first moment in Norwegian literary history when aesthetic advance is tied to an anti-progressive sociopolitical position. In this way, the early Hamsun presents an original configuration of literary politics in Norway that, while not *necessitating* his later turn to fascism, certainly makes it more understandable and not enigmatic. A key part of European modernism was just this decoupling of literature and aesthetics from idealistic ethics and politics of any stripe.[92] As Toril Moi has explained in connection to Ibsen, the aesthetic idealist demand for an ethically satisfying or uplifting authorial position was reflected in the Nobel Prize committee's original criteria for the literature award.[93] The case of Hamsun can be understood as an episode in modernism's post-idealist aesthetic development—an extreme case that emerges out of this process of decoupling. His career as a whole represents a brilliant and unsettling answer to the question of how far the modernist author's political positions can be taken toward the reactionary-radical, the inhumane, the willfully contrarian. Today we sometimes still witness the non-modernist desire for great writers or artists to guide, uplift, and equip us with weighty normative ideals to live by. But just as modernism often rejects traditional notions of beauty, harmony, and coherence, it also disposes with any conception of the great author as a purveyor of ethical ideals. The case of Hamsun should be seen not as an exception to a more satisfying or reassuring modernist culture but rather as the working-out of one of modernism's key internal logics.

Hamsun's modernist text expresses a deeply troubled literary and aesthetic response to the conditions of modernity, fantasizing alternatives located in primitive, unconscious, or intoxicated experience. In the attitudes communicated by its abject hero as well as its anti-realist narrative form, *Mysterier* displays key aspects of early fascist ideology, particularly its negations—its rejection of liberalism and parliamentary democracy (which was first instituted in Norway in 1884), its anti-bourgeois and romantic anti-capitalist stances, and its anti-positivism and irrationalism. Later in his career, Hamsun's nonfictional texts build on this ideological foundation to express fascism's bellicose and youth-obsessed discourse—as well as its preoccupation with Europe's degeneration and ethnic rebirth, as studies of Hamsun by Monika Žagar, Tore Rem, and Jørgen Haugan have all shown.[94] Though it was not a foregone conclusion, Hamsun's fin-de-siècle faith in the blood's subjective logic later developed into a revolutionary devotion to pan-Germanic revitalization.

CHAPTER 3

Wild Spring

Åsmund Sveen's Homoerotic Vitalism and Nazi Collaboration

In *The Queer Art of Failure*, Jack Halberstam remarks, "It is odd that we want to continue to connect gay sex, wherever we may find it, to political radicalism," and later adds, "We have to be prepared to be unsettled by the politically problematic connections history throws our way."[1] We should bear this in mind as we approach a remarkable figure from the archive of Norwegian literary modernism, the gay vitalist poet and Nazi collaborator Åsmund Sveen. In many ways, Sveen saw his politics as radical, but it was a radicalism of the right. He justified his work for Norway's fascist party during the occupation as part of a historically destined idealism that would supersede rationalist and materialist modernity.[2] At the same time, Sveen's poetry and politics were informed by a utopian vision of an emerging culture of erotic liberation, in which a less repressive and healthier relationship to sexuality and the body would prevail. This chapter examines how the erotic—and homoerotic—vitalism of Sveen's interwar poetry was enmeshed in his imagination of fascist revitalization. I will also discuss how Sveen's postwar poetry handled issues of guilt, punishment, and the sense of martyrdom that came as a result of his treasonous collaboration.

In thinking through these issues, we should be cautious to avoid prejudicial clichés about the sexual orientation or erotic character of Nazism. Scholars such as Laura Frost and Andrew Hewitt have examined the problematic ways in which the postwar period linked homosexuality and fascism, or drew connections between Nazism and other forms of sexuality considered deviant or abnormal. In

Sex Drives, Frost examines eroticized representations of fascism and Nazism, discussing not only fascist characters in literature and film but also an intellectual tendency to think of fascism in terms of sexual deviance. She analyzes how fascist dictatorships came to be understood "as a libidinal phenomenon" and why fascism came to be seen as a sexually significant ideology.[3] In *Political Inversions*, Hewitt rejects the surprisingly common "homosexualization" of the totalitarian libido. He examines the rhetorical work performed by "the identification of homosexuality with fascism in the order of our political imagination" and finds that sexual interpretations of fascism reveal more about the discourse producing them than about fascism itself.[4] An example of this identification at a theoretical level is Adorno's assertion in *Minima Moralia* that "totalitarianism and homosexuality belong together."[5] Klaus Theweleit also criticizes Adorno for this unfortunate aphorism in *Male Fantasies*, his influential study of fascist masculinity.[6]

For Hewitt, the rhetorical construction of "Homo-Fascism" results from a double fear that a non-fascist social order might result in fascism and that homosocial relations might verge too far on homosexuality. Linking fascism to homosexuality functions as a way of representing fascism's supposedly mysterious or unthinkable appeal. "Homo-fascism" makes fascism readable as a political inversion with a safely "other" psycho-erotic structure, in which narcissism, aestheticism, and masculinism all play an excessive role.[7] Previous commentary on Sveen has in fact portrayed his homosexuality as partly explanatory of his turn to Nazi politics. One scholar suggests, "The masculine orientation of Sveen's poetry can also be seen in connection to the masculine orientation of Nazi ideology. Nazism was an ideology created by and for (strong) men, and it is not unlikely that this was a contributing factor in Sveen's attraction to it."[8] The poet's attraction to men is here employed to explain his attraction to National Socialism. Sveen's biographer, Jan Olav Gatland, resists such an explanation, voicing doubt that a fascination with the masculine body as an expression of Germanic spirit was a significant motivation for his politics. He calls it "incomprehensible that, as a homosexual, he voluntarily enters this system," and expresses the awareness of Sveen's contradictions that this chapter addresses.[9] Being gay is neither a sufficient nor a necessary condition for a fascist fascination with the virile masculine body.

At the same time, a figure like Sveen challenges any assumptions we might have about the automatic political progressivism of queer modernists. Sveen emerges from what Halberstam calls "a contradictory archive filled with loss and longing, abjection and ugliness, as well as love, intimacy, and survival."[10] Certainly not a pleasing model for gay and lesbian identity politics, Sveen offers no narrative of overcoming but rather one of complicity and failure, and especially in the postwar era, obsession with shame, guilt, and punishment. In addition to moments of luminous erotic and sensual vitality, much of his poetry models a queer negativity that engages in diverse shades of "abjection and ugliness." It is often antisocial, disaffected, suicidal, suspicious, paranoid, masochistic, shame-obsessed, and death-driven. There is no way to make Sveen's modernist poetry or his fate as a collaborator into something inspiring. But we don't need to—we can learn more by acknowledging and exploring his contradictions and complicities than by attempting to emphasize only his successful or uplifting side.

Before the war and his Nazi collaboration, Sveen was in many ways a success story. In the 1930s he was a young poet and critic writing in *nynorsk*, a gay man living in Oslo with his partner (a photographer named Conrad Bringe), and a pacifist interested in what we might now call new-age spirituality. Acclaimed as an important voice of literary modernity, a "bold and strange talent," Sveen was received enthusiastically by influential figures such as Sigurd Hoel, who was his publishing consultant at Gyldendal.[11] Beginning in 1932 with his first collection, *Andletet* (The Face), Sveen's poems alternate between ecstatic awakenings into sun-drenched sensual pleasure and disturbing, even violent, darkness. Three poetry collections—*Jordelden* (Earth Fire), *Eros syng* (Eros Sings), and *Såmannen* (The Sower)—followed over the next eight years, as well as one novel (*Svartjord*) and one lost novel (*Vinduet og vaaren*), which was not published because Hoel found its depiction of its homosexual characters insufficiently psychoanalytic. For Hoel, who was married to a psychiatrist and whose cultural radicalism was influenced by Wilhelm Reich's blend of Marxism and psychoanalysis, *Vinduet og vaaren* did not conform to a proper social and psychological treatment of homosexuality. Hoel criticized the novel for representing "what we might call delayed puberty fantasies" in a style that he compared to the worst excesses of fin-de-siècle romanticism.[12] This description suggests that Sveen's novel was written in a decadent tradition of disproportionate ornament, impressionistic moods, and focus on exquisite surfaces. This was all quite different from Hoel's own pared-down, "masculine" style and unresponsive to his psychoanalytic preferences for character depiction.[13]

At its best, Sveen's poetry blends the pantheistic and the erotic in intense images and captivating verse. While it was admired for its novelty, Sveen's body of work also shows the disparate influences of both Sufi mysticism and the traditional rural songs (*bygdeviser*) he published along with his formally innovative poems. Ultimately, Sveen's literature was overshadowed by his commitment to National Socialism, which prevented him from publishing any of his complicated and troubling postwar work until *Brunnen* (The Well) appeared in 1963, the year he died, followed a few years later by *Tonemesteren* (The Master of Tones). Despite having been a marginal and little-known figure since World War II, today Sveen's importance in the context of a vitalist-expressionist modernism is increasingly recognized by Norwegian scholars.[14] Vitalism, a central concept of early twentieth-century art and literature in Scandinavia, lay behind Sveen's poetic eroticism, which included same-sex desire.[15]

Understanding how Sveen's erotic vitalism was connected to his Nazism may require modifying received assumptions about the ideology's sexual puritanism. Susan Sontag once asked in her influential article on Leni Riefenstahl, "Why has Nazi Germany, which was a sexually repressive society, become erotic?"[16] The historian Dagmar Herzog has more recently argued that German fascism "perpetuated and intensified certain aspects of the sexually liberalizing tendencies underway since the early twentieth century."[17] In addition to seeing fascism as an anti-rationalist, anti-materialist form of idealism destined to save Europe, Sveen also saw it as compatible with his own unconstrained and spiritual attitude toward the erotic. Herzog's *Sex After Fascism* shows how this recognition was possible, by revealing overlooked aspects of Nazi thinking about sex and love. Herzog also argues that the erotic in secular modernity functioned as a substitute for traditional religion and that National Socialist views of sexuality reflect this larger cultural shift.[18] Sveen made a cult out of a regenerative, procreative, and functional male sexuality, even though this seems to go against his own nonreproductive sexual desire. It is useful, therefore, to notice the tension in Sveen's erotic vitalism: on one hand, there is a biopolitical vitalism of sexual reproduction and natural fertility (which is inherently heterosexual and closer to the Nazi sexual ideology described by Herzog), and on the other, there is a more expansive vitalism that praises erotic desire as an indication of life and vigor (which can include nonprocreative and queer desires).[19]

"THE NAKED AND THE PURE"

Jan Olav Gatland's 2003 biography, *Det andre mennesket: Eit portrett av Åsmund Sveen*, directed new attention to Sveen's poetry and his miserable fate, and it offers a wealth of personal, literary, and historical details and documents. Gatland explains Sveen's turn to fascism with reference to his positive experiences in Germany in 1934, his political naiveté or ignorance, his romantic-nationalist values, and his economic concerns or opportunism. Like Hamsun, Sveen was a writer of many apparent paradoxes; both his poetry and his politics were heterogeneous to the point of incoherence. Gatland sketches him as a romantic pacifist, an apolitical but basically social-democratic thinker, and an idealistic poet seduced by features of fascist ideology but never genuinely engaged by it.[20] In 1937, for instance, Sveen published a pacifist poem called "Jord og blod og ære" (Earth and Blood and Honor) in *Dagbladet*, the leftist paper for which he wrote literary reviews. (*Dagbladet* would later become a primary force against Sveen during his postwar trial and punishment for treason.) In this poem, Sveen mocked the Third Reich's militaristic call for blood and honor. How, one wonders, could this leftist-pacifist poet end up greeting the Nazi occupation as a willing collaborator with their cultural and ideological mission?

When the young Sveen moved to Oslo from his home region of Elverum in the late 1920s, he initially shared a room with the then-unknown painter Kai Fjell, whose combination of expressionism with traditional folk motifs might be compared to Sveen's poetic output. By the end of the 1930s, he had become an acclaimed figure in Norwegian literature and a respected literary critic, and he was about to publish his fourth collection of poetry, *Såmannen*.[21] In a twist that surprised his family and undermined his future, Sveen joined Quisling's Nasjonal Samling party in November 1940—half a year after the Nazi invasion.[22] Throughout the war, Sveen worked as a cultural administrator and theater director for the Nasjonal Samling government. He wielded a significant influence on the cultural projects and programs that were part of Norwegian fascism, most notably by constructing the fascist literary canon in the anthology *Norsk ånd og vilje*.

These developments appear especially surprising given that Sveen was located on the political left in the 1930s and that he wrote boundary-breaking poetry that did not fit the artistic vision of the Nasjonal Samling. In their view of art and culture, the party wished to promote what it considered "healthy" and to forbid degenerate, insufficiently nationalist, or communist expressions. The party's program from 1933 stated that "press, theater, broadcasting, film, and other organs of culture must advance the interests of the nation. Antisocial propaganda and the spreading of class hatred are forbidden."[23] Although Sveen's work was not typical of this vision, it was also not wholly at odds with the nationalist rhetoric of health, nature, and origins. Sveen's poetry collections were hybrids of the transgressive modern and the traditional, containing expressionistic homoeroticism as well as folk ballads. In 1943, Sveen published a collection of *bygdeviser* that fit well into the Norwegian fascist-ruralist aesthetic mode. As my reading of the poem "Til dei unge menn" (To the Young Men) will make clear, a counterintuitive aspect of Sveen's story is that same-sex desire played a role in his imagination of "pure" Norwegian nature and ethnonationalist revitalization.

One of the Norwegian scholars to have written at length about Sveen calls his case "one of the strangest and sorriest" among the collaborators who were tried for treason after World War II.[24] Sveen's sentence for treason included over four years of forced labor and the forfeit of his civil rights. The court described him as "moderate," not ill-willed, but still guided by a deep conviction, and they also pointed out that he should have known better given his intellectual talents and status in the literary culture.[25] Sveen wasn't disturbed by losing his right to vote, however; he wrote, "Jeg har dømt meg selv til livsvarig taushet i politiske spørsmål, det skjønner jeg meg åpenbart ikke noe på" (I have condemned myself to lifelong silence about politics, I obviously don't know anything about it).[26] It is easy to concur with this self-judgment because the motivations for Sveen's politics were not political, at least not in a limited sense. Sveen, like other fascist intellectuals, was motivated by grandiose perceptions about the decline of "spirit" in the modern age and the need for cultural-spiritual (*åndelig*) revitalization at both a national and European level. Sveen also voiced fears of racial decline and imagined rebirth in terms of a mythic biological and cultural purity, which clearly places him in the orbit of Nazi racial ideology.[27]

Sveen's interwar poetry has been considered modernist because it eschews traditional lyrical structures and forms in a way that was perceived as an innovation in the *nynorsk* tradition and in Norwegian poetry more generally. He denigrated the expressive capacities of "eit stivt skjematisk vers" (a rigid, schematic verse) and preferred instead "rimlause, rytmefrie former" (rhyme-free, rhythmless forms).[28] Additionally, his work relies on a rejection of conservative sexual morality that was an important feature of the modernist and cultural-radical turn against bourgeois values in interwar Norway. As he wrote in 1933, "Det er noko skite ved den gamle generasjonen, dette strevet deira med aa løyne burt og klæ paa. Det nakne og reine er det friskaste" (There's something rotten about the older generation, with all their effort to keep things out of sight and cover things up. The naked and the pure are the healthiest).[29] Sexual liberation movements and youth movements of the early twentieth century often saw themselves as a return to a natural morality that was less bound by the hypocrisy and repressive decorum of the older generation.

The erotic attitude of Sveen's poetry is ecstatic and rapturous, celebrating the body and the senses, although there are also moods of extreme disharmony and neurotic self-torture. Matter and spirit merge in Sveen's expressionistic landscapes; the typical Sveen poem from the 1930s presents intensely resonant and stylized nature imagery, pervasive and sometimes masochistic eroticism, and frequent references to glowing sunshine and the vibrations of the forest. For example, consider this hypnotic and panerotic section of *Andletet.* (My literal translation follows.)

Varmedirrande
vill står skogen.
Glødd i solglo
og brend i solbrand—
med brusande bras
av barlaug og lauvbragl
og gnistrande greiner
i hungrig hete.

Lynblenkblakrande
blikrar lauvet.
Solskinsilande
vingjer greinene.
Kvåesveittande
brunkar borken
innmillom moldtunge
skuggar i barhanget
. . .
Eg bøygjer armen

mot bjørkegreina,
eg bender halsen
attende i mòsen,
eg krøkjer kroppen
i krevjande solgir
eg vrid meg naken
i vaken ørske.

Eg vrid meg naken
og solgiren tek meg,
eg opnar fanget
og opnar munnen.
Eg krøkjer kroppen—
og krafter fløymer
og safter strøymer
or livsens røter.

Eg bøyger armen,
og bender halsen
og brenner munnen
mot berre steinar.
Eg stryk min lekam
med heilage kvister,
og strekkjer meg djupt
i det varme jordfang.[30]

(Warm-vibrating / wild is the forest. / Glowing in sunshine / and burning in sun's fire— / with a roaring rush / of spruce and glimmering greenery / and flashing branches / in hungry heat. // Lightning bright shining / rustling leaves. / Sunshine-filtering / swinging branches. / Resin-sweating / the trunk darkens / between soil-heavy / shadows of hanging spruce // . . . I bend my arm / toward the birch branch, / I bend my neck / back in the moss, / I curve my body / in aching sun-lust / I strip naked / in a waking daze. // I strip naked / and sun-lust takes me, / I open my arms / and open my mouth. / I curve my body— / and forces flood / and juices flow / from the roots of life. // I bend my arm / and bend my neck / and scorch my mouth / on bare stones. / I stroke my body / with blessed branches, / and stretch deep / in the earth's warm embrace.)

It has often been suggested that *nynorsk*, the written form of Norwegian used in Sveen's interwar poetry, has greater resources than *bokmål* for the creation of evocative nature poetry, with more precise shadings and a broader landscape vocabulary. Sveen wrote that *bokmål* was not capable of providing "de typiske norske naturbetegnelser" (typically Norwegian descriptions of nature).[31] In this poem, he goes beyond such typical descriptions to a level of eco-erotic intensity rarely seen before in Norwegian poetry.

While remarkably eroticized, Sveen's landscapes also possess a clearly pantheistic or nature-mystical dimension. Such a worshipful attitude toward the sun and forests is found in the works of many twentieth-century Norwegian writers, although it is not always as red-hot and passionate as in Sveen. The Marxist critical tradition tends to associate nature worship in Hamsun's novels with fascism or reactionary discontent with the social.[32] However, it is important to recognize that Norwegian nature mysticism, like artistic vitalism in general, has a broader array of ideological ramifications. As Monika Žagar has observed, mystical reverence for nature is a traditional Scandinavian attitude that was co-opted by Nazism for its own purposes: "Nazi propaganda exploited and lauded the Nordic/Germanic link to Nature as a sign of primordial vitalism."[33] Although nature worship or vitalism is not automatically fascist in every case, by the 1930s it was an important part of fascist iconography and discourse, and a central aspect of the Nazi imagination of the "pure" North.

Andletet consists of fifty-seven untitled poems in three sections. Hoel interpreted the collection as a single poem cycle with a therapeutic narrative that he compared to a psychoanalytic progression through uncomfortable insight toward health. The two extremes of experience for the speaker in the poems are blissful erotic union (with nature or with people) and harsh alienation (from nature and from others). After the opening sections portray the young man's erotic unity with "wild spring," there follows a stage of crisis, fear of annihilation and suicide, and a growing awareness of non-heterosexuality. The young man emerges from a suicidal crisis, however, with an affirmative view of existence justified by the presence of divine beauty and sacred Eros. Interestingly, Hoel found this pantheistic resolution to be a flaw in the collection's otherwise remarkable and visionary poetry, which indicates his own distaste for the redemptive.[34]

Sveen's homoeroticism, as seen in poems about male romantic friendship or loving addresses to a second person, was unusually direct in the Norwegian poetic tradition. However, the literary theme of same-sex desire was not unexampled in Norway at this time. Depictions of homosexuality appeared in several novels written around 1930, including Cora Sandel's *Alberte og friheten*, Rolf Stenersen's *Godnatt da du*, and Gunnar Larsen's *I sommer*.[35] In the wake of such representations of deviant sexual proclivities, the early 1930s witnessed a renewed moral debate centered on homosexuality, a topic that was largely excluded from the Scandinavian Modern

Breakthrough's *sedelighetsdebatt* (debate about [sexual] morality) in the 1880s. For example, Stenersen's novel was among those attacked in an article by the cultural-conservative journalist Fredrik Ramm, titled "En skitten strøm flyter utover landet" (A Dirty Stream Is Flowing over the Land). In the same article, Ramm objected to Hoel's gloomy satire of bourgeois marriage and sexuality, in *En dag i oktober* (One Day in October, 1931).

Unafraid of such a reaction, Sveen boldly let the speaker in his poems engage in sexual activities with partners of both sexes or of grammatically indeterminate sex. He exploited linguistic ambiguities, employing the masculine *nynorsk* pronoun to create a homoerotic connotation. In the following excerpt from *Andletet*, the pronoun "han" refers to its antecedent "vårdagen" (spring day), but Sveen is also using it to describe an erotic encounter with a man.

Vårdagen—villande vårdagen lær
imot meg frå alt som eg kjenner!
Han femner meg fast—og han tek meg og bèr
på sterke, ustyrlege hender.
—Eg legg med innåt han, eg kjenner med all
så viljug til eitt å gjera:
gjeve meg lykkeleg livet i vald—
livet og vårdagsferda![36]

(The spring—the spring day leads me astray / from everything I know! / He embraces me tightly—carries me away / with strong and savage hands. / —I lay myself against him, I feel completely / willing to do one thing: / give myself happily to the grip of life— / of life and the journey of spring!)

The speaker in this poem celebrates his naked submission to the purity and ecstasy of spring—"him"—and also to "the grip of life" (*Livet i vold*—here spelled "livet i vald"—was also the title of a 1910 play by Hamsun). Another poem, "Guten låg i graset," equally nature-erotic but much more disturbing, imagines a man ominously approaching an adolescent who is sunning himself outdoors.

Naken låg guten i graset under solhimlen.
Han låg med attlatne augo mot solskinet,
men munnen var halvopen i ein undrande smil.
Sola låg på den høge bringa og i opne fanget hans
og fór med heite fingrar over håret og andletet
og lemene på han.
. . .
—Mannen kom vadande nærmere gjenom enga

og tung og kald var skuggen hans—
Safter steig op av avgrunns røter,
og blodraude blømer bruste og brann,
og guten vreid seg under solriset.
Og op or avgrunnen i han steig det ein storm,
og stormen sleit i hans livsens røter,
og guten strekte seg tungt under solhendene—[37]

(The boy lay naked in the grass under the sunny sky. / He lay with eyes closed facing the sunshine, / but his mouth was half-open in a wondering smile. / The sun glistened on his tall chest and his open arms / and ran its hot fingers over his hair and face / and limbs. . . . / —The man came wading closer through the meadow / and his shadow was heavy and cold— / Juices rose up from roots in the abyss / and blood-red blossoms burst and burned / and the boy twisted under the whip of the sun. / And from the abyss inside him came a storm, / and the storm ripped up the roots of his life, / and the boy spread out slowly under the sun's hands—.)

The image of the boy twisting "under solriset" (under the whip of the sun) offers a glimpse of the masochistic element in Sveen's eroticism. The poem concludes with the boy's ecstasy interrupted by the encroaching shadow of the "tung og kald" (heavy and cold) man from the forest. Norwegian scholars have shown a notable interest in this text: Pål Bjørby reads it as a "shocking, bold, erotic, unafraid description of 'the boy's' autoerotic orgasm" that is unparalleled in Norwegian literature.[38] Eirik Vassenden suggests that the central issue is the opposition between the boy's carefree bodily ecstasy and the presence of a guilt-inducing figure of moral authority.[39] Whether we read this text as a psychoanalytic allegory of the child's polymorphously perverse body being disciplined by the unfeeling law of the father, or even as a barely encrypted recollection of traumatic sexual abuse, it shows that Sveen's imagination of taboo eroticism is not merely a sunlit and shame-free liberation of the senses but also has a darker and disconcerting side. As Bjørby observes about *Andletet* in general, the reader "meets shame, self-torture, desperation, sorrow, longing, and resignation" and experiences "a view of sexuality as violent, regressive, aggressive, animal."[40]

After gaining recognition with *Andletet* and *Jordelden*, Sveen was selected to spend the summer of 1934 at the Deutsch-Nordisches Schriftstellerhaus in Travemünde by Lübeck, as a Nordic literary ambassador to Germany. This writer's institute was part of the Nordische Gesellschaft, which originally aimed to promote common Nordic and Germanic cultural ideals but eventually became a vehicle of the Nazi propaganda ministry led by Alfred Rosenberg.[41] The summer of 1934 was Sveen's introduction to Nazi Germany, and although he remained opposed to German militancy for most of the decade, he began to appreciate "the new mentality" and the enthusiasm of the young Germans. He wrote at the time, "Jeg ser annerledes på meget av nasjonalsosialismen siden jeg virkelig har truffet den nye mentaliteten 'ansikt til ansikt'—så å si" (I have a different view of much of National Socialism now that I've actually met the new mentality "face to face"—so to speak).[42] When commenting in private correspondence on the Night of the Long Knives—the purge of the Sturmabteilung on June 20, 1934, when Ernst Röhm was murdered—Sveen wrote that the Third Reich had nonetheless managed to secure peace and order. He refrained from expressing adverse judgment on the murders (in which gay men were targeted). During his time in Travemünde, Sveen also gave a speech about Hamsun. Perhaps this lecture anticipated his later wartime articles, in which he claimed Hamsun as a vanguard figure of fascist cultural revitalization.

VITALISM AND *EROS SYNG*

In the Scandinavian context, *vitalismen* is a cultural historical term that refers to a current of art and literature produced in the several decades before World War II, much of which had no specific connection to fascism.[43] This cultural usage contrasts with a narrower meaning of the term in English or French, where it often refers to the idea of a life force or principle behind organic life, in contrast to a mechanistic view in the philosophy of science. For example, Henri Bergson referred to an *élan vital*, while the German philosopher Hans Driesch developed a modern notion of entelechy to refer to the metaphysical element that made organic life distinct.[44] Such philosophies of life were accompanied by a broader set of social and cultural movements throughout Europe, which envisaged some form of revitalization to alleviate the onslaught of urbanization and industrialization in the late nineteenth century. As Griffin has observed, the many life-reform movements that emerged around 1900 occupied a specifically post-Darwinian context; by "radically undermining the metaphysical claims of Christianity, [Darwinism] had also created the cultural space for a cult of biological life."[45] Cultural vitalism was secular in this sense, but it was also a surrogate form of religiosity in a post-metaphysical environment. Scandinavian artistic *vitalisme* was in many respects a replacement religion that preserved spiritual ecstasy in the natural, earthly experience of vitality.[46]

Eirik Vassenden has described Sveen's poetry in relation to vitalist aesthetics, showing that it exemplifies typical motifs and themes such as sun worship, nature mysticism, the ecstatic body, and self-dissolution.[47] These occur with such frequency in Sveen's poetry that it seems impossible to understand it without such an aesthetic concept. The moods of Sveen's poetry shift rapidly and drastically in an expressionistic manner, from what Vassenden calls "ekstatisk glede over å være en del av livsstrømmen til en melankolsk fortvilelse over å være overgitt til individuasjonen og sin egen endelighet og smerte" (ecstatic joy in being part of the stream of life to melancholic despair in being given over to individuation and one's own finitude and pain).[48] Both sides of this dichotomy are rendered with intense and often disturbing images that suit the violence of the limit experiences that are central to Sveen's poetry.

Sveen's vitalism can be understood in relation to the various idealistic and utopian movements emphasizing youth, health, or natural bodily experience, which arose around the turn of the century and continued to influence modernist culture into the interwar period. As the German names *Lebensreform* and *Lebensphilosophie* suggest, a new emphasis on the joy of life, health, and bodily experience began to replace the perceived stultification or decadence of the bourgeois era. The German Wandervogel youth organization was founded 1896, and the Freikörperbewegung (Free Body Movement) appeared in the same decade. Vitalist painting in Scandinavia emphasized the natural, simple, and healthy, which also entailed a cult of youthfulness.[49] Griffin suggests the term "social modernism" to refer to such naturist or body-centered activities, which were an important aspect of the larger generational revolt against the constraints or discontents of bourgeois civilization in the early twentieth century.[50] Sveen was engrossed in this new gospel of the body; he owned magazines and photography books about *nakenkultur* (nudism), and he shared its anti-intellectualism, its interest in the primitive, and its aversion to industrial modernity. Sveen's poetry glorifies animal corporeality as a reaction to the modern surfeit of civilization, offering what his biographer Gatland calls "ein sanselig religiøsitet" (a religiosity of the senses).[51]

The cultural vitalist mind-set, with its prioritization of the sensual and the erotic, conflicts with the Enlightenment or humanistic conceptions of progress and culture that characterize liberal modernity. Because it stresses pre-reflective and immediate life as opposed to rationality and reflection, normative notions of truth, beauty, and morality all become less important in vitalism.[52] However problematic or simplistic its emphasis on unconscious life and the body may be, vitalism is not merely a reactionary and self-blinding escape into natural harmony (as in the Marxist interpretation of Hamsun). Vitalist artworks can offer "a potent point of departure for cultural criticism," although it is not clear that vitalism offers many resources to move far beyond that point.[53] The basic cultural criticism of Scandinavian vitalism is found in its skepticism about urban and bourgeois life forms, and about the project of modernity in general.[54] Of course, skepticism or hostility to bourgeois modernity is so widespread in the history of modernist art and literature that this is hardly a distinctive attitude. Yet perhaps vitalism's combination of intuitive intensity and limited critical precision is what allows it to inhabit a variety of political positions. The human individual in a vitalist framework is not the autonomous and rational subject of Enlightenment humanism but is instead subordinate to the heteronomous power of natural or unconscious life.

In Sveen's case, this power was Eros. Around the time he published *Eros syng* (1935), Sveen was developing an interest in Sufi mysticism. The Indian philosopher Inayat Khan, who founded a movement based on an interpretation of Sufism outside of Islam, held a lecture in Oslo in 1924. Sveen learned about universal Sufism through acquaintances who attended this event, and he was fascinated by its devotion to sacred love without limits and its inclusive attitude toward same-sex desire.[55] Because the Sufi tradition depicted love between men with apparent acceptance (especially in the works of the Persian mystic poets Hafez and Rumi), it offered Sveen a resource for self-understanding and acceptance. This was not an unusual use of these poets in Sveen's time. The *ghazal* form used by Rumi and Hafez had acquired a homosexual connotation in Europe in the nineteenth century, as did the Shakespearean sonnet. Heinrich Heine even proposed the term "ghaselig" as a new way to refer to men who loved men.[56] Although Sveen never became a serious devotee of Sufi mysticism, it provided an precursor for his own beliefs about divine Eros. In the collection *Eros syng*, he alluded to Sufi mystical poetry by including a poem titled "Ruba'i," after the Persian quatrain.[57]

Sveen's concept of Eros connects universal biological life and individual sexual longing, while also acting as an immanent divinity. Eros designates a primordial drive for Sveen, both a source and regenerator of life. He placed this religious interpretation of Eros in opposition to contemporary psychoanalytic thought. Here is Sveen commenting on *Eros syng* in a letter.

> Det jeg vil med samlingen som helhet er å påvise Eros som alle verdens dypeste kilde, i trangere betydning å identifisere det religiøse med det erotiske. Men i motsetning til de fleste psykoanalytisk overbeviste forfattere, som for så vidt stiller seg innenfor den borgerlig kristelig-ideologiske forestillingskrets som de ved denne "identifisering" forsøker å redusere det religiøses verdi—i motsetning til disse vil jeg i min lyrikk gi uttrykk for tanker om det guddommelige i det erotiske.[58]
>
> (What I would like to do in this collection as a whole is to show Eros as the deepest source of everything in the world, and in a narrower sense to identify the religious with the erotic. But in contrast to most psychoanalytically oriented writers, who remain within the bourgeois Christian-ideological frame of understanding to such an extent that they attempt to reduce the value of the religious by way of this "identification"—in contrast to these writers, I would like my poetry to express the idea of the divine in the erotic.)

Sveen pointedly distinguishes his own understanding of the erotic from a supposedly reductionistic psychoanalytic explanation, which he unexpectedly accuses of being trapped in a Christian worldview that holds a low estimation of erotic life. This shows that Sveen saw the contemporary psychoanalytic moment as an extension of the bourgeois rather than its radical challenger, as it is usually understood in relation to this period of Scandinavian cultural radicalism. This quotation also suggests that Sveen did not simply internalize Freudian or other medical theories about (homo)sexuality; he seems to have been more influenced by mysticism than by therapeutic or scientific discourse. For Sveen, to say that the religious has its roots in the erotic does not reduce religion to an expression of individual sexual psychology; it elevates the erotic as a sacred principle of life, which transcends individual desire.

This idea formed the basis of the erotic spirituality explored in *Eros syng*. In the five-part poem of the same title, Eros itself speaks to humanity, calling the individual person "a mirror fragment" that reflects and channels its divinity. Man's desire is the gift of Eros, whose omnipotent drive flows through and animates all life.

> Liksom mold i den svarte åker
> sender ei kraft til det levande korn

som tenjar seg med sine høge stylker
mot sommarshimlen
. . .
såleis sender eg duld lengsel
op i ditt liv og alt livet
så det kan tenja seg høgt i sola
og ringe mot himlen![59]

(As soil in the black field / sends a force through the living grain / that stretches its high stalks / toward the summer sun / . . . so do I send a hidden longing / through your life and all life / so it can stretch high in the sun / and ring toward the heavens!)

In an organic image, human life and sexual behavior are governed by the workings of an unseen natural divinity, whose power resides in all living things. As the poem continues, the voice of Eros explains that individuals may perhaps discover the "open secret" (Løyndomen min er open) of its mystical omnipresence. In the fourth section, Eros likens its own life-giving power to a river flowing through a landscape. The individual (male) subject is the riverbed, while Eros is the animating stream.

Såg du dei sterke åer
som fyller med krefter
skjerutte gråberg-lægjet?
Såg du dei milde elvar
som løyner med venleik
bolkutte raudjords-lægjet?
Såleis kan livet mitt i deg
full-liknas.

Det som du sjøl-deg kallar,
ditt skaltronge sinn,
er som det fattige elvelægjet
er som det steinberre åfaret.[60]

(Did you see the mighty rapids / that fill worn-out granite / riverbeds with force? / Did you see the mild streams / that cover rough red earth / riverbeds with care? / Thus can my life be / complete in you. / What you call your self, / your restricted mind, / is like the meager riverbed / is like the stone-bare course.)

These lines suggest Sveen's view that the self and the intellect are empty and arid without the vitalizing stream of universal erotic life. As the poem ends, Sveen's analogy emphasizes the reciprocity of individual form and the stream of life: "elvelægjet hadde kje vore / utan elva, / og åa var ikkje å i verda / åtte ho ikkje / åfaret" (the riverbed would be nothing / without the river, / and the stream would be / no stream without / its course).[61]

It is easy to understand why this mystical view of sexuality would appeal to Sveen more than the moral constraints and unhealthy guilt he associated with the Christian or bourgeois denigration of the senses and the body. By building loosely on Sufism and contemporary European revitalization movements, Sveen's erotic vitalism reconfigured the sacred in secular modernity as sexual desire—a universal principle that governs all life. This eroticism offered a way to transcend the soulless individual of bourgeois modernity. As we will see in "Til dei unge menn," Sveen's gospel of desire was also a gospel of the virile masculine body, which instantiates the will of universal Eros in the automatic and healthy unfolding of its desires.

The attractions of cultural vitalism for an early twentieth-century poet seeking sexual acceptance and expressiveness are apparent enough, but the idea that National Socialism could be seen as sexually liberating challenges the predominant view of totalitarianism as sexually repressive or puritanical. Postwar interpretations of fascism in particular have frequently imagined the fascist as sexually repressed or deviant. The stereotype's distorted sexuality signifies the ultimate unhealthiness of fascist repression, not a greater freedom of expression. If Nazism was fundamentally conservative in sexual terms, it would seem that Sveen's emancipatory erotic vitalism was simply in conflict with his support for fascism. However, Nazi sexual ideology was more complicated, not as uniformly sexually repressive as many assume. Herzog's *Sex After Fascism* argues that "the conventional periodization suggests that the Third Reich's sexual politics can best be understood as a reactionary backlash against the freedom and openness of the Weimar Republic."[62] She claims that this view results from postwar interpretations made by the New Left, which theorized a connection between sexual emancipation and sociopolitical justice. This perspective underestimated fascism's "sexually liberalizing tendencies" and overlooked the conflicts between the Nazi regime and the Christian church over sexual morality.[63] According to Herzog, the New Left perspective did so because theoretically it could not countenance the fact that "advocacy of sexual expression coexisted with virulent racism and mass murder."[64] Crucially and obviously, only certain forms of sexual expression were officially advocated and tolerated—healthy, racially correct ones; homosexuality was not among them.

Herzog contends that these new sexually liberating attitudes were linked to the process of secularization, which led to the attribution of greater existential significance to romantic love and sexuality. She quotes Nazi authorities who saw the sexual drive as "holy" and "sacred," placing it at a transcendental level of "eternal values."[65] Secularization did not mean only the diminished authority of traditional religious beliefs and decreasing church attendance. It was also "a reworking of languages and attitudes, a sort of compromise formation in which this-worldly matters were described as having divine significance."[66] Herzog sees the sacralization of sex and love as important aspects of Nazism's secular reconfiguration of sexual morality, as witnessed in the words of Nazi pedagogues and psychotherapists and even in the SS journal *Das Schwarze Korps*. She labels such attitudes "a kind of proto-New Age sentimentality that intersected with both deistic nature-loving Nazi racism and with what people genuinely experienced as involving their . . . supreme experiences of happiness."[67] Here we can discern an affinity with the erotic and nature-worshiping vitalism Sveen developed in his modernist poetry.

Sveen's overlap with National Socialist sexual ideology consists in the vitalistic sacralization of the erotic. The palpable difference is that while Sveen used a sacred notion of universal erotic desire to legitimate same-sex relations (among other forms of sexual expression), Nazism did not seek to expand the array of approvable sexual identities. On the contrary, it strengthened the compulsory nature of heterosexual marriage and reproduction, even as it used liberalized sexuality as a tool of manipulation.[68] Nazism was only emancipatory insofar as sexuality was bridled to the cause of the biological and social reproduction of the nation, which excluded any acceptance of same-sex relations.[69] Aspects of sexuality that were not considered racially hygienic or healthily procreative were not only discouraged, they were projected onto the demonized figure of the Jew.[70] Nation, race, and sexuality were clearly linked in fascist ideology, as expressions of sexuality were "subordinated to the biopolitical design of the state," both to amplify the racially approvable population and to make it fitter and healthier as a bulwark against degeneracy.[71] In the peculiar poem I will analyze next, masculine sexual virility is both glorified and racialized.

EROTIC AND SPIRITUAL VIRILITY

In the poem "Til dei unge menn" (To the Young Men), Sveen's representation of heterosexual reproduction merges uncomfortably with fascist biopolitics, even as the poem itself enacts a voyeuristic form of same-sex desire. The poem appeared in his fourth poetry collection, *Såmannen*, which was published the day before Nazi Germany invaded Norway (April 9, 1940), seven months before he joined Nasjonal Samling. "Til dei unge menn" was also the poem Sveen later chose to represent his own contribution to the Norwegian literary canon in his propaganda anthology *Norsk ånd og vilje*. He evidently considered it a literary expression of the utopian social vision he saw in National Socialism. Here is the poem in its entirety, followed by my English translation.

Når de kjem byksande liene ned i somarkvelden
—eikestres lår, bjørketres bringe, hender av einerrot—
ned til eit gamalt dansarhus på furumoen ved elva,
og stig-inn i stuga og speiar i møybenken
så huldrene fjetrast under augstålet,
og når de skrid gjenom sal
—raude og gule skjeft ikring harde halser—
og leikar med lamungan dykkar og dansar på bjørnlegger,
da liker eg dykk,
og når du raudmynte kvinnfolk-røvar raskar på heimveg
vadande gjenom engen føre dag
med grasfrø på skorne, søte i anden, doggperler i hår
og dansen enno duvand i mjuke leder,
å da liker eg deg!
Dansar sjela di og i solrenninga?

Og når de vitjar gjenten i bu og kammers
—ei ny, ei ny kvar laurdagskveld—
og kjenner undringa deira i det gode mørker,
ja nør de ligg med bringene berre liksom solbakkar
der vårgras brydder,
og freistar og elskar dykkar eigen manndom,
da liker eg dykk,
og når du har funne henne blodet ditt leiter etter
og luter deg mot, så håret ditt skygger anletet på ho
—siv over vatn, bar over sjø—
å da kjenner eg deg.
Da øygnar eg ljosken av den fyrste kjærkleiken!
Ein gong skal han loga igjenom alt ditt verande.

Nordavinds søner! Synnavinds elskarar!

Riddarar av flog og renn!
Når de kjem susande stavlaust ned over hengande skavlar
og skriv med løypene djerve ord i undrande snø,
når de kjem ridand i langkut gjenom den grisne skog
øvande hestar av edelt blod i haustdagen,
og når de fer med leande munn i lynvognar
—oljestrek over ivrig pann, flygande hår—
da liker eg dykk,
og når du, ørnevilje, vinn i rømda
og fyk med din pilsnøgge stålfugl vidt over fjell og hav
og borar deg einspissa opp til iskalde høgder—
å da likar eg deg!
Kjenner du og det svimrande floget inn—inn
i hjartehimlen?

Såmenn for Gud og verda!
Ser eg dykk utpå opne marker våronndagen
—sol over sveitte andletsdrag og mold på hand og fot—
når kornet drys ifrå hendene dykkar i sågiddret
og dagen legg gull i dykkar råa plogskjer,
undrast eg glad:
røkjer de og ein åker i det dulde?
Og når de tømrar heim til born og kvinner,
og nør de reiser byrge murar i aulande byar
—store hus, strålande hus, mykje nyttelege åt samfundet—
å da elskar eg dykk!
Byggjer de samfund av ånd?

Og du som spenner bru over svortnande klufter,
borar ganger i berg og kjelder i øydemark
og reiser sigrande tårn på ville fjell—
takk for auga dine!
Kanskje du sjølv ein gong skal stige
liksom eit fjell av velsigning millom aude sjeler.
Å born av sol og ljos,
de som har fått slik hyllest av natura!
Eg ser dykk på gule strender ved grøn sjø,
de dyrkar lekamen dykkar og elskar sola.
Eg likar dykk.
Kjenner de og den sannings sol
som brenn ved midnatt?[72]

(When you come bounding down the hillsides in the summer evening / —thighs of oak, chests of birch, hands of juniper root— / to an old dancing house on the pine heath by the river, / and step into the room and peer at the maidens

so the hulders [figures from Scandinavian folklore] are spellbound under the stable, / and when you slip through the hall / —red and

> yellow scarves around strong necks— / and play with your lambs and dance on bear's legs, / I like you then, / and when you, red-mouthed woman-robber, hurry homeward / wading through meadows before daybreak / with grass seeds on your shoes, a sweetened spirit, dew drops in your hair / and the dance still swaying in gentle rhythms, / how I like you then! / Does your soul also dance at the break of day? // And when you visit a girl in her bedroom / —another, another each Saturday night— / and sense their wonder in the blessed darkness, / yes, when you lie with chests bare like sunlit slopes / where spring grass sprouts, / to test and love your own manhood, / I like you then, / and when you've found the one your blood longs for
>
> and drives you toward, / so that your hair shadows her face / —reeds over water, pine needles over sea— / I understand you then. / And I see a spark of the first love! / One day it will blaze through your entire being. // Sons of the north wind! Lovers of the south wind! / Knights of skiing and running! / When you come buzzing briskly down over hanging snowdrifts / and write with a bold language in the astonished snow, / when you come riding in a race through the sparse forest
>
> training horses of noble blood in the autumn day, / and when you rush by with a smile in your speeding wagons / —a streak of grease on an eager brow, hair flowing—/ I like you then, / and when you, eagle-willed, take to the air / and dash like an arrow-quick bird of steel high over mountains and sea / and penetrate to ice-cold heights— / how I like you then! / Do you also know the dizzying flight—into / the heart of heaven? // Sowers for God and the world! / I see you out on open fields in spring / —sun over your sweaty faces and soil on your hands and feet— / when your hands scatter seeds in the vibrations of sowing / and the day puts gold in your raw plowshares, / I ask myself gladly: / are they also tending to an unseen field? / And when you build homes for women and children, / and when you raise solid walls in swarming cities / —great buildings, radiant buildings, quite useful to society— / how I love you then! / Are you building a spiritual society? // And you who span bridges across gaping abysses, / drill pathways through mountains and wellsprings in the wasteland / and victorious towers in the wilderness— / thank you for your vision! / Perhaps you one day yourself shall rise / like a mountain of benediction among desolate souls. // O children of the sun and light, / who have been so favored by nature! / I see you on golden shores by green seas, / you revere your bodies and love the sun. / I like you. / Do you also know the sun of truth / that burns at midnight?

This eccentric text brings together a catalogue of Sveen's political and artistic concerns, including mystical eroticism, a deliberately archaic lexicon, and the hope for a spiritually revitalized nation. In a seasonal progression, the male speaker voices his visual enjoyment of the virile sowers (*såmenn*), occasionally pausing to wonder if these men share his spiritual knowledge and the power of erotic ecstasy. At the beginning of the poem, in summertime, the men's bodies are likened to trees ("thighs of oak, chests of birch, hands of juniper root") and thus depicted as a natural force of the forest. This sense of natural vigor is reinforced as the men "dance on bear's legs" while seducing passive women. In addition to this animalization, the speaker awkwardly poses a spiritual question to one of the men: "dansar sjela di og i solrenninga?" (does your soul also dance at the break of day?). This line introduces the speaker's repeated curiosity about the interior life of the men, in addition to his interest in the naturalized unfolding of their sexuality.

The second stanza continues to depict the men as part of nature. With a body-landscape of "bringene berre liksom solbakkar / der vårgras brydder" (chests bare like sunlit slopes / where spring grass sprouts) they revel in their own masculinity, and their blood leads them to a heterosexual object choice. Although the speaker repeatedly exclaims his enjoyment in viewing these men, this attraction is not reciprocal; the men's sexual activity in the poem remains heterosexual even though the speaker's gaze upon it is voyeuristic and homoerotic. When the second stanza continues to portray the men's desire as a force of nature and the blood, the spiritual dimension of the erotic also returns: the "undringa . . . i det gode mørker" (wonder of the blessed dark), and more emphatically, the love that "ein gong skal . . . loga igjenom alt ditt verande" (one day will blaze through your entire being).

In the poem's third stanza, the speaker watches the men performing winter athletics and riding "horses of noble blood," a line that indicates an ideological concern for ethnic or racial purity. In the second half of this stanza, the speaker zooms in on an individual "eagle-willed" man as he "dash[es] with [his] arrow-quick bird of steel high over mountains and sea / and penetrate[s] to ice-cold heights." The phallic nature of this futuristic imagery is self-evident, and as usual, a question about inner experience accompanies the physical act: "Kjenner du og det svimrande floget inn—inn / i hjartehimlen?" (Do you also know the dizzying flight—into / the heart of heaven?). In such moments, the speaker seems to seek identification with the young men in a common experience of the mystical erotic.

Sveen's poem reaches spring in the fourth stanza, as the "sowers for God and the world" work on farms and build cities. These activities remain sexualized in a double sense. The homoerotic gaze on the men continues to configure them as robust and alluring masculine bodies as they work, with the "sun [on their] sweaty faces" plowing the fields. Also, the men themselves continue to possess erotic agency, scattering seeds "in the vibrations of sowing" (*når kornet drys ifrå hendene dykkar i sågiddret*) and reproducing. As we saw in the case of in "Eros syng," Sveen imagined the individual's sexual desire as an instantiation of the larger mystical force of Eros. Similarly, the sowers in "Til dei unge menn" are vehicles for the erotic principle of life.

In this manner, the poem envisions a utopian society constructed and reproduced by erotically potent men. The final stanza praises "kjelder i øydemark" (wellsprings in the wasteland) and "sigrande tårn på ville fjell" (victorious towers in the wilderness), contrasting the heroic fertility of the men to the surrounding desolation and barrenness. The speaker hopes that the virile men will remain sources of spiritual and social regeneration—that they will rise up "liksom eit fjell av velsigning millom aude sjeler" (like a mountain of benediction among desolate souls). This odd poem manages to run the gamut of fascist aesthetics, from the national-romantic glorification of farm labor to a futurist image of speed and metal in the winter sports section. At the end, the poem praises "children of the sun and light . . . on golden shores," which suggests two pictorial associations: the work of the early twentieth-century Danish vitalist painter J. F. Willumsen, but also a fascist propaganda poster by the illustrator Harald Damsleth, which shows a naked Nordic family on a beach, heralding a sun glowing with the Nasjonal Samling insignia.

"Til dei unge menn" raises some interesting questions about the homoerotic surface of fascist masculinity. Although fascism rejected effeminacy and sexual deviance quite violently in practice, its representational connection to homosexuality is strangely ambivalent.[73] Fascist representations of masculinity often have a homoerotic charge that seems at odds with the ideology's oppressive enforcement of compulsory heterosexuality. Such representations tend to glorify the virility and fertility of men while suppressing the influence of femininity, even fantasizing biological and social reproduction without women, as in Italian Futurism.[74] Sveen's masculinist aesthetic does not offer the fantasy of male self-sufficiency and misogynistic violence associated with Futurism or with Theweleit's analysis of the German Freikorps. However, his poetry does imagine an idealized and eroticized male figure of regeneration: "The Sower" (*Såmannen*). This figure of the sower can be contrasted with another fascist hero of masculinity, the soldier. Rather than glorifying the martial vitality of the trenches and the struggle of battle, Sveen's virile sower embodies the erotic, agrarian, and spiritual reproduction of the nation.

"THE LAND OF THE CENTAUR"

In its opposed images of the regenerative sower and the wasteland of desolate souls, "Til dei unge menn" suggests a narrative of contemporary history as fascist regeneration after bourgeois decay. Indeed, Sveen was seduced by the widespread fantasy that National Socialism was a revolutionary project whose destiny was to reinvigorate the West and save it from decline. As we see in his writings on authors like Knut Hamsun and Tarjei Vesaas, Sveen thought modernist literature belonged to a century of fascist revitalization, which would restore a materialistic and repressed civilization to the health of the pure and naked body.

Although Sveen did not identify as a National Socialist in the 1930s, he seems to have been drifting in that direction throughout the decade. In 1934, he wrote home from the Deutsch-Nordisches Schriftstellerhaus in northern Germany: "Jeg er ikke blitt nasjonalsosialist, hele ånden er en annen en min—jeg er pasifist og det er nærmest et skjellsord her nede" (I haven't become a National Socialist, the whole idea of it is different from mine—I'm a pacifist and that's nearly a dirty word down here).[75] But he also wrote that he was beginning to understand "the new mentality" and that if he revealed his true opinion about contemporary German politics to the leftist *Arbeiderbladet*, they would refuse to print it.[76] While Sveen's eventual decision to align himself publicly with Nazism might be explained in terms of his difficult economic conditions, his opportunism, or his political ingenuousness, it would be wrong to ignore the more substantial ways in which it captured his imagination.

Sveen's articles from World War II fit Griffin's model of nationalist "palingenesis" (rebirth) very well, with their critique of liberal and Marxist materialism in favor of a cultural-spiritual revitalization. Sveen described the appeal of fascism in terms of a utopian project that would embrace the premodern and the primitive as models for a future alternative to the capitalist and materialist present. In an article called "Hvorfor jeg er medlem av NS" (Why I am a Member of Nasjonal Samling) from 1944, he explained National Socialism as the revival of an authentic European culture after four hundred years of desiccating materialism and rationalism. It was a spiritual politics tinged with racial sentiment and fear of degeneracy, as he writes: "Jeg er spiritualist og idealist og ser på oppgjøret med materialismen som vårt århundredes historiske innebyrd. . . . Denne bevegelse må gjenføde den hvite manns verden, ellers er aftenlandene dømt til undergang" (I am a spiritualist and an idealist, and I see the revolt against materialism as the historical meaning of our century. . . . This movement must regenerate the white man's world, or the West is condemned to destruction).[77] Like Mussolini and Giovanni Gentile, the Italian philosopher of fascism who described it as a revolutionary "total conception of life," Sveen saw fascism as more than an ordinary politics.[78] He saw it as an "original historical idea" that would save the "white man's world" from decaying liberalism and the threat of Bolshevism. His fascism was based on a melodramatic, metaphysical, and racist view of European history.[79]

The naïve argument that poetry and politics are separate and unrelated activities would be especially odd to apply to Sveen, who was probably the Nasjonal Samling member who did the most to find antecedents for National Socialist ideology in Scandinavian art and literature. His published explanations of fascist politics were couched in conspicuously cultural and literary, even modernist, terms, rather than in a more limited political or economic discourse. In an article called "Kunsten og tiden" (Art and the Modern Age), which appeared in the Nasjonal Samling organ *Fritt Folk* in 1943, Sveen praises fascist art for its quasi-religious imagination, which addresses the fundamental and universal mysteries of life. He writes that the spiritual or cultural life (*åndsliv*) of the new fascist age is already visible in the works of certain literary figures such as Knut Hamsun and the sculptor Gustav Vigeland but also, less predictably, Henrik Ibsen and the Finnish Swedish modernist poet Edith Södergran.[80] In general, as the art historian Mark Antliff has written, the fascist method of dealing with cultural tradition was to "selectively plunder their historical past for moments reflective of the values they wished to inculcate for their radical transformation of national consciousness and public institutions."[81] This was precisely the manner in which Sveen edited *Norsk ånd og vilje*, a canon that collected texts from Eddic poetry through Bjørnson and Ibsen and even included speeches by Quisling.

Anti-realist and modernist literature in particular embodied for Sveen the values he saw as part of fascism's historical wave. In an article written for an anthology about Northern Norway, Sveen praised Hamsun for his "revolusjonær og konservativ . . . [kamp] mot forflating og utarming og mekanisering" (revolutionary and conservative . . . [fight] against banalization and impoverishment and mechanization).[82] In Sveen's hands, Hamsun's example points the way forward to a nationalist and vitalistic triumph over the banal and mechanized modern age. In a 1942 lecture about other fascist cultural figures, Sveen wrote that the task of contemporary poetry was to show the way back to "den opphavelige åndelige innsikt og den symbolstyrken som er gått tapt i så meget av den nyere sivilisasjons kunst" (the original spiritual insight and the symbolic power that has been missing in so much of modern civilization's art), and he distinguished this new poetry from both "den dekadente borgerlige privatpersonlige lyrikken og den rasjonalistisk-borgerlige tendens-poesien" (the decadent bourgeois lyric poetry of the private individual and rationalistic bourgeois tendentious poetry).[83] Modernist literature for Sveen reconnected with the mysteries and wisdom of the distant past, while rejecting the individualism and shallow rationalism of the recent past. This search for primordial values to revitalize the modern age was, according to Griffin, a central aspect of fascist literary modernism.[84]

When Sveen reviewed Tarjei Vesaas's novel *Kimen* (The Seed, 1940), he revealed the influence of both Hamsunian anti-realism and aesthetic vitalism in his conception of literary modernity. For Sveen, the novel showed the current need to recognize the value of the animal in man (*dyret i menneskja*).

> Dei som trur at den nye europeiske diktninga skal bli borgarlege idyllar, misseromaner, bollelitteratur—tek i miss. Det skal bli den evige diktinga om menneskja, men meir enn nokon gong diktinga om heile menneskja, om sind og blod, om kjærleik og gru, om visdom og drift, om ljos og mørker. Vår tid er den timen da kentauren lyfter hovudet i menneskja og openberrar sin universelle visdom og sitt avgrunnsdjupe vanvit. . . . Den nye diktinga må hjelpe til å gi nytt liv å verda ved å opne vegane inn til den åndelege røyndom. Og dei vegane går gjennom kentuar-landet.[85]

> (Those who think that the new European literature will include bourgeois idylls and sentimental novels are mistaken. It will be the eternal literature of mankind, but more than ever it will be literature about the whole person, about the blood and the mind, about love and horror, about wisdom and desire, about light and darkness. Our age is the hour when the centaur rears its head in man and reveals

> its universal wisdom and its abyssal madness. . . . The new literature must help to give new life to the world by opening paths to spiritual mysteries. And those paths lead through the land of the centaur.)

Sveen's future-primitive liberation of the animal in man was part of a broader urge toward sexual revolution and a new culture of the body in the early twentieth century. In this passage, the centaur raising its head against modern rationalism and against the repression of the animal-in-man supplies a dynamic image for the historical narrative of primordial reconnection that Sveen saw in his own time. He praises the "wisdom" of animalistic desire, which matches the sacralization of the erotic and the sensual upon which much of his poetry was built. But he also acknowledges its other side—its "abyssal madness." This dual image of revelation—the centaur unveiling its divine wisdom along with its demonic terror—suits Sveen's portentous reading of fascism as a vehicle for the spiritual and erotic revitalization of European modernity, and as a world-historical force embracing the mystical energies of nature and sex explored in his own poetry.

For Sveen, the utopian dream of overcoming the rationalist paradigm of bourgeois modernity was so intoxicating that it obscured the glaring problems of Nazism, even from his homosexual perspective as a potential victim. We should recall, however, that Sveen did not perceive National Socialism as a homophobic threat but rather as a movement of synthesis and harmony that would not exclude his marginal sexuality. It is chilling to read Sveen, deluded that a new fascist age is imminent, write in "Kunsten og tiden" that "viljen til sammenføyning, syntese, harmoni . . . først må bevirke en rensningsprosess, en storm i verden, [som] er historisk nødvendig. At stormen virker på oss nærsynte mennesker som kaos og vold er også naturlig" (the will to integration, synthesis, harmony . . . must first bring about a cleansing process, a storm in the world, [which] is historically necessary. That the storm seems chaotic and violent to us nearsighted people is also natural).[86] This is one of Sveen's most disturbing statements; he employs a typical fascist rhetoric of apocalypse and palingenesis to justify the storm around him from a perspective of historical necessity.

After his actions during World War II, it is difficult to see Sveen's work from the 1930s in a neutral political light, although it is worth remembering that he was not perceived as a fascist poet before his collaboration and that vitalism was not an exclusively fascist aesthetic. Rather, Scandinavian vitalism in the early twentieth century was a politically multivalent discourse of anti-rationalism, erotic liberation, sensual utopianism, and generational revolt. Sveen's literary vitalism envisioned a neoprimitive attitude toward the body and a religious understanding of sexuality, which he sacralized in his mythopoetic figure of Eros. As a Norwegian writer, Sveen belonged to a peripheral European culture that has sometimes been exoticized as a primitive and healthier location by continental Europeans, and also by Scandinavians. In her book on Hamsun, Žagar notices the parallels "between Scandinavian primitivism and that projected onto the Orient and other exotic locales"—each location has been constructed as an authentic, sexually vital, and natural escape from an over-civilized continental Europe.[87] This construction of Scandinavian primitivism shows how Sveen's literary vitalism could have coalesced with his romantic nationalism and his interest in forms of Norwegian folk art. By including traditional *bygdeviser* in his collections along with his boldly experimental works, Sveen achieved the primitivist synthesis of traditionalist and modernist artistic forms that was typical of fascist cultural production in other national contexts.[88] By looking to Sufi mysticism and to early twentieth-century revitalization movements, Sveen found sources of sensuality and religiosity that were supposedly absent in the repressive "iron cage" of modern Europe. Sveen's embrace of fascism, though related to the infatuation with masculine virility and mystical eroticism that we find in "Til dei unge menn," was not simply a political expression of homosexual desire. Sveen was obsessed with the spiritual crisis of secularized societies in the early twentieth century, and he viewed communism and capitalism as twin expressions of a godforsaken modern materialism that fascism would overpower.

FIGURES OF NARCISSISM AND PUNISHMENT

How did Sveen react to the failure of his utopian and idealistic revitalization politics and the catastrophes of World War II? Sentenced for treason, made to forfeit his civil rights, and excluded from publishing, Sveen moved into an even more dejected outsider position, becoming in many ways a figure of "inner emigration."[89] Writing in the wake of his collaboration and punishment, his poetry turned from the sun-drenched invocation of life forces and erotic ecstasy to more grim and enigmatic work that often focuses on punishment and persecution. In the postwar poetry, Sveen used two mythological figures to imagine his punishment and to weave together his divergent experiences of sexual and political deviance: Narcissus and Marsyas.

Sveen's final two poetry collections, *Brunnen* and *Tonemesteren*, are intimately connected. Most of these poems were originally written in the immediate postwar years, although they did not see publication until the 1960s. Sveen died in 1963, merely a few days after submitting the complete manuscript of *Brunnen* to his publisher. *Tonemesteren* was assembled as a posthumous collection and published in 1966; it is his only collection written in *bokmål* rather than *nynorsk*. The title of *Brunnen* alone (The Well) announces Sveen's engagement with the Narcissus tradition. As he wrote in 1962, "Jeg har kalt den *Brunnen*, og Narcissos-symbolet, utvidet og gitt ny dybde, er gjennomgangsmotivet" (I have called it *The Well*, and the Narcissus symbol, expanded and given new depth, is the leitmotif).[90] A young man staring into a well or pond, desiring his own reflection, is often accompanied by disturbing images of drowning or punishment, as in the epigraph Sveen selected for *Brunnen* (from *Jordelden*).

> Småguten sprang over vollen
> så berrføtt og blid til brunnen.
> Han likte å ligge på steinane der
> å sjå seg sjølv ned i grunnen.
>
> Somtider låg han og sørgde
> og stundom så kom han på låtten.
> Men ein gong var steinen hål etter regn
> og kjelda var djupt til botn.
>
> Mor hans hadde ein klebleik
> på groren bortafor brunnen.
> Ho kom og fekk sjå han og drog han opp.
> Og vatnet valt utor munnen.[91]
>
> (The little boy ran over the field / barefooted and joyful to the well. / He liked to lie on the stones there / to look at himself down in the bottom. // At times he would lie there in grief / and sometimes he did so with laughter. / But one time the stones were slippery from rain / and the well was quite deep to the bottom. // His mother had a bleaching spot / on the ground beyond the well. / She came and found him and drew him up. / And water ran out of his mouth.)

Sveen often takes a malicious pleasure in recounting such abrupt transitions, from the natural "barefooted and joyful" child, through the specular moment of narcissistic pleasure, and on to the drowned body. As an entrance to *Brunnen*, the text promises a dark and disturbing use of the Narcissus motif—and the poems that follow do not disappoint.

Some recurrent themes of the Narcissus tradition include "beauty, arrogance, pride, confusion of identities or ontological strata, metamorphosis, homosexual love, just punishment."[92] The most influential rendering of the Narcissus story—in Ovid's *Metamorphoses*—removes the issues of defiance and just punishment that were found in earlier versions and focuses more on aspects of mirroring (the gaze, reflection, doubling).[93] However, in Ovid's Greek contemporary Konon's version, it is Narcissus's arrogant and defiant attitude toward Eros and his dismissal of loved ones that lead to his drowning—a just punishment for his guilt.[94] Sveen's recurrent use of the Narcissus motif entails a complex set of issues, including the mirroring themes of selfhood and subjectivity in a universal sense, the autoeroticism that has often been linked to homosexual identity, by both gay artists and in developmental discourses such as classic psychoanalysis, and, lastly, the deviance and punishment that preoccupied Sveen after his treasonous collaboration.

Brunnen alternates between a sense of just punishment for pride or hubris and feelings of persecution and superiority. The bleak poem "Skogkjelda" (The Forest Spring) explicitly imagines narcissistic self-involvement as a suicidal escape from persecution by others, the speaker's "brothers." It begins, "Dei andre forfølgjer meg / brørne mine jagar meg gjennom skogen / noken er etter meg" (The others are following me / my brothers hunt me through the forest / someone is coming after me).[95] The speaker recounts his escape from the other people into the forest, where he plans to hang himself in an old birch tree. The motivation for this suicide is narcissistic in the classic sense: "så eg kan spegle meg i vatnet når eg døyr / og sjå i spegelen kven som kjem og henter meg når eg døyr" (so I can mirror myself in the water when I die / and see in the mirror who comes to get me when I die).[96] The poem ends with the speaker's rediscovery, in death, of a lost image of his child self. This specular image is revealed from under fragments and mirrored back in the water of the forest spring.[97]

One of *Brunnen*'s most fascinating uses of the Narcissus motif occurs in the metrically conventional little poem that follows "Skogkjelda," called "Nykken." Sveen boldly uses a figure from Norwegian folklore, the dangerous aquatic shape-shifter called *nøkken*, in a suggestive scene of violent homoerotic drowning.

I olderlunden ein soldag ølen
der åa vidgar seg ut i hølen
låg eg og godna min gutekropp.
Da kom ein fole or vatnet opp.

Han bykste månekvit inn på grunnen
og la seg ned der i skuggelunden
og byrja velte seg vill og kåt
og viste buken som blenkte våt.

Eg lystra ri på han, ville leike,
eg skreva over den ryggen keike,
da brått han bredgast og la på laup
og ut i djupaste hølen staup.

Han skifte ham i den skume skòre
og smilte mot meg med siv i håret,
og da eg svimra i sælesang
tok måneprinsen meg fast i fang.

Og dernå under dei døkke strender
vart eg ei harpe i nykkens hender.
Han spela på meg, det gret og log,
og låten skremte den lye skog.[98]

(In the alder grove on a blazing sunny day / where the river widens into a pool / I lay and let my young body ripen / then came a colt from out of the water // He leaped onto the ground, white as the moon / and lay down in the shade of the grove / and began to roll around, wild and horny [*kåt*] / and showed me his stomach, flashing wet. // I wanted to ride him, wanted to play / I climbed astride his bended back / then suddenly he changed and started to run / and plunged right into the watery depths. // He shape-shifted in the half-lit water / he smiled at me with reeds in his hair / and as I grew dizzy in the blessed song / the moon-prince took me in a firm embrace. // And down there under the murky strands / I became a harp in the hands of the *nøkk* / he played me, there were tears and laughter / and the song frightened the calm forest.)

This poem is another example of Sveen's distinctive brand of enigmatic homoerotics. "Nykken" echoes the poem "Guten låg i graset," from the interwar collection *Andletet*; we see the same passage from a carefree young male body in a harmonious natural landscape to a fantasized encounter with a figure of sexuality and death. Sveen employs the folkloric figure of the *nøkk*—already a potential figure of sexual violence and drowning—in an innovative way here. This is a far cry from the Norwegian Romantic poet Johan Sebastian Welhaven's tranquil and sentimental presentation of the *nøkk* as a figure of melancholic recollection (in *Digte*, from 1838). Sveen's *nøkk* is a force of unbridled, destructive sexuality, and the speaker finds the pain of being taken by him exquisite. The poem's queer appropriation of folklore and Romantic tradition should not conceal the fact that the speaker is another Narcissus figure, enjoying his body at the water's edge before being taken into the water for a frightening yet thrilling encounter with the "moon-prince." "Nykken" offers a surprising blend of Greek myth and Norwegian folklore in a tale of spontaneous homoerotic possession.

If this poetic imagination of a Narcissus figure drowning in sexual frenzy with the *nøkk* seems strange, we have only to look to a second figure of punishment for further eccentricity. Sveen's postwar identification with the figure of Marsyas was overt and overdetermined, pertaining both to his political deviance as a Nazi collaborator and to his sexual dissidence as a gay man in midcentury Norway. There are several versions of the Marsyas myth; the most well known is from Ovid's *Metamorphoses*. Sveen provided his own summary: "I den greske myten fortelles det at skogguden Marsyas med sin panfløyte utfordret Apollon, lyrens trålende gud, til en tonenes tvekamp. Driftsguden Marsyas tapte i dysten med bevissthetsguden Apollon og ble til straff for sin formastelighet flådd levende" (The Greek myth tells of how the forest god Marsyas, with his pan flute, challenged Apollo, the probing god of the lyre, to a musical duel. The god of instinct, Marsyas, lost in the fight against the god of consciousness, Apollo, and was flayed alive as a punishment for his presumptuousness).[99] In this account, Apollo's harmonic rationalism triumphs over the earthly passion embodied in the satyr Marsyas.

Marsyas is a figure of failure, humiliation, and over-the-top suffering—"a failed artist turned grotesque," as Ellis Hanson calls him in an article on Oscar Wilde.[100] Additionally, Marsyas is an enemy of the state and of the cultural hierarchy upheld by Apollo; he is persecuted for his hubris and for his deviance. As though the idea of persecution or martyrdom weren't explicit enough, Sveen selected the preposterous pseudonym Marsyas Christ as the name under which he tried to publish *Tonemesteren* after the war.[101] At one level, we might understand Sveen's identification with Marsyas in relation to his fascism. As this chapter has shown, Sveen understood fascism as a grand form of neo-primitivism that would reinvigorate the overly rationalized modern world. In aligning himself with the part-human/part-animal Marsyas, whom he explicitly links to Dionysus, Sveen continues this construal of fascism as a vitalistic revolt against modern rationalism. He thus politicizes the Dionysian-Apollonian distinction and again interprets fascism as a Dionysian politics, while also identifying himself with the defeated and punished "forest god."

At the same time, Marsyas is another instance of Sveen's penchant for violent and disturbing homoeroticism. Like Saint Sebastian—and of course Narcissus—Marsyas has also served as a figure of gay sexuality, and Apollo's horrible flaying of Marsyas has been imagined as a sadomasochistic homoerotic scenario. For example, the Italian Baroque painter Guido Reni suggestively depicted the punishment as a rape by Apollo.[102] In the context of Wilde, Hanson remarks, with memorable phrasing, that "Marsyas is in hot competition with Saint Sebastian as the favorite classical emblem of gay male masochism."[103]

Sveen's poem "Jeg-Marsyas" (I-Marsyas) from the collection *Tonemesteren* presents an alternative to Marsyas's failure, in a fantasy version of his victory over Apollo. Instead of challenging Apollo to a duel and then being flayed alive, Marsyas uses flattery to trick the conceited Apollo and steal the source of his music. Sveen presents Apollo as incapable of comprehending the "dark cry" of Marsyas's flute—Apollo stops playing his own music and listens "forundret og begjærlig som til noe han ikke kunne forstå" (astonished and desirous, as with something he could not understand).[104] Marsyas breaks his flute, casts himself down before Apollo, and flatters the god's vanity in order to keep him playing. Apollo is so enraptured by his own music that he doesn't notice as Marsyas carefully covers him in vines. Vine leaves grow into Apollo's skin and merge with his body and blood; he is eventually incorporated into the forest, his feet grow into the ground. The next morning, when Marsyas wakes up in the bright forest, he sees the ripe grapes that have grown from the vines that Apollo has become. Naming himself "Marsyas Dionysus," he drinks the grapes and appropriates Apollo's musical power.

In *De Profundis*, Wilde remarks observantly, "Apollo had been the victor. The lyre had vanquished the reed. But perhaps the Greeks were mistaken. I hear in much modern art the cry of Marsyas." At the end of "Jeg-Marsyas," Sveen writes, "Ingen hører i dag Apollons lyre. Bleke tanker lytter forgjeves efter dens klanger, råtnet er den forlengst i skogen" (No one today hears the lyre of Apollo. Pale thoughts listen in vain for its tones, but it has long since decayed in the forest).[105] Wilde was indicating a tendency toward the Dionysian and the pan-like that would only grow greater in subsequent modern art. In "Jeg-Marsyas," Sveen was staging in poetry a fantasy victory for Marsyas, a triumph for the Dionysian values of his forest vitalism, while in actual life he identified with the satyr's defeat and horrific punishment.

On the occasion of Wilde's 100th birthday in 1954, Sveen published a piece in the newspaper *Morgenbladet* that praised Wilde as evidence that the greatest artists are exceptions and deviants: they are "verdiskapende i samme grad som de avviker fra det regelrette forløp" (capable of creating new values to the extent that they deviate from the ordinary course).[106] Sveen defended Wilde's homosexuality while also identifying with his punishment and imprisonment. "Verst var den *fortsatte* straff etter fullbyrdet soning" (The worst part was the continued punishment after the sentence was served completely), he contends, speaking from experience.[107] The continued punishment was presumably the public's neglect of Wilde's artistic output and his inability to publish—a fate that Sveen shared in the postwar decades.

Sveen apparently felt that he had served his time in the immediate postwar years and thus saw his failure to publish or be recuperated as evidence of unfair persecution by others. Of course, the causes of punishment in the two cases differed greatly. Wilde was punished for so-called sexual "immorality," but Sveen was punished for treason for his Nazi collaboration. While it could easily be charged that Sveen is irresponsibly conflating two very different matters, it is evident that his postwar interest in Oscar Wilde was doubly motivated: Wilde was both a gay figure and a punished figure. Similarly, Sveen employed the figures of Narcissus and Marsyas both to explore a sexual subjectivity including autoerotic and masochistic fantasies and to express the intensity of the actual punishment that marked his postwar existence.

CHAPTER 4

Modernist Ragnarok

Rolf Jacobsen's Poetic and Political Anti-Nihilism

Of all the midcentury modernist poets in Norway who experimented and innovated in lastingly significant ways—including Paal Brekke, Gunvor Hofmo, Tarjei Vesaas, and Olav H. Hauge—Rolf Jacobsen has remained the most adored: Norway's "most popular modernist."[1] This persistent popularity is due to some arresting and elegiac late work from the 1980s, to his institutionalized status as the signal figure of interwar poetic modernism, and to the ways his anti-consumerist and environmentalist messages have resonated broadly in late modern Norwegian culture. Despite the publicly available record of his Nazi collaboration and sympathies, Jacobsen's name does not conjure up the fraught wartime issues and difficult legacy that Hamsun's does. There is no memory complex around Jacobsen, perhaps for the simple fact that his Nazism is not remembered. More quietly than Hamsun, and with less obvious ideological dedication, Jacobsen served the occupying regime's regional press and propaganda goals, aligning himself with National Socialism for a five-year period that has frequently been disregarded in scholarship and left silent in memory.

Jacobsen's interwar poetry exemplifies the modernist impulse to create a new artistic language in response to the transformed conditions of urban and technological modernity. The two collections he published in the 1930s, *Jord og jern* (Earth and Iron, 1933) and *Vrimmel* (Swarm, 1935), broke with the Norwegian poetic tradition by drawing motifs from the banal surface of the modern city: asphalt, plate glass, railroads, airplanes, telephone poles, power lines, and newspapers.[2] This literary encounter with the machine age might initially suggest an aesthetic of speed, power, and mechanical form along the lines of other technophilic modernisms, such as Italian Futurism. But, as commentators on Jacobsen's poetry invariably observe, rather than a one-sided fascination with the machine aesthetic, a fundamental ambivalence lies at the heart of this encounter with technological modernity. For instance, the Danish critic Torben Brostrøm underscores Jacobsen's alienation in "modernity's double-world of quick satisfactions and deep lack."[3] Others have emphasized the sense of melancholia, foreboding, and apprehension that accompany any enthusiasm for the new.[4] Over the course of Jacobsen's poetic career, the initial ambivalence grows into a patently pessimistic stance toward modern technological civilization. This shift is noticeable already in *Vrimmel*, which was followed by a sixteen-year hiatus before his postwar poetic return, with *Fjerntog* (Distance Train, 1951) and *Hemmelig liv* (Secret Life, 1954). These collections began to consolidate Jacobsen's position as a major Scandinavian writer and an ecological poet known for his critique of consumerism, or what he saw as the Americanized *reklamesivilisasjon* (culture of advertising).[5]

The facts of Jacobsen's support for National Socialism during the hiatus in his authorship—a troubling past that he refused to discuss honestly—were finally made clear to the public with the appearance of two biographies in 1998, four years after his death.[6] As the editor of *Kongsvinger arbeiderbladet*, renamed *Glåmdalen* during the war, Jacobsen published almost sixty pro-Nazi editorials, and he was also the propaganda leader for his local division of Nasjonal Samling. He was sentenced for treason after the occupation, although the judge found that he "belonged to the moderate wing of NS."[7] The biographical accounts give the sense of a sudden reversal after the German invasion, when Jacobsen joined the Norwegian fascist party despite his earlier leftist orientation. Although this shift seems perplexing, Jacobsen's radical politics of both left and right were based on consistent underlying concerns: his opposition to Anglo-American liberal capitalism, his anxiety about present technological-industrial developments, and his qualms about a modern culture of nihilism.

Jacobsen's National Socialist sympathies have been bewildering to admirers of his poetry, which is hardly legible in terms of fascist aesthetics or ideology. Critics have rarely seen Jacobsen's fascism as anything more than an untoward blunder, with little relevance for his career as a poet. From this perspective, it comes as a surprise that Jacobsen was featured in the wartime propaganda work

Nasjonalsosialister i norsk diktning (National Socialists in Norwegian Literature). The article on Jacobsen there focuses on the metallic and modern functionalist aesthetic of his interwar work, using his example to claim that National Socialist art is multifaceted, encompassing not only nostalgic ruralist national romanticism but also the work of "Rolf Jacobsen, the spokesman of the city, industry, iron, and metal."[8] While this description epitomizes the superficial reading of Jacobsen's relation to technology, it also inclines us to ask how his poetry was connected to his political support for National Socialism. In what way might we understand Jacobsen's fascism as something more than a temporary aberration with no relevance to his literary output? How are Jacobsen's concerns as a modernist poet—his encounters with technology, modernity, and nihilism—connected to his political engagements, including his National Socialism?

To the extent that questions like these have even been raised, they have not been answered persuasively in discussions of Jacobsen. Critics and commentators have often been reluctant to pursue any lines of continuity between Jacobsen's poetry and his politics.[9] This is partly because Jacobsen is a beloved figure, while fascism is an unsettling topic, but it also reflects the fact that his poetry differs stylistically from what is usually considered fascist. As a poet, Jacobsen produced complicated and image-rich texts with multiple meanings; his work cannot be unmasked as essentially proto-fascist through any type of suspicious reading method. In fact, a critical method that attempts to detect features of fascist ideology or aesthetics will not yield much of interest in Jacobsen's poetry. However, the prevailing narrative of Jacobsen's career is inadequate, because it is unable to account for his fascist interlude.

Instead of locating fascism *in* Jacobsen's modernist poetry, this chapter underscores the concern with nihilism—the lack of a foundation for beliefs and actions, the lack of direction and commitment—that underlies both his poetry and his political engagements. I aim to reconsider Jacobsen's political activities and their indirect relationship to his poetic imagination, without glossing over his National Socialism, but also without reducing his poetry to any single political discourse. To that end, this chapter discusses Jacobsen's wartime support for National Socialism as more than a meaningless hiatus; it was based on his poetic critique of modernity's nihilism and it was part of his search for a way to overcome this cultural paradigm.

As Jacobsen himself admitted after the war, his political radicalism was motivated by a displaced religiosity, and following the war he ended up converting to Catholicism after his disillusionment with redemptive politics. Many of the pessimistic reservations about the culture of nihilism that motivated Jacobsen's grand political visions of the 1930s and 1940s migrate into his postwar stance, a hybrid of Catholic and environmentalist critiques of (post)modernity. The difference is that the messianic longing no longer resides in secular politics but is now housed in an actual religious discourse. In what follows, I examine how Jacobsen's interwar poetry encounters and recoils from what he perceived as the nihilism of technological modernity, how this was followed by his search for secular redemption in the form of utopian politics, and how his postwar poetic stance emerged from disillusionment with political forms of salvation.

TECHNOLOGY, SPEED, NIHILISM

Jacobsen's work offers a variety of modernist poetic impulses, with strong hints of imagism, futurism, and expressionism. The poems in *Jord og jern* and *Vrimmel* contain concrete and precise images of both urban spaces and natural landscapes; this has led critics to link Jacobsen to both imagism and "the new objectivity."[10] Jacobsen's sober poetic perception of undistorted objects, even when it becomes somewhat mystical, offers a counterpoint to Sveen's intoxicated verse and to the early Hamsun's probing of the unconscious. Instead of exhibiting psychological depth, his literary imagination is strikingly geographical and spatial, as some of his titles suggest: "Reise," "Avstand," "Europa," and "Erosjon" (Travel, Distance, Europe, and Erosion). Futurist symbols and images appear frequently in Jacobsen's poems, for example, "Flyvemaskiner" (Flying Machines), but not with the Futurists' unequivocal admiration for speed and machines over and against nature. His work from the 1930s also shares many thematic features with expressionism, including its fixation on angst and alienation in urban and technological spaces (examples include "Signaler" in *Jord og jern* and "Lysreklamen i skumringen" in *Vrimmel*).

Jacobsen's interwar poetry has been called a literary exploration of "technology's secret significance for modern life."[11] The early collections show that he was indeed captivated and disquieted by the material surface of the industrial urban environment. Occasionally, his work attempts an imaginative synthesis of nature and technology, as in the incredible final poem in *Jord og jern*, "Jernbaneland" (Railroad Country), which visualizes trains rhythmically stretching over the earth, bringing a "et lite vers av stål og sten / i veiens store sang" (little verse of steel and stone / in the railway's mighty song).[12] However, the same text also expresses profound doubts about the ultimate impact of machinery and a growing awareness of the distress caused by technical-industrial advancement. In the culminating section of "Jernbaneland," the railroad itself speaks the following prophetic words to mankind.

For det kommer nok en dag og det kommer nok en tid
da den jord hvor du trår er en brennende jord.
Og du rømmer fra dig selv og da kommer du til mig
på min flukt over syngende spor.

Og du finner ikke ro og du leter overalt
gjennem tider og land i en rivende strøm.
Og du hører mine hjul som en tromme i ditt blod
på din jakt mot den ytterste drøm.

(For there will surely come a day and there will surely come a time / when the earth underfoot will be burning coals. / And you'll flee from yourself and then you'll come to me / in my flight over singing rails. // And you won't find any peace, you'll be searching everywhere / across ages and lands: a torrential stream. / And you'll listen to my wheels like a drumming in your blood / while you hunt for the ultimate dream.)[13]

The railroad is a means of escape both from the self and from a future catastrophe ("brennende jord"). It is spatially and temporally unhinged, but at the same time a seductive machine in an ideological quest for the new. Jacobsen suggests here that modernity's technological utopianism—its "ultimate dream"—creates a feverish march ("en tromme i ditt blod"), an unmanageable process of disruption and mobility, a hunt that leads nowhere.

The dawning cultural critique in Jacobsen's interwar work reflects his concern that technology, despite its enthralling facade, has become an uncontrolled and out-of-balance force, and that modernity, despite its seductive freedom, actually entails a loss of meaning—an uneasy cultural condition of nihilism in which something has been forgotten. Later, from his postwar environmental perspective, Jacobsen understands this loss as the collective forgetting of humanity's profound dependence on nature.[14] For instance, the lovely 1956 poem "Grønt lys" (Green Light) declares, "for dette har vi glemt, at Jorden er en stjerne av gress, / en frø-planét, rykende av sporer som skyer, fra hav til hav, / et fokk" (for we have forgotten this: that the Earth is a star of grass, / a seed-planet, swirling with spores as with clouds, from sea to sea, / a whirl of them).[15] I will return to Jacobsen's haunting postwar work later in the chapter.

Jord og jern (1933) announced its cutting-edge style and subject matter with a sleek functionalist cover design. This collection is divided into two parts that correspond to the title's nature/culture contrast: "Skyggene" (The Shadows) contains timeless natural landscape poems, while "Morgenfrost" (Morning Frost) consists of present-day technologized landscapes. Readers as early as the ubiquitous Sigurd Hoel have noted that the two kinds of landscape are treated in parallel.[16] Jacobsen claimed that the collection, with its juxtaposition of primordial landscapes inspired by the Poetic Edda and metropolitan, industrial landscapes, emphasized similarity rather than contrast.[17] Along with his use of new industrial motifs and poetic rhythms, commentators have focused on Jacobsen's linkage of natural and technological imagery as an original and characteristic feature of his modernism.[18]

Looking back at *Jord og jern* in 1978, Jacobsen said that readers had neglected that it is a kind of creation narrative ("en slags skapelsesberetning").[19] The collection was originally called "Begynnelsen" (The Beginning), and the first several poems evoke a mood of awe and astonishment in a prehistoric landscape. "Regn" (Rain) commences the collection with these lines.

> Himmelen har stillet sin harpe på skrå mot jorden
> og rører de tusen strenger med døvende vellyd,
> løfter de store klemt over skog og sletter
> med lekende hender.
> . . .
>
> Regn var det første. Øglene bet mot regn.
> Langsmed de støvgrå sumper gynget de fuktige trær.
> Papegøiene kaklet. Himmelens flyvefisker
> rodde sig skrikende frem
> gjennem regn.
> . . .
>
> Regn var det første sansene skjønte på jorden
> —susende regn.

> (The sky has rested its harp aslant on the earth / and is moving the thousands of strings in deafening harmony, / lofting great chords above forest and steppe / with playful hands . . . Rain was the first thing. The dinosaurs snapped at rain. / Humid trees swayed beside dust-gray swamps. / Parrots cackled. The flying fish of the sky /

paddled forward, shrieking / through rain . . . Rain was the first thing the senses grasped on the earth / —rushing rain.)[20]

After "Regn" comes "Floden" (The Flood), and then the poem that Åsmund Sveen selected for his fascist propaganda anthology *Norsk ånd og vilje*, "Ophav" (Origin). The second half of "Ophav" calls to mind a silence at the world's beginning and portrays the forest as a location that preserves this ancient wonder.

Jeg våknet i frost
og så i halvdrøm en fugl lette mot himlen.
En fugl med tordnende vinger.
Granen.

Og det var ingen annen lyd på jorden.

—Det var bare skogen som snakket til mig
om det som var hendt her,
fra tidens morgen og frem til den
ytterste dag.[21]

(I awoke in frost / and, half-dreaming, saw a bird rising toward the sky. / A bird with thunderous wings. / The spruce. // And there was no other sound on the earth. // —It was only the forest speaking to me / about what has happened here, / from the dawn of time and forward on / to judgment day.)

Perhaps Sveen chose this poem for his National Socialist anthology because of its forest mysticism, one of his favored topics, which could be invested with nationalist significance. In contrast to Sveen's and Hamsun's forest intoxication, however, Jacobsen's poetry does not involve the vitalistic body or the unconscious. As translator Roger Greenwald notes, it is about attunement to one's surroundings and reverence for the natural world.[22] Rather than Dionysian abandon in the eroticized wilderness, Jacobsen's nature poems offer a more sober mood of contemplation and deep recognition. "Ophav," with the image of the spruce tree as a gigantic bird rising, confers on the forest a kind of subjectivity and also a language of its own. The forest will speak of its enduring secrets, the poem suggests, if you are silently receptive to its language. Later, in Jacobsen's uncollected wartime poetry, the theme of dawn and the end of time takes on new significance in relation to fascist apocalypticism—this time through the lens of the mythological Ragnarok rather than the Christian judgment day ("den ytterste dag").

In *Jord og jern*, a less obvious type of creation narrative involves the techno-industrial landscapes. Jacobsen's placement of images of technological creation in parallel to primordial nature implies that the machines, power lines, and trains also belong to a creative force beyond human subjectivity. The poems bring an awareness that, among the machines of iron, as in the extra-human workings of nature, something is happening, emerging, creating itself; this process exceeds the limits of the human subject's knowledge or intentions.[23] Asbjørn Aarnes writes that in its depictions of both natural and technological landscapes, *Jord og jern* "reveals an area where consciousness is absent, the subject-independent world of things."[24] Such a parallelism of the primordial and the technological is perhaps most apparent in the poem "Industridistrikt" (Industrial District).

Det er i jordens oldtid
—at ditt vindu lukkes op mot morgenen
i murbergene
og knirker på sine hasper
og slipper inn lukten av kalk og ny brand
mot dine varme laken,

—at ditt øre fanger den langsomme lyd
av en dampmaskin like i nærheten,
lufthamrenes gjø over taken
den hule hoste fra gater du ikke kan se gjennem røken,

—at ditt øie møter de store
marker av ull,
jernvanger, tomter med koks
under sparsom sol. Fabrikk-
skorstener med kroner av gul røk,
—at ditt hjerte brister i drøm:
Dinosaurene, hornøglene,
løfter de tynne halser over for-
stenede sumper
og gresser
i skyenes tak av løv,

—at din tanke med ett fylles av lys og våkner:
"Idag skal jeg ut og kjøpe nye sko."

(It is in the earth's prehistory / —that your window is opened to morning / amid mountains of walls / and creaks on its hinges / and lets the smell of lime and new fire drift in / toward your warm sheets, // —that your ear catches the slow sound / of a steam engine nearby, / of jackhammers barking over the roofs, / the hollow cough from streets you can't see through the smoke, // —that your eye meets the vast / fields of dust, / iron meadows, lots with coke / under thin sun. Factory / chimneys with yellow crowns of smoke / —that your heart

> bursts into dream: / The dinosaurs, the horned lizards, / raise their thin necks over / petrified swamps / and graze / in the canopy of leafy clouds, // —that your mind is filled at once with light and awakens: / "Today I'm going out and buying new shoes.")[25]

The poem opens in the primordial phase of the world, but it is soon revealed that this dawn is actually just the start of a modern day in an urban-industrial locale. The addressee of the poem awakens to the noisy sounds of machines and the sight of factory smoke choking the streets—lines that suggest the dystopian possibility of industrial society. This person, upon seeing the "fields of dust, / iron meadows, lots with coke," dreams up a landscape populated by dinosaurs and ancient lizards, creating the parallel between the technological modern and a prehistorical moment of the past. A similar image of machines as large creatures returns in the well-known poem "Landskap med gravemaskiner" (Landscape with Steam Shovels), from *Secret Life* (1954). In the postwar poem, technology has become an unambiguously destructive force: the deformed creatures are "eating up my woods" and creating "some sort of hell."[26] In "Industridistrikt," however, the dystopian possibility fades away—or is repressed—as the awakening person decides to fulfill a banal commercial task in the space of the modern city by purchasing new shoes.

Another poem from the second half of *Jord og jern*, "Speilglass" (Plate Glass), describes the dreamlike experience of a new urban commodity space as its main theme. The speaker likens a trip through the city on a streetcar to an underwater journey into an uncanny but congenial world of artificial satisfactions.

> På vår seilas med trikken
> ut til løvetann og syriner
> ble vi sittende fast i speilglass
> i en lang osende kanal.
> Vi la et blått kjølvann bak oss
> gjennem rutenes blinkende brenning
> da vi ble hyllet inn i skygge
> og så var vi på byens havbunn.
>
> Over takenes bølgetopper
> så vi maisolen lyse,
> men i de hemmelighetsfulle sunkne paradiser
> så vi unge piker av voks.
>
> I de strålende, fortyllende akvarier
> lå gaudaostenes gule møllestener,
> røkelaks

og sprø, duftende roquefort med grønne perler.
Og bak de stirrende speilglass-øine
(fuktige av gatens gjennemtrekk)
korseletter, min herre,
og bysteholdere av silkerips.

La løvetannen lyse.
La trikken seile med sitt kjølvann.
—Jeg er strandet på et koralrev
og lar havets champagne bevifte mine gjellespalter.

(On our sailing trip by trolley / out to dandelions and lilacs / we got stuck in plate glass / in a long streaming canal. / As we left a blue wake behind us / through the glittering swell of the panes, / we were enveloped in shadow / and ended up on the city's seabed. // Above the wave-crests of the roofs / we saw the May sun shining, / but in the mysterious sunken paradise / we saw young girls of wax. // In the sparkling, bewitched aquariums / lay yellow millstones of Gouda cheese, / smoked salmon, / and crumbling, fragrant Roquefort beaded with dew. / And behind the staring plateglass eyes / (watering from the draft) / corsets, dear sir, / and brassieres of ribbed silk. // Let the dandelions shine. / Let the trolley sail on with its wake. / —I am stranded on a coral reef / and let the sea's champagne flutter the slits of my gills.)[27]

"Speilglass" is one of Jacobsen's few carefree depictions of the pleasures on offer in the urban landscapes of modernity. Through the defamiliarizing glitter of reflective glass, the speaker experiences an unreal undersea paradise, in which the shop-window mannequins are seen as "girls of wax." Being "stranded" in this eroticized world of fashion and consumption, with its gourmet delicacies and silken undergarments, may even be preferable to nature's dandelions and lilacs. The text's lighthearted aestheticization of the city's "sunken paradise" of champagne and boutique windows stands in stark contrast to other interwar poems that feature a darker expressionist treatment of urban angst and nihilism.

While the surface enchantments of the city's commodity culture are unreal in a positive, enchanting manner in "Speilglass," this very unreality becomes the target of Jacobsen's sociopolitical critique in "Virkelighet" (Reality) from *Vrimmel.*

Dagen vi klynger oss til:
Butikkene hvor vi kjøper vakre klær. Reiser vi skal
gjøre om en tid.
Gatenes tummel. Regnet som faller på fortauene i
skumringen er drøm.

Natten og søvnløsheten.
Pengesorgene.
Lykken som ikke kommer er virkelighet.

Tryggheten fra de store, brusende forsamlinger.
Farten.
Orkestrenes brøl og de tykke spennende aviser er drøm og skygge.
Øinene på ham som ber.
Hendene på ham som fryser.
Trampet fra alle de masser som driver
sultne omkring i storbyene
er virkelighet.

De langvarige, interessante debatter. Argumentene
(på den ene side og på den annen side).
Katetrene, prestene, trompetfanfarene.
Trommen, takten, strømmen som driver oss fremover er drøm.
Maskingeværene.
Blod-engene og sølen. Skriket da du
en aften våkner til smertene.
Lasarettenes sne.
Massegravene, er virkelighet.

Torven som gror.
Gresstråene som bøier sig mykt i vinden.
Bølgenes sang
er virkelighet.[28]

(The day we cling to: / Shops where we buy nice clothes. Journeys we will / soon take. / The clamor in the streets. The rain falling on sidewalks / at dusk is a dream. / The night and sleeplessness. / Worries about money. / Happiness that doesn't come is reality. // Safety in the large, roaring crowds. / Speed. / The orchestras' howling and the thick exciting newspapers are dream and shadow. / The eyes of the praying man. / The hands of the freezing man. / The trudging of all those masses that wander / around starving in the big cities / is reality. // The long, interesting debates. The arguments / (on one hand and on the other hand) / The lecterns, the priests, the trumpets' fanfares. / The drumming, the rhythm, the rush driving us forward is dream. / The machine guns. / The bloody fields and mud. Your cry when / one night you awake suffering. / The snow on field hospitals. / The mass graves, are reality. // The turf growing. / Leaves of grass bending softly in the wind. / The song of the waves / is reality.)

In this solemn text, the pessimistic reservations about modern culture that hover tacitly over Jacobsen's first two collections receive direct expression. Shopping, travel, leisure, speed, news media, public assemblies, political debates, the stream of progress—all are part of the phantasmagorical exterior of modern life. Such phenomena are reduced to smoke and mirrors covering over desperation, hunger, and terror. "Virkelighet" reveals Jacobsen's perception of the true, annihilating core of modernity—that underneath all the chatter is a violent emptiness. The rush of progress is a fantasy; what's true according to this 1935 poem is Europe's barbaric regression in the rawness of war. The concluding reference to bloody fields, military hospitals, and mass graves shows the lingering impact of the collective trauma of World War I and the trench experience, even in the imagination of a younger poet from a neutral country. But, in its final statement of what is real, the poem turns to the enduring remedy of the unpeopled natural landscape: the grass blowing softly in the wind, the song of the waves.

That nature outlasts the vacuous hustle and bustle of modern civilization is also the message of the final poem in *Vrimmel*, "Myrstrå vipper." This poem mocks the vain world of toothpaste and gramophones, of crowds and routines, in cities "hvor menneskene stimer på fortauene og ser hva de andre har på sig" (where people swarm on the sidewalks and look at what others are wearing). In a typical *vanitas* manner, the poem looks toward death and imagines empty fields—"ødemarkene"—that will outlive the annihilation of a bankrupt modern culture. An abrupt temporal shift forward in the middle of the poem evokes a future in which technology is in ruins and people are absent.

> —Femti år og andre bor i husene,
> sporvognene har nye skilt og nytt
> skinn på setene.
> —Hundre år og bilene er stanset i lange
> rekker, side om side står de i evige
> karavaner, dynger sig op i store hauger,
> ligger med hjulene i været som døde insekter.
> —Tusen år og jernbjelken er en rød
> stripe i sanden.[29]

> (—Fifty years and other people live in the houses / the streetcars have new signs and new / leather on the seats. / —A hundred years and the cars have come to a halt in long / rows, side by side they stand in eternal / caravans, piling up in great heaps, / lying with their wheels in the air like dead insects. —A thousand years and the iron beam is a red / stripe in the sand.)

Jacobsen uses this imagined perspective from an uninhabited future to unveil the transience of the modern life the poem derides. His fast-forward effect shows automobiles—futurist symbols of modernity's intoxicating speed and freedom from the past—as rusted remains of a vanished civilization.

In a little-known work from 1931 titled *Modernisme*, the Norwegian author Haakon Bugge Mahrt claimed that speed (*farten*, *hastigheten*) was central to the experience of the modern. He wrote that "vor mentalitet er uophørlig rettet mot hastigheten" (our mentality is relentlessly directed toward speed) and that this obsession, along with technology, produces an existential unease in our lives.[30] Mahrt compared speed to an addictive substance that caused people to overestimate their own capacities. When Jacobsen relegates "speed" and "progress" to the realm of false fantasy, as he does in "Virkelighet," he unmasks two major ideals of modern technological culture. The poem "Nitti Kilometer" (Ninety Kilometers) shows how distinct Jacobsen's work is from any technophilic form of modernist poetry, even as it depicts the intoxication of speed.

Å stupe ned
gjennem aftenrøden
mot andre lande
på flukt mot dagen
mens stunden brenner
til aske bak dig
med høie flammer.

Å høre glefset
av motormunnen
mot veiens kurve
mens landet kommer
med favnen åpen,
med nye steder
du ikke kjenner
med trær og tårner
imot ditt hjerte.

Å flenge natten
med gylne kniver
og jage skyggen
til døde forut
til dagen løfter
de hvite bryster
imot din lebe.

—Den lyst er iskold
og dyp som døden
og ensomheten.

. . .
Ja, skynd dig skynd dig
og favn det heftig
ditt bleke bytte
med lydløs jubel,

—for bak dig brenner—
en drøm til aske
med røde flammer—[31]

(To plunge down / through the sunset glow / on to other lands / in flight toward day / while the moments burn / to ash behind you / with tall flames. // To hear the bark / of the motor's mouth / toward the curving road / as the land approaches / with open embrace, / with new places / you do not know / with trees and towers / against your heart. // To slash the night / with golden knives / and hunt the shadow / to death until / the day lifts up / its white breasts / against your lips. // —That pleasure is ice-cold / and deep as death / and solitude . . . So hurry up, hurry up / embrace it fiercely / your pale plunder / with soundless joy // —for it's burning behind you— / a dream to ashes / with red flames—)

As in "Jernbaneland," the initial exhilaration of speed sours in the course of the poem into a violent and ghostly pursuit; the dream of escape devolves into an existential nightmare. The motorcar racing through an endless landscape, always fleeing ("på flukt") toward the seduction of the new, presents an image of what the Futurists called simultaneity.[32] While the poem imagines the car as an assertive animal ("glefset" is a dog's noise) in search of novelty and power, it does not simply praise the eroticized violence as beautiful or liberating. Instead, the poem focuses on the destructive effects of the machine's flight. As John Brumo observes in an article about speed in interwar Norwegian poetry, "In the wake of the intoxicating and erotic experience of speed there clearly follows an element of loss and destruction."[33] This flight, though sexy, is an "ice-cold" pleasure, compared to death and solitude, and it is burning "a dream to ashes" behind it. "Nitti Kilometer" does not celebrate the futurist wish to escape history and destroy the past. Rather, it allegorizes uprooting and destruction in a movement forward that is both hyperactive and passionless. The intoxication is over: modernity's speed reveals itself as perpetual loss, oblivion, and disaffection.

Whatever initial ambivalent fascination Jacobsen's interwar work expresses is eventually overshadowed by his grave doubts. A blunt critique of technological modernity supplants his poetic infatuation with metropolitan space in "Speilglass" and with the railway journey in "Jernbaneland." In the course of the 1930s and after, Jacobsen adopts an anxiously pessimistic stance toward the culture of nihilism, the degradation of life saturated by speed and noise. This critical view becomes increasingly apparent after Jacobsen's postwar poetic return, in collections such as *Hemmelig liv* and *Stillheten efterpå*. While establishing Jacobsen as one of the major Scandinavian poets, these works also begin to cement his ecological critique of postwar Western consumerist culture.

What has been missing from the usual narrative of Jacobsen's career is an account of the connection between this sort of poetry and his political engagements. I do not mean that we need an ideologically suspicious method of reading that reveals an inbuilt fascist tendency in Jacobsen's poetry before or after the war. Rather, what we need is a more continuous narrative—one that can explain his wartime collaboration as something other than a baffling or insignificant deviation. Ivar Havnevik's 2002 history *Dikt i Norge* (Poetry in Norway) typifies the standard approach to the issue:

> [Etter *Vrimmel*] kommer det ikke flere bøker før krigsutbruddet, og Jacobsen arbeider da som journalist. Og plutselig finner vi ham som nazi-innsatt redaktør for avisen Glåmdalen på Kongsvinger. Selv sa han i et intervju mange år senere at det var om å gjøre for ham å drive den vanlige sosialdemokratiske journalistikken videre inne i avisen, selv om han brukte forsiden til nyheter fra NS-regimet i Oslo. Dette er bare delvis riktig, og han ble dømt til straffarbeid i 1945.[34]

> ([After *Vrimmel*] there are no more books before the war breaks out, and Jacobsen then works as a journalist. And suddenly we find him as a Nazi-appointed editor of the newspaper *Glåmdalen* in Kongsvinger. He said himself in an interview many years later that it was important for him to carry forward the newspaper's standard Social Democratic journalism, even though he used the front page for news from the NS regime in Oslo. This is only partly true, and he was sentenced to hard labor in 1945.)

The description then jumps ahead to 1951, when *Fjerntog* was published. The reader never hears in what sense Jacobsen's statement was only "partly true" or what his collaboration, trial for treason, imprisonment, hard labor penalty, and eventual conversion to Catholicism meant for his work, if anything. The latter are evidently considered to belong to "the private Rolf Jacobsen," not his poetry.[35] This quotation also makes it seem like Nazism is something that happens *to* Jacobsen, not something that he chooses for reasons that we might investigate.

Havnevik reasonably points out that neither Jacobsen's National Socialism nor his Catholicism appear often as explicit themes in his poetry, and he stresses that "diktene er blottet for nazistiske holdninger" (the poems are devoid of Nazi attitudes). But why assume that the only way for Jacobsen's National Socialism to be relevant to his literary career is for something called "Nazi opinions" to surface unmistakably in his poems? It seems that Jacobsen's extratextual politics are relevant only when *safe*—when he is the youthful socialist or the later "critic of Western consumer society . . . and of American, imperialistic warfare."[36] (These positions are by no means inherently non-fascist.) Havnevik's conclusion is that Jacobsen's National Socialism was a "wrong choice during the occupation—five years of a life" and merely "the result of a temporary deviation, along with a kind of opportunism completely separate from his 'real' opinions before and after the war."[37] This perspective reflects a larger pattern of response to Jacobsen's wartime collaboration; it is inadequate because it implies that Norway's principal twentieth-century poet can "suddenly" become a fascist for several years without this exerting some contextual pressure on our understanding of his work.

By situating Jacobsen's poetry and politics in a narrative sequence of uneasy nihilism followed by a vision of redemption—modernist chaos followed by fascist recentering—we can see how the normally glossed-over National Socialist hiatus fits into his career. The continuity in Jacobsen—including his fascist politics, his modernist poetics, and his later hybrid Catholic-green stance—lies in his sustained response to modernity's culture of nihilism. Jacobsen sought to resist or overcome nihilism in two ways: one poetic, one political. In the rest of this chapter, I will first consider the idea that the aesthetic itself, and especially a certain type of poetic language, offers a type of resistance to nihilism. Following that, I explain Jacobsen's turn to fascism as a form of anti-nihilism: a post-Death-of-God attempt at metaphysical and moral regrounding.

POETIC ANTI-NIHILISM

Literary modernism set its mode of aesthetic perception in opposition not only to tradition but also to modernity's rationalist and instrumentalizing approach to the world. It offered instead a model of heightened sensitivity that could "take in" more than the everyday consciousness.[38] In Norway, both Knut Hamsun and the poet

Sigbjørn Obstfelder were proponents of an early modernist literature of the nerves. Obstfelder wrote that he worked "med alle Dele af min Organisme, med Sanserne, som direkte forholder sig til Materien, med Nervene—ja med altsammen" (with all parts of my organism, with the senses, which relate directly to the material substance, with the nerves—indeed, with everything).[39] Similarly, Jacobsen described his poetic activity in terms of receptivity and attunement. Using a radio metaphor, he wrote that poets are attuned in an unusual way, with an "extra-receptive disposition, a slightly longer antenna that can receive other stations," and he claimed that "the poet is a person with twice as many nerves."[40] Jacobsen's self-description builds on the fin-de-siècle idea of artistic perception as a form of neurasthenia, which he interestingly combines with the technological trope of the radio that can receive unfamiliar stations.

Norwegian scholars have repeatedly read Jacobsen's work in terms of Martin Heidegger's later writings on poetry, technology, and Being. They suggest that, as a poet, he replicates many of the philosopher's concerns. Although Jacobsen did not share Heidegger's philosophical critique of modernity in any detailed way, there are some interesting parallels that these interpretations have brought to light. Jacobsen's poetry attempts to overcome the modern paradigm of nihilism by using language as a vehicle that registers awe and astonishment at being itself. From a Heideggerian perspective, technological nihilism refers to the *absence* of such a primal encounter with being. The situation of technological nihilism is about "the human distress caused by the technological understanding of being, rather than the destruction caused by specific technologies."[41]

Heidegger locates nihilism in the forgetting of the difference between Being itself and "beings" as objects (nihilism as *Seinsvergessenheit*). The modern technological organization of the world represents the culmination of this objectification of Being in the tradition of Western metaphysics. In "The Question Concerning Technology," Heidegger describes the essence of technology as an "enframing" (*das Gestell*) that organizes the world—nature and the human—into a "standing reserve" (*Bestand*) of measurable and manipulable objects. As the most widely used English translation reads,

> Enframing does not simply endanger man in his relationship to himself and to everything that is. As a destining, it banishes man into that kind of revealing which is an ordering. Where this ordering holds sway, it drives out every other possibility of revealing. Above all,

> Enframing conceals that revealing which, in the sense of *poiesis*, lets what presences come forth into appearance.[42]

For Heidegger, "enframing," with its dangerous capacity to alienate and uproot humanity further from "Being," is a result of the modern metaphysics of the subject. In his writings on language, dwelling, and thinking, Heidegger elevates poetry as an essential activity of language that offers a space of resistance to the technological. The poet is the one who makes room in language for the "unconcealment" of Being; that is what poetry is for. This poetic way of using language stands in opposition to the technological danger of the total ordering of Being in *das Gestell.* Heideggerian "poetic thinking" counteracts the nihilism of calculative, technological thinking and prepares a space for a new, more authentic relationship to Being.[43] Heidegger's understanding of the poetic can be seen as an instance of a more widespread phenomenon in modern aesthetic thought: the attempt to describe the value of art in terms of its power to resist nihilism.[44]

In accordance with this theorization of the poetic, the Norwegian Heideggerians have interpreted Jacobsen's poetic activity as a form of anti-nihilism. They often rely on the above-mentioned idea of the poet's different kind of aesthetic "attunement," and they explain Jacobsen's poetic stance of "listening" or "receptivity" in terms derived from Heidegger. Andreas Lombnæs argues that Jacobsen's poetic discourse endeavors to resist modernity's technological snowball of noise and acceleration by remaining attuned to what has been forgotten: the lost wisdom of being and nature.[45] Asbjørn Aarnes claims that Jacobsen's poetic stance toward technology is basically identical to Heidegger's in "The Question Concerning Technology." Aarnes reads Jacobsen's poetic project as a form of what Heidegger called *Gelassenheit*—the stance of "letting things be" in their uncertainty rather than representing and mastering them as objects of technological manipulation. Jacobsen's poetry enacts this sort of meditative thinking and offers the non-humanist insight that "there is something that transcends subjectivity, something we must relate to by 'letting be' or listening."[46]

Lastly, the Norwegian scholar Erling Aadland has written a book-length study of Jacobsen's poetic thinking.[47] He argues that Jacobsen's fundamental project as a poet was to listen in astonishment for the event of Being—its "unconcealment": "the poem arises in silence, and the poet is a listener."[48] Jacobsen's poetic receptivity differs from the traditional understanding of poetic creativity, according to Aadland, in that the poetic act is not one of imagination originating and centered in a particular subject but rather an attempt to listen for something more primary than the subject-object split: the phenomenon of being itself. This argument echoes Heidegger's pastoral stylization of the authentic poet as the "shepherd of Being"—the one who watches over Being, makes dwelling possible, the opposite of the technological subject.

My brief summary of the Heideggerian readings shows how Jacobsen's poetic activity has been understood as an attempt to counteract the nihilistic forgetting of Being and to offer an alternative to the degradations of technological reason. Jacobsen's stance of poetic listening implicitly challenges the paradigm of technological nihilism, which Heidegger saw as the total forgetting of being in the modern, instrumentalizing approach to the world. Compelling as they are, these readings, like most studies of Jacobsen, neglect to consider political aspects of his historical context, even as they employ the ideas of a thinker with comparable fascist baggage. In 1933, the year that Heidegger became the rector of the University of Freiburg, he understood National Socialism as a means of overcoming nihilism. Hubert Dreyfus suggests that Heidegger's diagnosis of nihilism led him to expect a "renewing event" that would overcome the crisis of the West and provide it with an understanding of Being that involves awe and mystery.[49] Heidegger's political engagement was in this sense "predicated upon his interpretation of the situation in the West as technological nihilism, and of National Socialism as a new paradigm" to counteract this situation.[50] In 1936, Heidegger even referred to Mussolini and Hitler in a lecture as "the two men who in different ways introduced a countercurrent to nihilism."[51] However, by the late 1930s and the time of his Nietzsche studies, Heidegger abandoned this understanding of fascism, or any type of politics, as such a countercurrent, and he eventually came to think of National Socialism not as a solution to but as "the most extreme expression" of technological nihilism.[52]

POLITICAL ANTI-NIHILISM

What I would like to preserve from this limited comparison of Jacobsen with Heidegger is the narrative arc of an encounter with modern European nihilism that sets the stage for a temporary vision of National Socialist redemption. In April 1940, Norway was invaded by Nazi Germany, and the leader of the miniscule Norwegian fascist party, Vidkun Quisling, was announced as the new chief of government. After the fall of Norway, all political parties except Nasjonal Samling were banned, but not all Norwegians joined the party, as Jacobsen did on his own initiative in October 1940.[53] By the beginning of the new year he was the editor of a Nazified newspaper, which received instructions from the German press directorate; during the war he also worked as the press and propaganda leader in the Kongsvinger division of Nasjonal Samling.

Like Sveen, Jacobsen was located politically on the left in the interwar period. In the early 1930s, he was a member of the socialist organization Clarté and involved with the radical Mot Dag group, which at the time included many of Norway's leading intellectuals. During his visit to Germany in 1934, Jacobsen reacted positively to Berlin as a cultural metropolis but negatively to the new Nazi regime. He attended an anti-Nazi seminar shortly after his return. Although he shared certain interests with the Mot Dag communists—he was actively engaged with social issues, working conditions, poverty, and "the industrial question"—he never became an orthodox Marxist intellectual.[54] Jacobsen's poetry rarely reflected his leftist stance openly, as did the work of other Norwegian poets such as the key interwar figures Arnulf Øverland and Nordahl Grieg. His engagement was only occasionally visible in his literature, as in the poem "Brosten" (Bricks) from *Vrimmel.* In the second half of the decade, Jacobsen published a few tendentious and formally conventional poems in the manner of Øverland.

One of these uncollected texts, published in *Kongsvinger arbeiderbladet* in 1936, speaks of red flags, solidarity, and a bright future to come after the burning night of the world's struggle and despair.[55] In contrast to the later fascist context of his images of renewal, at this point Jacobsen's invocation of "den nye tid som gryr" (the new age that is dawning) still referred to a dream modeled on the Soviet Union. In the 1937 article "Comrades" (Kamarater) he called Soviet Russia "et veldig håpets land som vokser i styrke og rikdom for hver dag som går" (a great land of hope whose strength and wealth are increasing every day).[56] This was the time of Stalin's Great Purge and the Moscow show trials, but Jacobsen probably would have viewed descriptions of these events as part of a conspiracy against the Soviet Union.

Another of Jacobsen's tendentious poems, "Konjunktur" (Conjuncture), was printed in the newspaper *Dagbladet* in February 1937.

The poem depicts exhausted workers leaving a steel factory as the mechanized production rushes along according to its own schedule.

> Dag efter dag og natt efter natt
> jager fabrikkenes hjul som besatt.
> Arbeiderne raver dødstrette hjem
> men nye tusen tar fatt efter dem.
> . . .
> Stål noteres i 175 prosent i New York og Berlin.[57]

> (Day after day and night after night / the wheels of the factory drive as if possessed. / The workers stagger home dead tired / but thousands of new ones set to work after them . . . Steel is quoted at 175 percent in New York and Berlin.)

The second half of the poem describes the production of cotton, which it suggests is related to steel as bandages are related to weapons of war. The poem presents a stark commentary on international industrial-capitalist preparations for warfare in a time of international crisis. In 1938, Jacobsen celebrated May Day at a worker's parade by reciting Øverland's poem "Guernica," an anti-Francoist text about the Spanish Civil War. The same year, after Hitler's annexation of Austria, he published a protest poem against the German war machine, called "Fredens Festning" (Fortress of Peace).[58]

All these examples show that Jacobsen was positioned on the pacifist, anti-capitalist left well into the late 1930s. How could he have performed such a drastic political about-face? One of his former friends called it "a political turnaround the likes of which I have never seen."[59] Both biographers explain the change by pointing out aspects of his socialist anti-capitalism that Jacobsen apparently hoped to preserve in his National Socialism: his concern for workers' interests and his hatred of imperialist England.[60] The importance of the latter should not be underestimated: Jacobsen claimed that his decision was *against* England at least as much as it was *for* Germany.[61] A turning point may have come when the Norwegian Labor Party (Arbeiderpartiet) formed an alliance with Great Britain in 1940, which sorely disappointed Jacobsen. It was not unheard of at this time in Norway for leftists to join Quisling's party during the occupation, in the belief that there was a true "socialism" to be found within National Socialism.[62] While important to consider, the view of Jacobsen's fascism as an extension of his earlier socialism fails to capture something crucial: the quasi-religious and anti-nihilistic dimension of his political commitments. This poet expected radical anti-bourgeois politics to address not only social and economic injustice but also the existential predicament of modern technological nihilism that he explored in his interwar poetry. As we will see, Jacobsen's wartime writings contain an undeniably affective and messianic dimension.

In January 1941, Jacobsen took over as the editor of *Kongsvinger arbeiderbladet*—later renamed *Glåmdalen*—which received instructions from the Deutsche Pressabteilung specifying everything from layout to content.[63] After the war, Jacobsen claimed that he wanted to direct the paper as a local news source and to keep it from becoming a pure organ of Nazi ideology. He also argued that the editorials he signed did not reflect his own personal opinions, because they were sent from the German authorities. However, his biographer Ove Røsbak has compared the published articles with the ones sent by the Nazis, and he concludes that Jacobsen added significant content and that the final design was his own.[64] For instance, a lyrical voice emerges in some of them, such as "Vissent Lauv," published in *Kongsvinger arbeiderbladet* on February 19, 1941. Here, the titular "withered leaves" being blown away by the wind symbolize the old political and social illusions—liberalism, democracy, and other "bourgeois" relics—giving way to the "new growth" ("nytt lauvspring") to come. It is an organic and mild image of fascist regeneration. Other articles contain a more aggressive and militant style that Røsbak views as the language of the official German press directions.[65]

These editorials formed the basis for Jacobsen's sentence for treason of over three years of forced labor after the war, when the court found him personally responsible for their published form.[66] Articles such as these must be treated with caution, since they are not necessarily Jacobsen's original work. Yet they do sometimes provide a glimpse of his priorities and convictions. One of them describes an ideological battle between young nations, which were free from the "iron grip of capitalism," and older nations, namely Great Britain, which was the center of imperialist capitalism.[67] Others are more damning in terms of their ugly anti-Semitism: "Krigens årsak" (The Cause of the War) from October 1942 describes a struggle between capital and labor, depicting Hitler as a fighter for social justice against "de tyske finansjøder, men også deres brødre i alle land" (the German finance-Jews, but also their brothers in all countries).[68] Another from 1944 mocks the democratic press for being "kjøpt og betalt . . . til å vedlikeholde den jødeimperialistiske hydras hypnose overfor de små folk" (bought and paid . . .

to maintain the hypnosis in which the Jewish-imperialistic hydra holds the common man).[69]

In "Barbarenes storm" (The Barbarian Storm), which was written in response to the Allied bombing of a monastery in Italy, the author writes that the barbaric American capitalists have no appreciation of European civilization. The term "culture" has "en ganske annen betydning her i Europa enn i Amerika, og dens helligdomer lar seg ikke bygge opp igjen på 14 dager slik som filmkulissene i Hollywood" (quite a different meaning here in Europe than in America, and its sacred places are not easily built up again in fourteen days like a Hollywood film set). The article goes on to state that there is no difference between primitive America and the "robot state in the east"—in fact, "kulturnegrene i vest og kulturnegrene i øst i virkeligheten er en og samme fiende, nemlig den kapitalistiske barbar" (the cultural negros in the west and the cultural negros in the east are one and the same enemy, namely capitalist barbarism), and they share the same "sadistisk ødeleggelseslyst" (sadistic lust for destruction).[70] The overt racism and anti-Semitism of these statements are some of the most offensive aspects of the articles that Jacobsen published and signed. Regardless of any discrepancies in perspective or style, it remains the case that Jacobsen was legally and morally responsible for these articles, even though his newspaper was controlled by the occupying Nazi authorities.

The fact that Jacobsen was able to shift his vision of "socialism" to the Nasjonal Samling party should prompt us to ask what he was looking for in political radicalism in the first place. In 1946, he wrote in his diary that "alle politiske massebevegelser er i virkeligheten miniatyr-avbildninger av den store Kirke, og surrogater for den kristne tro" (all political mass movements are in reality miniature-depictions of the great Church, and surrogates for Christian faith).[71] Both of Jacobsen's political engagements, with the Mot Dag left and with Nasjonal Samling, later appeared to him as phases on the way back to the Christian God.[72] He wrote to his wife in 1946 that "det tiden lengter efter—og som skapte *nasjonalsosialismen* blant annet—er en fast tro, en *stor* livstanke og en trygg lærebygning som menneskene kan lene sitt hode til. Det er i dag etter min mening bare to ting å velge mellom: Katolisismen eller Kommunismen. Det andre er ferdig" (what the age is longing for—and what led to *National Socialism* among other things—is a firm belief, a *great* view of life, and a secure doctrine that people can rest their heads on. In my view there are only two things to choose between today: Catholicism and Communism. The second one is over).[73]

In another postwar reflection, Jacobsen wrote that people are longing for "en befrielse fra noe ondt man ikke selv vet" (a liberation from something evil they don't even know about) and they are stuck in a situation of divine lack: "verdens krise skyldes at Gud er borte" (the world is in crisis because God is absent).[74] He imagined a violent storm that was about to consume the nihilistic, disintegrating world: "En etsend vind blåser over verden og varsler Ragnarokk [*sic*]. . . . Vindene, de skarpe og fortærende som jager over jorden, foran Dommedag" (A corrosive wind is blowing through the world, and omen of Ragnarok. . . . The winds, the severe and destructive ones that hunt the earth, before Judgment Day).[75] Such remarks shed light on the apocalyptic mentality in which Jacobsen greeted the redeeming power of National Socialism. One of his comments even refers to Nazism as "det første utslag av denne messiasforventning. Dens mystiske kjennemerker var et surrogat, en erstatning for det drepte mysterium, for den døde Gud, etter kirkens og Gudssamfundets ødeleggelse" (the first product of this expectation of a messiah. Its mystical signs were a surrogate, a replacement for the demolished mystery, for the dead God, after the destruction of the church and religious society).[76]

Years later, in a 1984 interview, Jacobsen continued to explain mass politics in terms of salvation: "Både kommunismen og fascismen er verdslige religioner, med klare paralleler til jesuittismen. De har syndere og frelste, himmel og helvete" (Both communism and fascism are worldly religions, with clear parallels to jesuitism. They have sinners and saved, heaven and hell).[77] Twentieth-century totalitarianisms have often been interpreted as political religions, or at least as political ideologies that expressed themselves in religious terms of belief, sacrifice, and redemption in order to address the anomie of contemporary society.[78] Retrospectively, then, Jacobsen explained his fascist commitment as a longing for salvation from the contemporary malaise.

Some of his wartime editorials fantasized an apocalyptic scenario of destruction and regeneration—"storm" followed by "spring." One of them explains the current world crisis and its coming solution with reference to the final battle of the Norse gods, saying that "after Ragnarok a social state will be built up" in which the interests and security of the workers would be assured.[79] Belief in a better world after "Ragnarok" also appears in "Disiplin" (Discipline), one of the articles that Røsbak claims was crafted personally by Jacobsen. This text describes the era in which Jacobsen's generation grew up as "den uroligste av alle tidsepoker, tiden foran og mellom de store kriger—da alt vaklet, alt var spenning, tvil, svakhet, angst for morgendagen" (the most troubled of all historical epochs, the period before and between the great wars—when everything was about to collapse, everything was tension, doubt, weakness, anxious waiting for daybreak).[80] Here we see the anticipatory tenor of Jacobsen's political discourse: the present epoch is a time of disintegration, confusion, and ambivalence before a new dawn.

In some little-known wartime poetry, Jacobsen also expressed excitement about participating in the dawn of a new age. While there may be uncertainty about the authorship of Jacobsen's editorials, in the case of the ones about "Ragnarok" we may safely consider the perspective his own, because they match the rhetoric and imagery of the poetry he published in the same newspaper during the war. Jacobsen's National Socialism may have been temporary, "moderate," and based on socialist and anti-English principles, but these poems also express his messianic expectation of a heroically and violently transformed world.

The first poem Jacobsen published during the war, "Tideverv" (The Age), appeared in the Christmas issue of *Glåmdalen* in 1943. The poem expresses hope for the rebirth of a new world after the storm of war. Printed in Gothic script, its language of collective struggle, daybreak, and rebirth is as close to fascist kitsch as Jacobsen's writing comes.

> Snart skal det stige bak skodden
> nyfødt en jord påny,
> demrende fram av vår lagnads unge,
> veldige morgengry.
> Snart skal dens lunder grønnske
> i lys av en nyfødt dag
> og løvkroner suse i tidevervets
> hastende vingeslag.
> Snart skal hver arm få løfte,
> snart skal hver hug i tru
> fylkes om dåd og tanker
> du ikke aner nu
> . . .
> Av sorg er søyler støpte
> under de nye velv,
> hvor du i høgtids-haller

atter kan finne deg selv.
Kom storm, kom snø, kom vårlys,
kom sommer med solskinnsfokk.
Vi veit at en verden grønnes
bak røken fra Ragnarok.[81]

(Soon it will rise up from behind the mist / a new earth born again, / shimmering forth in the young and mighty / dawn of our destiny. // Soon its groves will turn green / in the light of a newborn day / and treetops rustle in the quickening / wingbeats of the new age. // Soon each arm will be raised / soon each faithful heart will / rally for deeds and thoughts / you do not imagine now . . . Columns are cast of sorrow / under the new arches, / where in halls of celebration / you can find yourself again. // Come storm, come snow, come spring light / come summer with sunshine. / We know that a world is blooming / behind the smoke from Ragnarok.)

Whereas the newspaper editorials might reasonably be seen as the work of a forced hand, no one told Jacobsen to write a poem exemplifying fascist palingenesis. This poem anticipates a fated victory after the present hardships, a spring in which people will "return to themselves" and build the world anew in social harmony. Thematically, this text refers to the Poetic Edda, especially to its first poem, "Völuspá" (The Prophecy of the Seeress). The diction here is somewhat different from Jacobsen's ordinary *bokmål*, perhaps because he is borrowing from the rhetoric of the Norwegian fascist party, with words like "fylke" (assemble for battle, rally) and "lagnad" (fate, destiny).[82] "Tideverv" reveals Jacobsen's genuine hope that National Socialism would achieve a new dispensation after the grand struggle currently being waged, similar to the reconstruction of the world after Ragnarok in Norse mythology.

The Christmas issue of the following year, 1944, also featured a new poem by Jacobsen, "Ring Klokke" (Ring Bells). This poem does not contain the same mythological imagery, but it continues to express hope for a new dawn, even though it was written at a time when the Third Reich was nearing defeat.

Ring klokke bak snøen.
Gjennom dens hvite flor
hører vi milevide
ditt bronseord.
Ring klokke i skogen
høgt over granens sus.
Ring for riker som kommer
og riker som går i grus.
Ring klokke bak natten.

Ring sorg. Ring lyst.
Ring for de ville drømmer
i mannens bryst.
Ring klokke i stormen.
Ton ut i nettenes hav.
Ring for de blåsende blomster
over en vissen grav.
Ring klokke bak døden
den sang vet jeg.
Løft dine bronselurer
mot evighet.
Ring klokke i hjertene
—stilt så det bærer frem.
Bryt ut som fugleskarer
på langferd hjem.
Ring alle verdens klokker
med rungende, sterke slag.
Ring med tusende tunger
mot dag, Mot Dag.[83]

(Ring bells behind the snow. / Through its white layer / we hear from miles away / your word of bronze. // Ring bells in the forest / high over the soughing spruce. / Ring for empires to come / and empires falling to ruin. // Ring bells behind the night. / Ring sorrow. Ring delight. / Ring for the wild dreams / in the breast of man. // Ring bells in the storm. / Sound out in the sea of nights. / Ring for the blossoms blowing / over a faded grave. // Ring bells behind death / I know that song. / Raise your bronze horns / to eternity. // Ring bells in our hearts / —calmly so it carries forth / Burst out like flocks of birds / on a journey home. // Ring all the world's bells / in resounding, strong strokes. / Ring with a thousand tongues / toward day, Toward Day.)

In this poem, the theme of an idealized new age is crucial again, but the tone is more elegiac and mild. The poem is not easy to decode in terms of its historical significance. Has Jacobsen given up on National Socialism at this point? Is the Third Reich one of the "riker som kommer" (empires to come) or one of the "riker som går i grus" (empires falling to ruin)? The plaintive tone suggests that Jacobsen has by this point become disillusioned about the redemptive potential or even the continued existence of National Socialism. Nevertheless, Jacobsen celebrates a more generic political idealism: mankind's utopian desires ("ville drømmer i mannens bryst") for liberation ("bryt ut som fugleskarer") and homeland ("på langferd hjem").

The poem concludes strangely, with the capitalized words "Mot Dag" (Toward Day), the name of the Communist periodical and organization Jacobsen was involved with in the early 1930s. Røsbak wonders whether this might be an instance of concealed propaganda for Jacobsen's earlier leftist stance. In my view, the repetition of "mot dag, Mot dag" unites Jacobsen's political radicalism of the left and the right under the banner of a generalized quasi-religious utopian longing, which accords better with Jacobsen's own retrospective view of his commitments. He wrote in hindsight that his age craved a new ethos—what he called "a firm belief, a *great* view of life, and a secure doctrine that people can rest their heads on."[84]

Jacobsen's postmortem of his fascism is saturated with what the Italian philosopher Gianni Vattimo calls "incomplete nihilism"—the desire for another ultimate ground of authority and paternal wisdom after the "death of God." Nietzsche's famous announcement of the "death of God" can be summarized as "the devaluation of the highest values," or in other words as the depletion of dominant metaphysical and moral ideas. In his 1887 notes on "European Nihilism," Nietzsche writes, "One interpretation has collapsed; but because it was considered *the* interpretation it now seems as if there were no meaning at all in existence, as if everything were in vain."[85] The resulting nihilism has two forms: Nietzsche distinguishes between a "passive" nihilism that mourns meaning and an "active" nihilism that affirms existence even in the absence of a foundational interpretation. Vattimo builds on this distinction between what he calls "incomplete" and "accomplished" versions of nihilism in works such as *The End of Modernity* and the more recent *Nihilism and Emancipation.* Accomplished nihilism is the post-metaphysical thinking of hermeneutics; Vattimo welcomes "the letting-go of foundationalism and the letting-loose of a conflict of interpretations" as a style of thought more congruent with a democratic, anti-authoritarian politics.[86] Incomplete nihilism, on the other hand, refuses to admit the absence of a metaphysical foundation of meaning. In Jacobsen's case, incomplete nihilism is all too ready for a commitment to a new savior, a utopian remedy against modern estrangement. Fascism spoke to this metaphysical urge to replace the deceased interpretation—Christianity—with a new foundation. As an incomplete nihilist, Jacobsen exemplifies what Terry Eagleton has called modernism's "phantom limb syndrome" and its frantic attempts to fill the "God-shaped hole at the centre of its universe" with new visions of totality, absolute foundations, and God-surrogates.[87]

The point of my investigation of Jacobsen's National Socialism is not to demonize him personally or to unveil his literature as fascist—which it is not. Rather, the goal is to better understand a key feature of the interwar period in art and literature: how certain types of modernist response to the situation of modernity end up complicit with regimes that seemed to offer utopian visions of renewal and solutions to the culture of nihilism. In this respect, Jacobsen's poetic encounter with modernity and nihilism appears as a prelude to his fascist utopianism. Jacobsen's fascist "hiatus" was indeed connected to his poetic production before and after the war, not in terms of ideological content but as part of his process of casting about in various places for a foundation of meaning to counteract the condition of nihilism. In the next, concluding section, I will show how Jacobsen reflected on this process in some of his postwar writings.

THE SILENCE AFTERWARDS

On May 9, 1945, the day after Nazi Germany's unconditional surrender, Rolf Jacobsen was arrested in the town of Kongsvinger. For several days he was imprisoned with other traitors, including volunteers from the Eastern Front.[88] Some of them may have been influenced by an article Hamsun published in 1941 encouraging young Norwegian men to volunteer in the SS—as his younger son Arild did.[89] At his hearing a month later, Jacobsen claimed that he joined Nasjonal Samling because he approved of "the social aspect" of the party's program.[90] He was not sentenced for treason until the following summer, when the court drew attention to his activity as the newspaper editor. They listed eleven incriminating editorials (focusing, of course, on what counted as grounds for treason, not on all expressions of ideological commitment).[91] In the five years immediately after the war, Jacobsen both served his hard labor sentence and underwent an existential crisis that led him back to Christianity. He had witnessed the collapse of political solutions to modernity's spiritual and social chaos, and in his guilt and disillusionment, he decided to return to the church. Following the Decadents of the 1890s, he converted to Roman Catholicism, a somewhat exotic faith in Norway's Lutheran context. After Jacobsen's metaphysical longings were diverted through a catastrophic episode of sacralized politics, they found more permanent habitation in a conventional religious discourse.

Postwar Europe as a whole saw an increase in the number of Catholics. Tony Judt argues that this was because the Catholic Church offered continuity and reassurance in a violently transformed world; its "association with the old order, indeed its firm stand against modernity and change . . . gave it a special appeal in these transitional years." Protestant churches could not exert a similar allure, suggests Judt, because they "did not offer an alternative to the modern world but rather a way to live in harmony with it."[92] Although Jacobsen's Catholicism is not regularly detectable in his later poetry, in the collection *Hemmelig liv* he published a remarkable poem about Norway's medieval wooden churches: "Stavkirker" (Stave Churches).

Jeg tror på de mørke kirkene,
de som ennu står som tjærebål i skogene
og bærer duft med sig som de dyprøde rosene
fra tider som kanskje eide mer kjærlighet.
De sotsvarte tårnene tror jeg på, de som lukter av solbrannen
og gammel røkelse brent inn av seklene.
Laudate pueri Dominum, laudate nomen Domini.

Øksene teljet dem til og sølvklokker klang i dem.
Noen skar drømmer inn og ga dem vinger å vandre med
ut gjennem tider og fjell. De velter som brottsjø omkring dem.
Nu er de skip, med utkikkstønnen vendt mot Ostindia,
Santa Maria, Pinta og Niña da dagene mørknet
mot verdens ende, årelangt fra Andalusia.
Laudate pueri Dominum, laudate nomen Domini.

Angst overalt, selv Columbus er redd nu
der hildringer lokker dem frem og vinden har slangetunger.
Stjernene stirrer urørlige ned med avsindige jernøyne,
alle dager er onde, det er ingen redning mer, men vi
seiler, seiler, seiler.
Laudate pueri Dominum, laudate nomen Domini.

(I believe in the dark churches, / the ones that still stand like tarred pyres in the woods / and like deep red roses carry a fragrance / from times that perhaps had more love. / Those jet-black towers I believe in: the ones that smell of the sun's heat / and old incense burnt in by the centuries. / *Laudate pueri Dominum, laudate nomen Domini.* // Axes shaped them and silver bells rang in them. / Someone carved dreams in and gave them wings so they'd wander / out across ages and mountains—which surge up around them like breakers. / Now they are ships, with crow's nest turned toward East India, / the Santa Maria, Pinta and Niña when the days grew dark / near the end of the world, years out from Andalucía. / *Laudate pueri Dominum, laudate nomen Domini.* // Everywhere dread, now fear takes even Columbus

> / as mirages lure them on and the wind has the tongues of a serpent. / The stars stare down impassively with demented eyes of iron, / every day is evil, there's no hope of being saved, but we / keep sailing, sailing, sailing. *Laudate pueri Dominum, laudate nomen Domini.*)[93]

This poem is a good example of Jacobsen's Catholic anti-modernity and his continued engagement with "the specter of nihilism." The text sets up a clear contrast between a morally superior past and an unredeemed present, characterized by nihilistic drift. At the beginning, the speaker expresses a preference for "the dark churches," as opposed, presumably, to the newer churches of modern Lutheran Norway. These stave churches, though black with soot ("sotsvarte"), are alluring to the senses (redolent of roses and incense), and they suggest a less hate-filled historical period ("mer kjærlighet"). The poem imagines their persistence as a heartening message transmitted through the ages.

In the middle of the second stanza of "Stavkirker," these emblems of the Old World transform into vessels on the way to a New World; they become Columbus's ships traveling to the Americas. As opposed to the poem's past moment—the time of love when dreams were carved—the present is a time of dread and depravity. The days have grown dark and the end of the world is approaching, while "mirages" tempt the vessels off course, and they are carried only by an evil wind. "Even Columbus" has succumbed to the present's lack of direction and orientation. The stars that should provide navigational guidance are of no help, with their "demented eyes of iron." In this world "there is no more salvation" (another way to translate "det er ingen redning mer"); there is just movement: "sailing, sailing, sailing." The repeated Latin lines from the Book of Psalms suggest an echo from a place outside of this directionless world, which claims that the only guidance to be found is in a religious tradition: "praise, servants of the Lord, praise the name of the Lord."

Around the time of his conversion to Catholicism, Jacobsen wrote to his wife and explained his interwar and wartime political commitments in terms of a spiritual search for therapy and solace.

> Jeg har søkt og søkt—i arbeiderbevegelsen, i det som kom efterpå . . . Jeg har lett efter en sikker grunn å bygge på . . . noe å hengi seg til . . . mon ikke all denne travelheten min i de siste ti årene var et slags bedøvelsesmiddel . . . Jeg kastet mig inn i organisasjonsarbeide og allskens elendighet. For å døyve uroen og for å vinne en vei fram—i denne forvirringens tid.[94]

> (I have searched and searched—in the labor movement, in what came after that . . . I have looked for a firm ground to build on . . . something to devote myself to . . . I wonder if all my activity in the past decade was not really a sort of anaesthetic . . . I have thrown myself into organizational work and all sorts of wretchedness. To deaden my feeling of anxiety and to find a way forward—in this age of confusion.)

Jacobsen interprets his Nazi sympathies—euphemized as "what came after that" and "all sorts of wretchedness"—as an anaesthetic to soothe his own anxiety, his own pain. By portraying himself as the sufferer of a confused age, Jacobsen sidesteps his actual political decisions and his culpability. This points to a pattern of avoidance that the poet continued for the rest of his life.

In his poetry of the 1950s and up until his death in 1994, Jacobsen extends his earlier critique of unrestrained technological development and Anglo-American liberal capitalism, while he also develops a more explicit environmentalist message. A central aspect of Jacobsen's earnest critique of consumerist culture is his notion that material wealth and technological comforts have a dark side: "Vi har mistet noe . . . Vi er kommet inn i enn tingverden og en kjøpeverden, som vi aldri har drømt om. . . . Maskinene hjelper oss ikke med alt" (We have lost something . . . we have entered a world of things and world of purchases, which we never imagined. . . . The machines can't help us with everything).[95] He spoke out against television as an instrument of Americanization, against the modern *reklamesivilisasjon* (culture of advertising), which he said produced empty, indifferent, atomized individuals who would follow any political leader but had no sense of solidarity or family.[96] It is ironic to see this particular poet faulting individuals in postwar liberal-democratic societies for being willing to follow any political leader because they feel spiritually empty.

In his later poetry and in interviews, Jacobsen offers a lot of general criticism of *the age* but no real recognition or condemnation of his own specific actions. He is vocal and preachy about the nihilistic culture of (post)modernity, but he is utterly silent about the victims of the regime he supported. Jacobsen's commitment to Nazism was a desperate failure, but an additionally frustrating thing was how he dealt with his wartime past: he lied about it. He refused to acknowledge it in any way, even as he accepted the role of a moralizing and politically clear-sighted public figure. The novelist Knut Faldbakken interviewed Jacobsen in 1975 and heard only denials of his involvement with Nasjonal Samling. Faldbakken later quipped that the poet's strategy was captured in the title of his 1965 collection *Stillheten efterpå*—"The Silence Afterwards."[97] Jacobsen's evasion of his wartime past was so thorough that his son published a book in 2007 called *Kjente jeg deg?* (Did I Know You?—the title of a poem Jacobsen wrote after his wife died in the early 1980s).

Much of the critical commentary on Rolf Jacobsen does not permit his National Socialism to be a serious issue—thereby repeating his own evasiveness. Jacobsen is often presented as a purveyor of simple wisdom, openness, and wonder. His Canadian translator, Roger Greenwald, describes him with hushed reverence as contemplative and religious in sensibility, combining "an ancient way of looking . . . with an openness to the new," and writing in a way that "evinces humility at every turn."[98] When Greenwald writes that "silence lies at the core of [his] work in more senses that one," he surely does not intend to refer to Jacobsen's avoidance of his fascist past, but perhaps this remark inadvertently indicates something important.

Some aspects of National Socialism that appealed to Jacobsen—what he saw as its "socialist" component, its promise of a balance of nature and technology—migrate into his stance after the war, but they are divorced from any political hope of redemption. Jacobsen's fascism gives way to the pessimistic-green stance of *Hemmelig liv*—sometimes considered a second debut but also a conclusion to the phase of his career that began with *Jord og jern* in 1933. *Hemmelig liv* contains several important ecological poems, including "Landskap med gravemaskiner," "Tømmer," and "Mørk Saga," a prophetic-dystopian poem about the age of oil. Despite his personal conversion to Catholicism, his postwar poems continue to address the disintegration of grand narratives and the resulting cultural situation of lack, fragmented meaning, and nihilistic drift (as in "Stavkirker"). In this regard, the poem I would like to spotlight is "De store symfoniers tid" (The Age of Great Symphonies), which expresses Jacobsen's continued preoccupation with the culture of nihilism, even after his disappointment with political solutions.

De store symfoniers tid
er over nu.

De steg mot himlen i stor prakt
som solskimrende skyer med torden i
over de store århundrer.
Cumulis under lyshimler. Corialan.

Nu stømmer de ned igjen som regn,
et stengrått, stripet regn over alle bølgelengder og programmer
og dekker jorden som en våt frakk, en sekk av lyd.

Nu faller de ned igjen som regn,
de pisker mot skyskraperne som elektrisk hagl
og drypper ned i bondens kammers
og trommer over villabyene or murstenshavet
som evindelig lyd.

Regn som lyd.
Seid umschlungen Millionen,
til å døve skrik

alle dager, alle dager
over jorden som er tørst og tar dem til sig igjen.

(The age of the great symphonies / is over now. // They rose toward the heavens in full splendor / like thunderclouds shimmering in the sun / over the great centuries. / Cumulus under clear skies. Coriolanus. // Now they're pouring back down as rain, / a stone-gray, streaked rain on all wavelengths and programs, / covering the earth like a wet coat, a sack of sound. // Now they're falling back down from the heavens, / they pelt the skyscrapers like electric hail / and seep down into the farmer's bedroom / and drum on the suburbs and the oceans of brick / as continuous sound. // Rain as sound. / Seid umschlungen Millionen, / to deaden screams // every day, every day / on this earth that is thirsty and drinks them in again.)[99]

In this poem, the symphonies of centuries pour back down from the sky as a nourishing rain. Perhaps like Jacobsen's healing Catholicism, they act as a musical narcotic that can "deaden the screams" of those living among "oceans of brick," in the wasteland.

CHAPTER 5

Unconscious Nazism

Sigurd Hoel's Psychoanalytic Antifascism

During the interwar period in Norway, psychoanalysis joins Marxism as a powerful tool in the leftist critique of bourgeois society. Psychoanalytic sophistication became a marker of the younger literary generation by the 1920s, enough so that Sigurd Hoel could ridicule its pretensions from an insider's perspective in his charming novel *Syndere i sommersol* (Sinners in the Summertime), from 1927. Hoel was Norway's leading cultural-radical intellectual of the interwar period, an influential conduit of modernist thought and literature not only in his novels and essays but also in his editorial and consulting work at the Oslo publishing house Gyldendal. It was in this capacity that Hoel advised against the publication of Åsmund Sveen's now lost experimental novel of homosexual life, *Vinduet og vaaren.*[1] Unlike Sveen and the other writers examined in this book, Sigurd Hoel never voiced any Nazi or fascist sympathies. He did not buy into the dream of a Germanic or Nordic ethnocultural rebirth that would counteract the negative aspects of modernity, and he viewed the notion that Nazism could be a vehicle for any sort of redemptive impulse as delusional. For years, Hoel was deeply absorbed in what he considered one of his central tasks: to destroy fascism intellectually and politically. He wrote during the war that "for mange av oss er det blitt noe av en livsopgave, dette å få nazismen tilintetgjort . . . . Den viktigste livsopgaven" (for many of us, it has become a mission in life, to eliminate Nazism . . . the most important mission in our lives).[2]

Hoel's antifascist orientation developed alongside his career as a novelist and critic, from his earliest responses to Italian Fascism and

Nazism in the 1920s, through the rise of Nazi Germany in the 1930s, and during the Nazi occupation of Norway, the latter part of which Hoel spent in exile in Sweden. After the war, Hoel adopted an antitotalitarian position founded on vigilance about the reappearance of Nazism under other names. In 1947, he published the important occupation novel *Møte ved milepelen* (Meeting at the Milestone), a probing, but necessarily partial, examination of the psychological roots of Nazism in the case of Norwegian collaborators. By using interwar psychoanalytic thought about mass psychology, patriarchy, and sexual repression, and in particular the works of the Austrian analyst Wilhelm Reich, Hoel produced midcentury Scandinavia's most significant literary reaction to Nazism.

Eli Zaretsky writes in *Political Freud* that it is useful to think of psychoanalysis as "an uneasy synthesis of three different projects: a therapy or medical practice, a paradigm for interpreting culture, and an ethical current in everyday life." [3] Hoel responded profoundly to psychoanalysis in all three of these ways. He was married from 1927 to 1936 to one of Norway's first female psychoanalysts, Nic Waal, who trained under Reich in Berlin in the early 1930s and later became one of the founders of child and adolescent psychiatry in Norway. Hoel himself spent several years in training analysis with Reich, when the latter was living in Denmark, Sweden, and Norway, after being expelled from the International Psychoanalytic Association in 1934. The couple's time in Berlin in the early 1930s was a period of not only increased exposure to contemporary psychoanalysis but also firsthand contact with Nazism. Already in 1931, Hoel wrote to his fellow left-Freudian novelist Aksel Sandemose that he was convinced of Hitler's eventual rise to power.[4] A decade later, Waal and Hoel, though no longer married, were both active in the Norwegian resistance movement during the Nazi occupation.

In the wartime magazine *Norges-Nytt*, which was issued from Stockholm by the Norwegian Legation during the occupation, Sigurd Hoel wrote the following in 1944.

> Sannheten om nazismen er ubehagelig, ikke bare fordi den handler om et ufyselig stoff, men fordi den krever en nærgående granskning i oss selv. Hvorfor hadde nazismen en slik evne til å ete om seg? Fordi det i noen hver—i noen hver av oss—fins et lite punkt, ofte et meget kjært lite punkt, hvor det sitter en liten kime til—ikke til nazisme, å langt ifra. Men til noe som ligner ganske betenkelig. Vi har ikke lyst til å sette lyset på det lille punktet. Det er ofte omgitt av såkalte hellige følelser.[5]

> (The truth about Nazism is uncomfortable, not only because it concerns something disgusting but because it requires an intimate investigation of ourselves. Why did Nazism have such an ability to devour everything? Because in each person—in each of us—there is a little place, often a cherished little place, where there is a little seed of—not of Nazism, far from it. But of something with a troubling resemblance to it. We don't want to cast light on this little place. It is often surrounded by so-called sacred feelings.)

In a publication whose readers were active in the Norwegian resistance, Hoel dared to identify the private seed of something resembling Nazism in each person. Similarly, in the article "Om den ubevisste nazismen" (On Unconscious Nazism), published in the journal *Tiden* in March 1945, Hoel claimed that no one is completely free of Nazi or fascist impulses.[6]

To understand the background for these provocative statements about unconscious Nazism, we need to investigate Hoel's Reichian views of patriarchy and mass politics. As Hoel saw it, Nazism was more than a question of ordinary politics or economics; it was a pathological symptom of patriarchal authority in crisis. Both before and after his encounter with Reich's thought, the critique of patriarchy was a major concern. Hoel refused to treat Nazism in dichotomous moral or ideological terms: he avoided reading its psychological and social problems as characteristic only of (Nazi) Germany. Sigrid Undset went to the other extreme, reading Nazism as an expression of a transhistorically pathological and specifically German character.[7] For Hoel, by contrast, what was so haunting about Nazism was the way it mirrored, in an extreme and grotesque form, common problems of patriarchal culture: intense sexual repression, longing for certainty provided by a strong father figure, a violent and cruel relationship to oneself and others.

Rather than being the exclusive property of Nazism, these features lived on as obstacles to liberation even in the social democratic postwar era. Because he understood Nazism as symptomatic of a more broadly repressive patriarchy, Hoel feared that other fascisms under other names might emerge from this common source. The Reichian view of the erotically warped character of Nazism thus incited Hoel's troubled examination of his own culture's fascist potential—which did not refer simply to the actual fascist party in Norway, Nasjonal Samling. From his influential position as a writer and a disseminator of modernist thought and literature, Hoel aspired to make resistance to Nazism an inner, as well as an outer, struggle. He used the challenge of Nazism as an occasion for a cautious form of self-reflection about the potentially authoritarian mentality in his society's repressive and patriarchal legacy.

To explore Hoel's psychoanalytic antifascism further, this chapter will take the form of a commentary on two significant essays: "Rebell og trell" (Rebel and Slave, 1934) and "Om nazismens vesen" (On the Essence of Nazism, 1945).[8] We will see how Hoel configures Reich's theories for a Scandinavian antifascist audience. Previous criticism has treated these essays as exercises in popularization, because Hoel is not adding anything at the theoretical level.[9] Although it is correct that Hoel's ideas largely are derived from Reich, it is also significant that he communicates these ideas in imaginative ways, employs them in a subtler and more exploratory manner, and puts them to use in a different national context.

Zaretsky calls Reich's *Mass Psychology of Fascism* one of "the landmark political-critical books of the last century" and views Reich as "exemplary of the political Freudian tradition."[10] Others have a less favorable view of Reich's contribution; for example, Roger Griffin has dismissed the same book as an example of "aberrant psycho-historical theories" of fascism.[11] With this in mind, I would like to specify that my approach here is literary and intellectual history—the goal is not to resurrect Reich as a theorist of fascism for today but to explore the ways in which his ideas had a purchase on the Norwegian cultural-radical imagination.

Sigurd Hoel, by employing Reich's views of unhealthy fascist sexual frustration, joins a larger field of midcentury Freudian social theorists who focus on the twisted erotic profile of the fascist personality. This category includes Erich Fromm's 1941 *Escape from Freedom* (with its emphasis on the "sadomasochistic personality") and the *Authoritarian Personality* study by Adorno et al., published in 1950.[12] Although the specific arguments of midcentury political Freudianism might be outdated—and at times guilty of homophobic and other sexual prejudices—Hoel at his best displays an attitude of cautious ethical self-reflection. By training his lens on internal obstacles to progress and emancipation, Hoel transcends a superficial radicalism in a way that deserves recognition as a model of alert literary and political engagement from a brutal era.

INTERWAR CULTURAL RADICALISM

Sigurd Hoel's basic aesthetic and ideological orientation in the interwar period has always been understood as "cultural radicalism" (*kulturradikalisme*). In the Scandinavian context, this term refers to a leftist critique of conservative society, patriarchy, Christianity, and capitalism. Hoel's version of this critique developed as a hybrid of Marxist, Freudian, democratic-socialist, and liberal-individualist strands of thought. In Norway, literary *kulturradikalisme* produced engaged works in many genres in the 1920s and 1930s. In terms of formal innovation, Norwegian cultural radicals tended to be either moderately modernist, like Hoel, or quite conventional and even opposed to literary modernism, like the poet Arnulf Øverland.[13]

The interwar cultural radicals, including Hoel, saw their project as a continuation of the Brandesian and Ibsenian critical realism of the 1870s and 1880s. In a self-positioning essay on the history of cultural radicalism from 1955, Hoel retrospectively described the interwar moment as a third wave—after the eighteenth-century Enlightenment, which was European, and the nineteenth-century Modern Breakthrough, which was more limited to the Nordic context.[14] The influence of psychoanalysis on the third wave of cultural radicalism provided a needed corrective to the overly rationalist assumptions of the earlier phases, according to Hoel. It is customary to describe interwar cultural radicalism as a synthesis of Marx and Freud; equally important in terms of literary history is Hoel's view that it was a synthesis of Brandesian rationalism and Hamsunian neo-romanticism.[15]

As a widely read essayist and critic, Hoel exercised public power in the creation of a modernist reading public as a publishing consultant at Gyldendal and editor of *Den gule serie* (The Yellow Series) of translated literature. While not enamored of all forms of modernist experimentation, Hoel set many of the premises for modern literature in interwar Norway.[16] Similarly, Hoel was never an orthodox Marxist, but he was often engaged with socialist and social-democratic organizations, working as an editor or literary critic in the publications *Mot dag*, *Social-Demokraten*, and *Dagbladet* in the 1920s and 1930s. Hoel has appropriately been called a "barometer" for the concerns of the Nordic interwar intelligentsia.[17] His essays and reviews bear the imprint of the signature intellectual debates of his time, as filtered through a melancholic, wry, and urbane sensibility.

As a novelist, Hoel had two main Nordic literary influences, Henrik Ibsen and Knut Hamsun, both of whom he wrote about on many occasions.[18] Hoel tended to view Hamsun, not unfairly, as a romantic aesthete-genius whose work appealed primarily to youthful rebels.[19] Similarly, he understood Hamsun's politics as a reactionary-romantic form of cultural criticism with a seductive allure that ought to be resisted by more sober and reflective minds. Hoel was quite willing to view Hamsun's bad ideas as a regrettable feature of an author who should remain prized for his stylistic brilliance.[20] Predictably, Hoel had an enormous appreciation for his cultural-radical predecessor Ibsen, especially the ethically alert and self-judging Ibsen obsessed with a burdensome past and its tragic consequences for a younger, progressive generation seeking liberation and justice. Hoel also shared Ibsen's cautious and liberal suspicion of fanaticism or idealism in the form of total solutions, which inspired his response to totalitarianism.[21]

The first novel Hoel published, *Syvstjernen* (The Seven-Pointed Star) from 1924, is a modernist allegory marked by a macabre and bitter view of war-ravaged Europe. With dark humor, the novel focuses on a traumatized European city's reversion to barbarism and sadism in the aftermath of the war. *Syndere i sommersol*, Hoel's amusing send-up of the intellectual pretensions of interwar youth, includes a few minor characters who can be considered caricatures of fascist masculinity. The evocative depiction of a rural boyhood in 1890s Norway, *Veien til verdens ende* (The Road to the End of the World, 1933), was Hoel's first novel to show a specifically Reichian influence, rather than the more general reception of Freudian thought shown in his earlier fiction.[22] In *Fjorten dager før frostnettene* (A Fortnight Before the Frost, 1936), Hoel employed Reichian ideas about the liberation of eros and the fear of happiness in what he later called a "figurative representation of an analysis."[23] Hoel even fictionalized Reich in this novel as the unsympathetic character named Ramstad.

Although Hoel's 1931 novel *En dag i oktober* (One Day in October) has sometimes been read as a collective novel, in that it follows a group of people in a shared urban space rather than a central character, it would be wrong to associate the work too readily with a collectivist sociopolitical ideology. A modernist spatial narrative, *En dag i oktober* illuminates the damaged relationships and quiet desperation of a group of married couples and younger single people living in the same Oslo apartment building. While clearly a critique of the repressive institutions and attitudes of bourgeois society, the novel's concerns are the frailties of human bonds and poisonous forms of self-righteousness and moral policing. Hoel was often wary of the ways collectivist political goals could override individual rights, and this led to a backlash against him in the postwar period from leftists who saw his focus on individual liberty as a sign that he had shifted rightward. However, Hoel's form of cultural radicalism was always a continuation of the individualist strand of Modern Breakthrough liberalism advanced by Ibsen and Brandes.[24]

In 1938, Hoel published the novel *Sesam sesam*, a document of the times in its portrayal of the insular intellectual and cultural life of the Norwegian capital on the verge of World War II. *Sesam sesam* is a satirical roman à clef about journalists, writers, and other cultural-radical and avant-garde figures in Oslo. The novel's central idea of "patentmedisin" (cure-all) refers to anything that acts as a surrogate-religious total solution that brings certainty and authority to the age's moral and intellectual chaos.[25] Hoel later reflected that Hamsun found this "patentmedisin" in Nazism, and the idea also applies to Jacobsen and Sveen.[26]

After spending the latter part of the war in Sweden, Hoel published a book of essays about Nazism in 1945 called *Tanker i mørketid* (Thoughts in a Dark Time). Many of these were written while he was working on the layered and complex novel *Møte ved milepelen*, which draws on Reichian character theory in its psychological depiction of Norwegians who became Nazi collaborators. The roots of Nazism are to be found in the "human structure that is engendered by sexual repression," wrote Hoel, and the main culprits of this repression are fathers, the men of the older generation.[27] While *Møte ved milepelen* harshly condemns patriarchy, it focuses less on the domination of men over women and more on the prohibitive and loveless domination of older men over everyone else.[28] One of the novel's National Socialist characters, Hans Berg, has had a strict patriarchal upbringing. The psychological portrait makes clear that his father, a brutalizing pietistic Christian patriarch, has had an influence on his later fascist submission. Hans Berg's fascism is also portrayed as an expression of a wide-ranging discontent with the bourgeois status quo, an oppositional rage, and a sheer desire to negate.[29]

One lesson of *Møte ved milepelen* is that there was no single motivation shared by all Nazi collaborators, although they are all men and certain key features do emerge in the novel's constellation of explanations.

Hoel includes an interesting chapter called "Galleri av fortapte" (Gallery of the Damned), which gives brief individual portraits of Nazi collaborators and hints at their varied motivations. Among the portraits are careerists, opportunists, men searching idealistically for a surrogate religious faith, as well as one motivated by a belief in nationalist rebirth.[30] In line with other midcentury imaginings of fascism as erotically deviant, a few of the "damned" characters are depicted as having uncommon sexualities, and at least one of them appears to be a repressed homosexual.[31] The Reichian point that Hoel's novel makes often is that young people under patriarchy are forced to deny and repress their true nature in ways that warp and twist them, creating the psychological preconditions for Nazism. Turning to Hoel's essays, we will see how the image of Nazism in *Møte ved milepelen* was developed over the course of the interwar period.

"REBEL AND SLAVE"

Wilhelm Reich was the century's "most influential theorist of fascist libidinal repression," who offered a radical blend of Freud and Marx in interwar works such as *Massenpsychologie der Faschismus* (1933).[32] His fundamental argument was to link the political phenomenon of fascism (including Nazism) to the character structure of the sexually repressed mass individual. Sexual liberation and pleasure, what Reich called "orgastic potency," were central to social and individual emancipation, so Reichian psychotherapy aimed for the release of this energy. In contrast to the sexual conservatism of some other working-class and social-democratic movements of the era, Reich called for the thoroughgoing sexual liberation of youth and women.[33] This put him in conflict with the German Communist Party, which expelled him in 1933; he was also expelled from the International Psychoanalytic Organization the following year, which attests to what a controversial figure he was in theory and practice.[34] After World War II, Reich became notorious for his cosmic-biological speculations on "orgone energy," but he was later revived as an intellectual authority for the New Left in the 1960s. At that moment, explains Dagmar Herzog, his interwar sex-political work "captured the imaginations of those who urgently hoped that the struggle for social justice and the pursuit of pleasure were mutually enhancing projects."[35]

Hoel's attentive reading of psychoanalytic theory began in the 1920s, but his personal interaction with Wilhelm Reich took place in the 1930s, when they saw each other "almost every day" between 1934 and 1939.[36] Hoel recalled first hearing of Reich in Berlin in January 1932 when his wife, Nic, was in psychoanalysis there. She came back from a lecture by Reich beaming with enthusiasm about his ideas. Hoel spent over two years in training analysis with Reich, first in Sweden, then briefly in Denmark, and after the fall of 1934 in Oslo, where Reich resided for the rest of the decade.[37] During and after this period of routine contact, Hoel began to employ Reichian concepts for the analysis of the fascist and authoritarian character in his essays and novels. Reichian analysis gave Hoel the notion that "character" itself was an armoring—a rigid protection for a fragile or vulnerable ego, as well as an artificial mask of self-control. For Reich, patriarchal authority was internalized in the character structure of individuals. Paul Robinson explains in his classic *The Freudian Left* that ideology for Reich was not to be accounted for "simply (vulgarly) in terms of the economic/political power of the ruling class" but as an internalized structure of the unfree psyche.[38] Since character structure was formed in childhood, it "embodied the ideological forms of an earlier era" and was essentially conservative. For Hoel, the rigidity of the bourgeois-patriarchal character construct was identical in kind if not in degree to the fascist's hardened character armor. Seeing fascism as basically a patriarchal counterrevolution, Hoel read its authoritarian character types as a rearguard intensification of features found in earlier historical periods.

Reich also described Nazism's character structure as grounded in the psychology of the German masses, especially the lower-middle class. Crucial to this account was the idea that the petty bourgeois (*Kleinbürger*) had an ambivalent relationship to authority, both desiring submission and maintaining the contradictory fantasy of possessing an elite power. For Reich, submission to the absolute authority of a dictator reassuringly resembled submission to the law of the father, while at the same time the submissive subject assumed an authoritarian and often sadistic power relation to those perceived as social or racial subordinates.[39] Hoel found this twisted relationship to authority all too easily visible in the psychopathology of Nazism. Just as importantly, however, he saw it as belonging to the character structure produced by the patriarchal family of his own childhood era (the 1890s). It was not a problem only of the German lower-middle class in the rise of Nazism; the potentially fascist character structure needed to be criticized wherever it resided, whether or not its habitat was an overtly fascist or Nazi regime or society. Whenever Hoel wrote about Nazism, he was also writing about patriarchy, about the psychology of authority and submission, and about the fear of freedom and anxiety about pleasure. These are the central concerns of his fiction of the 1930s, even when it has no apparent connection to politics.

An early and significant attempt to configure his thoughts on these matters came in the 1934 essay "Rebell og trell" (Rebel and Slave), which was written during the time of his close contact with Reich. Hoel begins the essay with a gesture of modesty, calling it "just a little glance out over the landscape."[40] He describes the period before World War I as a time when a naive idea of technoscientific and social progress still held widespread validity for the European left, as humanity moved harmoniously toward a democratic-socialist future. This age of innocence saw the eventual triumph of the working class as something automatic, necessitated by a faith in the laws of history. Everything was clear-cut and assured for this socialism, as Hoel paints it retrospectively, with gentle mockery, from the other side of the abyss of World War I. The essay then gestures toward standard leftist explanations of the catastrophic war: technical, imperialist, and capitalist development was out of control, following its own logic, while nationalism in the working class enjoyed a sudden and unexpected resurgence. According to the optimistic progressive logic Hoel voices ironically, the desperate situations of the interwar period—economic crises, unemployment, hunger, and so forth—should only have hastened the revolution or produced a decisive moment of working-class radicalization. "Rebell og trell" begins, then, by recognizing that fascist mass politics represented a challenge to conventional socialist notions of politics and history.

Hoel sketches a stock image of "der wild gewordene Kleinbürger" (the distraught [or crazed] petty bourgeois), a German phrase that he uses in the original. This phrase originally comes from an essay by Lenin, and it became a more widespread stereotype of the reactionary "other" in socialist discourse.[41] Precariously situated, angered and scared by the threat of proletarianization, "der wild gewordene Kleinbürger" will go along with *anything* to avoid downward social mobility and solidify his position.[42] Hoel summarizes some explanations offered by interwar leftists for the mass appeal of fascism: the spread of the petty bourgeois mentality into the working class destroyed the unity and solidarity needed for socialist struggle; the division in working-class politics between revolutionaries and social-democratic reformists widened. As a psychoanalytic literary intellectual whose ultimate goal is to explain Nazism's affective and erotic structure, Hoel summarizes these arguments only to move beyond them and take a different approach.

The essay then turns inward, from political and economic explanations to a Reichian model of dialectical conflict in each individual, between "en opprører og en trell" (a rebel and a slave).[43] Psychoanalysis, which for Hoel and his generation had shown the importance of childhood for the formation of patterns in later life, provided a new way to understand the adult's relationship to political authority. In this view, the child's experiences of parental authority at home, especially paternal authority, prefigure a later pattern of relationship to external state authority. The key to the slave-like part of the psyche, writes Hoel, is enjoyment in submitting, that is, enjoyment "å kunne bøye rygg for en stor og fin herre—som han forferdelig gjerne vil ligne. Så gjerne at han undertiden tror han *er* ham i det øyeblikk han bøyer rygg for ham" (in being able to bend down before a great master—whom he wants so terribly to be like, so much so that sometimes he believes he *is* the master in the moment he bends down before him).[44] What Hoel is describing is a male fantasy of obtaining power through a double act of submission to and identification with a glamorized father. This fantasy plays itself out not only in the bourgeois interior of the past but also in the repetitions and variations of childhood relationships to authority that, in this psychoanalytic lens, offer a key insight into the rise of fascist mass psychology.

Hoel is not merely describing the psychological structure of an ideological enemy. On the contrary, he exhorts the reader to acknowledge their own inner "småborger" (petty bourgeois, *Kleinbürger*). Further relying on a socialist stereotype, he explains the inner "småborger" as "the incarnation of conservative virtues"—the part of us that is dutiful, obedient, reliable, frugal, organized, always watchful, and never fun. Despite these "virtues," the inner "småborger" is also anxious and afraid, lacking in imagination and initiative, scared of free thought and creativity, with an underdeveloped sense of justice and solidarity. This part of us sees other people as superiors, competitors, or subordinates—or simply foreign. Hoel's aim is to bring his readers to an awareness of this figure in their own psyche—the obedient and unimaginative, productive and useful, rule-bound and hierarchical little authoritarian. This is the "little seed" in each of us that wants to submit to a leader's reassuring commands—in the double act of submissive identification that also gratifies our lust for power. Vigilance about this part of the psyche is the key to Hoel's politics.

Offering another Reichian image, Hoel locates the petty bourgeois "slave" in the middle of concentric circles of paternalized authority: first the actual family unit, then the state/fatherland, and finally the grandest father figure of all, the (Lutheran) God. These concentric circles surround a rigid cell—a prison that feels secure because the inner slave fears actual freedom. Again, the encircled petty bourgeois is not truly liberated but centered and made powerful through fantasy identification with the figure of paternal authority. The exact opposite in Hoel's essay is the revolutionary worker (*rebellen*, *opprører*). This figure's primary feature is a decentering feeling of solidarity, which removes him from the encircled center and makes him "et fnugg mellom utallige andre" (a speck among countless others). For Hoel's revolutionary *opprører*, "autoritetsfølelsen forandrer seg til solidaritetsfølelse—farsprinsippet erstattes av brorsprinsippet" (the feeling of authority changes into the feeling of solidarity—the principle of the father is replaced by the principle of the brother).[45] In Hoel's essay, the psychological dichotomy of the rebel and the slave corresponds to the class-political opposition of the revolutionary worker and the petty bourgeois. The former is characterized by an emphasis on brotherly solidarity as opposed to paternal authority, and a decentered political affect as opposed to concentric circles of patriarchal power extending outward from family to state to cosmos.

At this point in reading Hoel's 1934 essay, we might pause to ask whether his dichotomy excludes something important known from other familial figurations of totalitarian power: namely, the authority of the (big) brother, the surveillance of the peer, and the tendency of brotherly rebellion to stiffen into doctrinaire rigidity. The psychoanalytic feminist critic Juliet Flower MacCannell has argued that the modern "regime of the brother" was even more oppressive than the patriarchal regime it replaced.[46] Hoel, being the self-interrogating essayist he is, recognizes the potential corruption of the positive terms in his binary scheme. He remarks that "undertiden kan vi allerede i selve opprørsropet høre tyrannens røst" (sometimes we can already hear the voice of the tyrant in the cry of rebellion itself).[47] In this moment of precaution and self-deconstruction, Hoel's essay becomes especially interesting. The essay constructs an opposition between a positive political figure (worker, healthy rebel, free individual in solidarity with equally free brothers) and a negative figure (petty bourgeois, jealous and anxious competitor, submissive and obedient fascist with a fantasy power thrill). But because he views both figures as metaphorically contained within each person at a psychological level, the dichotomy collapses. The positive figure of the rebel is corruptible and liable to become its opposite, its scandalous mirror image. For Hoel, the cultural radical leftist, this potentiality of the inner fascist, becomes an object of fear and alertness, as well as a key theme in his fiction and essays on Nazism.

Years later, in *Møte ved milepelen* (1947), Hoel emplots this scandal of recognition, the shock of perceiving the self in the Nazi other. The novel's narrator, called "Den plettfrie" (the Blameless one), an anti-Nazi member of the resistance effort, realizes late in the story that his illegitimate child from years earlier has become a Nazi. At one moment, he recognizes his own face in the face of a Nazi soldier, and as he realizes that it is his child, he becomes morally implicated in the production of a Nazi. His guilt over betraying and abandoning the mother infects his ability to maintain ideological innocence. The Norwegian word for treason (*landssvik*) echoes the compound noun for "betrayal of love" (*kjærlighetssvik*), as both contain the word for betrayal (*svik*). This makes clear at a linguistic level how the narrator becomes complicit in the novel's network of linked betrayals. In a visionary fragment late in the novel, he writes, "Jeg så nazismen som vårt uekte barn. Avlet i blinde og i feighet, forrådt i mors liv og overlatt til seg selv, til lut og kaldt vann. Og jeg så oss, de plettfrie, og selvrettferdige, stå der og se på dette vesenet, vårt barn av kjøtt og blod, og si: Vi kjenner deg ikke!" (I saw Nazism as our illegitimate child. Begotten blindly and cowardly, betrayed in his mother's womb and left to fend for himself. And I saw us, the blameless and self-righteous ones, stand there and look at this creature, our child of flesh and blood, and say, "We do not know you!")[48]

TWISTED ECSTASY

Hoel's adherence to a Reichian analysis of fascist mass psychology was visible in the mid-1930s, as was his willingness to think beyond a clear-cut dichotomy of us (the socialists, social democrats, liberals) and them (fascists and Nazis) by shifting the ground of analysis to the shared psychology of authority under patriarchy. These ideas remained fundamental in the later essay "Om nazismens vesen" (On the Essence of Nazism) from 1945, Hoel's most significant statement on the topic.[49] Hoel begins his essay with characteristic vigilance, referring to "nazismen, som vi har sett den, og som vi under andre navn kanskje atter skal få se den" (Nazism, as we have seen it, and as we will perhaps see it again, under other names).[50] He then discusses modernity's tendency toward specialization and compartmentalization, in which a new form of longing emerges, "efter frihet, efter samhørighet, efter å forsvinne ut av vår lille bås og gå op i noe større, noe felles" (for freedom, for connectedness, to disappear from our little compartment and be dissolved into something larger, something shared).[51] Politicians and demagogues exploit this widespread sense of alienated longing, explains Hoel, but they appeal to the masses not to go beyond all compartments (*båser*) but to join a larger communal compartment—the cause (*saken*). In Hoel's account, the longing to escape atomized alienation combines with an ambivalent attitude toward freedom (it is both desired and feared). The result, in Nazism, is a strong identification with the racialized collective as well as the production of an enemy image.[52]

As in "Rebel and Slave," Hoel quickly summarizes Marxist arguments that Nazism results from the economic anxiety and precarious position of the lower-middle class under capitalism, with its recurrent crises, unemployment, and so on.[53] But again, his psychoanalytic background prompts him to plumb the inner life of the Nazi: "når disse krisene fører til nazisme, så henger det sammen med et sinnelag" (when these crises result in Nazism, it has to do with a mentality).[54] Hoel's ultimate goal is to account for Nazi ecstasy, which he claims we do not yet understand; he refers to the object of his interest as "heten i alt det som skjedde, avsindigheten i det, ekstasen i det" (the fever in what happened, the insanity of it, the ecstasy of it).[55] The Reichian answer, predictably, is that "det er stengte erotiske krefter som kommer til utbrudd i denne ekstasen. Krefter som er bundet og hemmet av angst og forbud og grått, ensformig liv" (it is dammed-up erotic forces that break out in this ecstasy. Forces that are bound and constrained by anxiety and prohibitions and a gray and monotonous life).[56] In Hoel's essay, the unhealthy erotic life of the Nazi masses is the key factor in an explanatory mixture consisting of longing for de-individuation in a religious and collective experience, ambivalence about freedom, fear of the other, and obsession with power as a replacement for love.

In a revealing moment, Hoel offers an image of the proto-Nazi as an (implicitly male) tiger made mad in captivity, tearing itself apart with claws and teeth, consuming and destroying itself in a frenzy of violence. Sexual repression in Christian-bourgeois and patriarchal society issues prohibitions, which obstruct and imprison the "animal in man," leading to an explosive and destructive situation.[57] When the supposedly natural and healthy sexual drives are restricted, the result is a rebellious release of sadism and violence. The Reichian model of erotic energy Hoel uses is hydraulic in the manner of early psychoanalytic explanation (which Freud himself had long abandoned): when the wholesome or proper outlet is unavailable, this sexual energy releases itself elsewhere in a distorted form.

Hoel argues that Hitler was able to co-opt the revolutionary mood and potential within Germany's crisis situation by addressing this toxic blend of sexual frustration, repression, and sadomasochism. He views Hitler as having performed a patriarchal counterrevolution. Patriarchy for Hoel (as for Reich) was the source of the private property system, of class division, of tribal thinking, of the warlike cult of masculinity, of torture, of the objectification and degradation of women, of the monetization of love and sex—the list goes on. The mechanisms of punishment and oppression instilled by patriarchy were both outward and inward: corporal punishment and social ostracism, yes, but also fear of pleasure, a guilty conscience about the body, and the distortion of open intimacy and natural love.

This world-historical account of the ills of patriarchy allows Hoel to offer a description of Nazism's neurotic psychopathology. Nazis are unhealthy fanatics, monological idealists, hatefully obsessed with fixed ideas, fearful of perceived decline, yet for that very reason prepared to be part of the salvation and overcoming that the moment of truth affords.[58] Nazism's emphasis on overcoming is in fact a patriarchal survival strategy in modernity, a pseudo-emancipatory movement that restores rigid adherence to an archaic mode of social and sexual organization. Nazism for Hoel is patriarchy sadistically reasserted, yet morally cleansed: "all medlidenhet skulde brennes ut av sjelen på disse unge mennene, og de skulde opdrettes til overmennesker uten skyldfølelse og uten synd" (all compassion was to be burned out of the souls of these young men, and they would be bred into supermen without feelings of guilt or sin).[59]

Hoel's Reichian critique of patriarchy relies on a noticeably utopian matriarchal counterimage. Both Hoel and Reich derived their ideas about a natural matriarchal society from Bronisław Malinowski's interwar anthropological studies of the Trobriand Islands (now part of Papua New Guinea). Malinowski portrayed life on the island as an example of non-authoritarian parenting and active and expressive sexuality for women and the young, with no neuroses or perversions.[60] Reich and Hoel thought that matriarchy entailed a harmonious "self-regulation of sexuality," in contrast to the oppressive, unjust, and guilt-inducing sexual economy under patriarchy.[61] This idea of the natural matriarchy in a prelapsarian state continued to influence Hoel's imagination of utopia; it appeared, for example, in the narrative fragments toward the end of *Møte ved milepelen*.

One reason Hoel offers a psychoanalytic explanation of Nazi ecstasy is that he thinks the Marxist left has underestimated the irrational and conservative forces in the human psyche, the ones that work in favor of patriarchal tradition, the ones imprinted through an authoritarian upbringing.[62] As we have seen, Hoel faulted earlier stages in the history of cultural radicalism, such as the Brandesian Modern Breakthrough, for being insufficiently attentive to the irrational. Evidently Hoel had absorbed the lessons of psychoanalysis as well as the writings of the early Hamsun, who in many ways lurks in the background of his essays on rebellion, patriarchy, and Nazism. As these essays reveal, Hoel saw the irrational and erotic aspects of psychological life as linked to both politics and the sacred. When he writes that everyone has the seed of something like Nazism inside, he adds that we tend to avoid casting light on it, because "det er ofte omgitt av såkalte hellige følelser" (it is often surrounded by so-called sacred feelings).[63] For Hoel, that "cherished little place"—the birthplace of the inner Nazi—can be traced back to a specific childhood location: the patriarchal home. At the end of "Om nazismens vesen," in a return to the start of his essay, Hoel suggests that the key to preventing the return of Nazism under other names is to work for a happier childhood/youth and a less brutalizing mode of raising children.[64] This concluding reflection connects his essay to his ex-wife's therapeutic work as a child analyst and to the fictionalized depiction of his own childhood in *Veien til verdens ende*.

This type of psychoanalytic antifascism can be criticized for leading to an overly eroticized understanding of mass politics, but it also promotes an ethical self-critique of the non-fascist subject, who is shaped by the same distorting forces of patriarchal authority, albeit in different proportions. Hoel claimed that his fellow radicals in Scandinavia accepted simplifications about Nazism—it was caused by unemployment, it was only a German problem—because they did not dare to perform the unpleasant task of looking for its roots inside themselves. As he writes in the statement quoted above, "Sannheten om nazismen er ubehagelig, ikke bare fordi den handler om et ufyselig stoff, men fordi den krever en nærgående granskning i oss selv" (The truth about Nazism is uncomfortable, not only because it concerns something disgusting but because it requires an intimate investigation of ourselves).[65] His struggle against the Nazi mentality, and also again "den ubevisste nazisme" (unconscious Nazism), was a struggle against the internal ghosts of patriarchal authoritarianism. Tying together the intimate and the political in his literary treatment of Nazism allowed Hoel to break down the black-and-white dichotomies that govern many analyses of the Nazi mind as aberrant.[66] For Hoel, as for other midcentury Freudian social theorists, the urgent and definitive opposition to fascist regimes and politics was not a time for self-congratulation. Rather, it offered an opportunity for penetrating self-reflection about repressive and authoritarian features of one's own psychology and culture. Though they are clearly artifacts of a Reichian moment in the interpretation of fascism, Hoel's essays and novels also remain valuable documents of a midcentury cultural radicalism, showing a different interface of Norwegian literary modernism and fascism.

Conclusion

In a 1967 essay titled "The Idea of the Modern," the Democratic Socialist critic Irving Howe identified the "specter of nihilism" as "the central preoccupation, the inner demon, at the heart of modern literature."[1] Howe meant the term "nihilism" both morally and existentially. He referred to the experience of losing belief in both "transcendent imperatives and secular values" as sources of moral orientation, and also to the feeling that existence has become meaningless. In the modern culture of nihilism—the condition of devaluation proclaimed by Nietzsche with the "death of God"—experience is reduced to a wasteland of boredom and drift. At its base, Howe claimed, "nihilism comes to imply a loss of connection with the sources of life."[2] The Norwegian literary modernists examined in the foregoing chapters all exhibit this encounter with the specter of nihilism. Excluding Sigurd Hoel, they perceived the condition of nihilism as a derailment of "life" under the rationalized and mechanized conditions of a recently formed and rapidly changing technological culture. As figures from a peripheral nation with a strong liberal-democratic consensus, Hamsun, Sveen, and Jacobsen were part of a subculture of pro-Nazi sympathizers who collaborated with the more powerful German center.

The careers of Hamsun, Sveen, and Jacobsen all show some kind of transition from a literary form of anti-nihilism to a political form of regeneration, a shift from an anxiety-ridden aesthetic encounter with modernity's chaos and reduction to a charismatic fantasy of renewal and rebirth via fascism. In each case, the attitudes that motivate their turn to fascist utopianism also lie behind their literary modernist urge to develop new post-traditional literary forms. This orientation includes a set of characteristic features: a neo-romantic and "reactionary-radical" dissent from the social, often urban, world of liberal modernity; an affective opposition to the culture, ethos, and style of secular rationality; the self-perception that one belongs to an aesthetic, sexual, or spiritual vanguard; and the understanding of the present as a time of disintegration that requires a totalistic solution to build a glorified future.

While the cultural-radical novelist Sigurd Hoel remained admirably alert to the fundamental sickness of this regenerative vision, the other authors imagined fascism as a vehicle for the secular redemption of European modernity. Hamsun, Sveen, and Jacobsen attached themselves to an absolute solution that spoke to a utopian desire for revitalization and idealistic overcoming. Fascism offered a novel form of salvation in the absence or exhaustion of conventional mythic frameworks. Whether the target was "positivism" (for the early Hamsun), "materialism and banalization" (for Sveen), or technological "nihilism" (for Jacobsen), the pattern of response was similar.

The case of Hamsun displays in a single figure the more general cultural development from a fin-de-siècle moment of reactionary-radical rebellion to an interwar moment of utopian faith in the fascist overcoming of Anglo-American materialism. As we see from a reading of Hamsun's carnivalization of realism and positivism in *Mysterier*, his early modernist fiction is quite revealing for the development of his later fascist worldview, even if the former does not foreshadow the latter teleologically. Hamsun formed an image of the Anglo-American as the nihilistic destroyer of "life" early in his career, and this mental construction of the ideological adversary stuck with him to the bitter end of his Nazi sympathizing.

The case of Hamsun's much younger admirer, the sexually and politically dissident Åsmund Sveen, also shows the role of vitalistic discourse in Norwegian modernist politics. Sveen's bold homoerotic vitalism overlapped with the cultural-critical foundation of his fascist allegiance. As with Hamsun, Sveen saw European politics in the interwar period as a battle between "life," ancient wisdom, and national or ethnic spiritual-cultural strength (fascism) and stultifying rationalism, restrictive bourgeois morality, and deracinated weakness (liberalism). Sveen crafted an unconventional religious framework with Eros as the central term, and he imagined fascism as the world-historical movement of a post-materialist regeneration. His utopian commitment to this regenerative vision apparently outweighed any consideration of his own status as a sexual minority and a potential victim of the Nazi regime.

The case of Jacobsen shows the most overt instance of totalitarian politics as a form of surrogate religion. Less concerned with aesthetic and cultural vitalism than Hamsun or Sveen, and more explicitly disturbed by the prospect of technological modernity as a form of nihilistic uprooting, Jacobsen latched onto fascism both as a way to assuage unresolved personal-existential anxieties and as a way to fasten modern culture to a secure foundation. When this "God" failed, Jacobsen went through a period of grief and eventually found his way to Roman Catholicism. To the extent that these modernist authors approached fascism not only as a source of public, social, and economic renewal but also as a form of inner transformation and even transcendence, fascism's appeal went beyond politics in a narrow sense. In his own way, Sigurd Hoel also recognized the transcendental and "metapolitical" aspects of fascism and Nazism. Of course, such a view of the authors' search for redemption should not obscure the racial dimension of their fears of degeneration and decline. They sought regeneration not for humanity in general but for Germanic Europe.

In *Thinking the Twentieth Century*, Tony Judt observes that the Norwegian context was "the outstanding case of a pro-German fascism" and that Norwegian fascists "saw themselves as extensions of *Deutschtum*, as part of the great Nordic space in which they could hope for a role in Nazi ambitions."[3] The potent Germanic center of National Socialism was a redeeming force that seemed to offer what peripheral Norwegian fascists desired: a political form of idealism that would reinvigorate Europe and counteract the desiccating materialism of both Americanism and Bolshevism. This imagination of a particular ethnic group as the custodian of authentic vitality and true wisdom stood in opposition to the uprooted cosmopolitan modernity, the "Jewish" influence, and the Anglo-American world. Indeed, America for Hamsun, as for many others on the European right, was contemptible not only for its rampant commercialism and unhistorical shallowness but also for its racial and ethnic mixing.

The racist sort of regeneration these writers imagined to be embodied in European fascism turned out catastrophically for their own postwar lives and compromised legacies. Beyond their own suffering, punishment, and disappointment with the modern age, however, were the millions of people they never knew who died as victims of the Nazi regime. Although anti-Semitism did not emerge as a fixed obsession in their literary works, it was an undeniable component of the regime they chose to support. As we have seen, Jacobsen, Sveen, and Hamsun all voiced distastefully racist or anti-Semitic comments at one point or another in a nonfictional context. Quite simply, to support Nazism was to think in terms of racial exclusion and purification. It is true that these authors could not have experienced their support for National Socialism as support for "Auschwitz" as it is remembered today. Yet their collaboration with the Nazi regime and its propaganda machinery during the occupation was part of Norway's role in the Holocaust. During the middle years of the Nazi occupation, from 1942 to 1943, 772 Norwegian Jews were deported to German camps.[4] Most of them were sent to Auschwitz, including the young diarist Ruth Maier, who was deported on the *Donau* in November 1942 with over 500 others. Only 34 of these deported Norwegian Jews survived. The total number of Jews registered in Norway went from 2,100 before the war to 559 in 1946.[5]

In the immediate postwar decades in Norway, memory of the war focused on Norwegian victimhood under the German occupation, and the persecution of Jews became part of that narrative.[6] The dominant story of the war in Norwegian historiography and memory culture was that of a small nation in resistance to the Nazis, with the chief dichotomy being between "good Norwegians" and the Nasjonal Samling and its supporters.[7] Within this nationally framed narrative, as Synne Corell has argued, Norwegian wartime society was constructed as monocultural, and the fate of the Jews and other minorities was often disregarded. This patriotic narrative was typical of an earlier phase of Holocaust and war memory, but it has since been questioned and challenged in both academic and public contexts. In the early twenty-first century, the Holocaust is recognized and memorialized as *the* central feature of World War II. As Tony Judt writes in *Postwar*, "The Holocaust today is much more than just another undeniable fact about a past that Europeans can no longer choose to ignore . . . the recovered memory of Europe's dead Jews has become the very definition and guarantee of the continent's restored humanity."[8] Norway, like the other Scandinavian countries, began to deal seriously with questions of guilt, complicity, and compensation in the 1990s, with the national commission that led to the establishment of the Center for Studies of Holocaust and Religious Minorities.[9]

In Scandinavia as elsewhere, the collective and public memory culture regarding World War II has shifted from nationally framed narratives to a more cosmopolitan and international form of Holocaust remembrance. This shift forms a larger context for Jens Stoltenberg's moving apology in 2012 for the deportation of Norwegian Jews and refugees seventy years earlier. Seen through this international memory context, the literary modernist collaborators Hamsun, Sveen, and Jacobsen appear not simply as "bad Norwegians" whose chief crime was treason but rather as misguided idealists at best, who publicly supported one of the worst genocides in history. The antifascist Sigurd Hoel, who also drew on fundamental aspects of modernist culture and discourse, remains an admirable example who shows that clear-sighted and sincere intellectual engagement matters, and is possible, even in dark times.

NOTES

INTRODUCTION

1. Stanley G. Payne, *A History of Fascism, 1914–1945* (Madison: University of Wisconsin Press, 1995), 459.

2. Bjarte Birkeland, "Forfattarmiljø og nazisme i trettiåra," in *Nazismen og norsk litteratur*, 2nd ed., ed. Bjarte Birkeland and Stein Ugelvik Larsen (Oslo: Universitetsforlaget, 1995), 21. See also Nils-Aage Sørgaard, *Fire forfattere og norsk fascisme* (Oslo: Forlaget Ny Dag, 1973).

3. Birkeland, "Forfattarmiljø og nazisme i trettiåra," 28.

4. Arnulf Øverland, *Vi overlever alt! Dikt fra krigsårene* (Oslo: Aschehoug, 1945).

5. Sigrid Undset, *Tilbake til fremtiden* (Oslo: Aschehoug, 1945).

6. For a brief discussion of Bjørneboe's work, see Ann Schmiesing, "Nazi Germany and the Holocaust in Norwegian Literature," in *German Studies in the Post-Holocaust Age: The Politics of Memory, Identity, and Ethnicity*, ed. Adrian del Caro and Janet Ward (Boulder: University of Colorado Press, 2000).

7. "About the Center," Center for Studies of Holocaust and Religious Minorities, http://www.hlsenteret.no/english/about/.

8. Antero Holmila and Karin Kvist Geverts, "On Forgetting and Rediscovering the Holocaust in Scandinavia," *Scandinavian Journal of History* 36, no. 5 (2011): 526.

9. Bjarte Bruland and Mats Tangestuen, "The Norwegian Holocaust: Changing Views and Representations," *Scandinavian Journal of History* 36, no. 5 (2011): 587–604.

10. Ibid., 598. In addition to Bruland's work and the research conducted at the Center for Studies of Holocaust and Religious Minorities, another publication worth mentioning is Marte Michelet's *Den største forbrytelsen: Ofre og gjerningsmenn i det norske Holocaust* (Oslo: Gyldendal, 2014), which won the prestigious Brage Prize for Non-fiction in 2014.

11. Vibeke Kieding Banik, "Holocaust i Norge," Store norske leksikon, 2015, https://snl.no/Holocaust_i_Norge.

12. Jan Erik Vold, *Ruth Maiers dagbok: En jødisk flyktning i Norge* (Oslo: Gyldendal, 2007).

13. Jens Stoltenberg, "Speech on the International Holocaust Remembrance Day," January 27, 2012, https://www.regjeringen.no/en/aktuelt/speech-on-international-holocaust-rememb/id670621/.

CHAPTER 1

1. Ingar Sletten Kolloen, *Hamsun: Erobreren* (Oslo: Gyldendal, 2004), 122.

2. Ibid., 137.

3. For a description of this event, see ibid., 271–74.

4. Ove Røsbak, *Rolf Jacobsen: En dikter og hans skygge* (Oslo: Gyldendal, 1998), 109.

5. "Krigen er uhyggelig, opprørende og motbydelig. Den er like opprørende og motbydelig som den samfunnsordning som er skapt av jødene og pengemakten." Rolf Jacobsen, "At ikke menneskene er kommet lenger!" editorial, *Glåmdalen*, December 27, 1943.

6. Jan Olav Gatland, *Det andre mennesket: Eit portrett av Åsmund Sveen* (Oslo: Det Norske Samlaget, 2003), 93.

7. Ibid., 96.

8. Åsmund Sveen, "Hvorfor jeg er medlem av NS," *Nationen*, January 29, 1944.

9. *Glåmdalen*, November 24, 1943.

10. Peter Sjølyst-Jackson, *Troubling Legacies: Migration, Modernism and Fascism in the Case of Knut Hamsun* (London: Continuum, 2010).

11. See Knut Hamsun, *Hamsuns polemiske skrifter*, ed. Gunvald Hermundstad (Oslo: Gyldendal, 1998), and Tore Rem, *Knut Hamsun: Reisen til Hitler* (Oslo: Cappelen Damm, 2014).

12. All of the biographies consulted for this book have appeared within the past twenty years. For Hamsun, see Ingar Sletten Kolloen's two-volume *Hamsun: Svermeren* (Oslo: Gyldendal, 2004) and *Hamsun: Erobreren*, which has been published in an abridged translation as *Knut Hamsun: Dreamer and Dissenter*, trans. Deborah Dawkin and Erik Skuggevik (New Haven: Yale University Press, 2009). For more detailed readings of the novels within a biography, see Jørgen Haugan, *Solgudens fall: Knut Hamsun—en litterær biografi* (Oslo: Aschehoug, 2006). For Jacobsen, there are two biographies from 1998: Ove Røsbak's *Rolf Jacobsen: En dikter og hans skygge* and Hanne Lillebo's *Ord må en omvei: En biografi om Rolf Jacobsen* (Oslo: Aschehoug, 2006). For Sveen, there is the engaging biography by Jan Olav Gatland, *Det andre mennesket: Eit portrett av Åsmund Sveen.*

13. Rottem wrote: "Hamsun-debatten [har] kommet til å ligne en forskutt og forlenget rettsak, en prosedyre—med aktorer, forsvarere og dommere, med innlegg der Hamsun blir angrepet . . . [og] med innlegg der Hamsun framstilles som nazist i hele sitt vesen og i hele sitt menneskesyn. Og på den annen side—med innlegg der Hamsun unnskyldes, der formildende omstendigheter trekkes fram, der mennesket, og ikke minst diketeren Hamsun blir frikjent, eller i alle fall blir gitt absolusjon og tatt til nåde" (The Hamsun debate [has] come to resemble a prolonged legal case, a hearing—with

prosecutors, defenders, and judges, with pleadings where Hamsun is attacked . . . [and] with pleadings where Hamsun is portrayed as a Nazi in his entire being and his entire view of humanity. And on the other hand—with pleadings where Hamsun is excused, extenuating circumstances are brought forth, where the person, and especially the writer of fiction, is acquitted, or in any case given absolution and restored to favor). See Øystein Rottem, *Hamsun og fantasiens triumf* (Oslo: Gyldendal, 2002), 9–10.

14. See, for example, the introduction to Richard J. Golsan, ed., *Fascism, Aesthetics, and Culture* (Hanover, NH: University Press of New England, 1992).

15. For a typical example, see Dominick LaCapra, *History, Literature, Critical Theory* (Ithaca, NY: Cornell University Press, 2013), 128.

16. Jobst Welge, "Fascist Modernism," in *Modernism*, ed. Astradur Eysteinsson and Vivian Liska (Amsterdam: John Benjamins, 2007), 548.

17. Golsan, *Fascism, Aesthetics, and Culture*, xv.

18. Lisi doesn't give much weight to the twentieth century at all, claiming that "the height of productivity in Scandinavian modernism spans two crucial historical events: Denmark's loss of Schleswig-Holstein to Prussia in 1864 and Norway's independence from Sweden in 1905." See Leonardo Lisi, "Scandinavia," in *The Cambridge Companion to European Modernism*, ed. Pericles Lewis (Cambridge: Cambridge University Press, 2011), 192. For more about Lisi's understanding of Scandinavian modernism, see also his *Marginal Modernity: The Aesthetics of Dependency from Kierkegaard to Joyce* (New York: Fordham University Press, 2013), 9–11.

19. See the chapters "Ibsen and the Ideology of Modernism" and "Rethinking Literary History" in Toril Moi, *Henrik Ibsen and the Birth of Modernism: Art, Theater, Philosophy* (Oxford: Oxford University Press, 2006).

20. In this regard, see Martin Humpál, *The Roots of Modernist Narrative: Knut Hamsun's Novels Hunger, Mysteries, and Pan* (Oslo: Solum, 1998).

21. For more on Cora Sandel and other female Nordic prose modernists, see Ellen Rees, *On the Margins: Nordic Women Modernists of the 1930s* (London: Norvik Press, 2006).

22. This debate has been overly central to the construction of modernism in Norwegian literary history. See John Brumo and Sissel Furuseth, *Norsk litterær modernisme* (Bergen: Fagbokforlaget, 2005), 33–34.

23. Stanley G. Payne helpfully explains debates around the terms "fascism," "modernity," and "modernization" in *A History of Fascism*; see especially 202–5 and 471–86.

24. Peter Fritzsche, *Life and Death in the Third Reich* (Cambridge, MA: Harvard University Press, 2008), 9.

25. Ibid., 14–15, 307.

26. Astradur Eysteinsson and Vivian Liska, eds., *Modernism* (Amsterdam: John Benjamins, 2007), 1:5.

27. Michael Levenson, *Modernism* (New Haven: Yale University Press, 2011), 8.

28. Ibid., 9. Emphasis added.

29. The emphasis on "disembedding" and the amplification of doubt comes from the work of Anthony Giddens, for example, *Modernity and Self-Identity: Self and Society in the Late Modern Age* (Stanford, CA: Stanford University Press, 1991).

30. For more on the idea of a "new consensus," see the preface to Roger Griffin, *International Fascism: Theories, Causes and the New Consensus* (London: Arnold, 1998). Here he contends that a common understanding of the definition of generic fascism has emerged in scholarship, with a focus on the ideology's utopian vision of an idealized and regenerated national community.

31. Daniel Woodley, a political theorist critical of "culturalist" approaches, writes that the new consensus was "founded less on scholarly agreement than a conscious rejection of historical materialism." See *Fascism and Political Theory: Critical Perspectives on Fascist Ideology*. (London: Routledge, 2010). He writes that the consensus is not shared by Italian and German historians but is more limited to Anglophone studies (10). *The Oxford Handbook of Fascism*, edited by R. J. B. Bosworth (Oxford: Oxford University Press, 2011), also rejects the idea of a consensus among scholars.

32. Woodley, *Fascism and Political Theory*, 2–10.

33. Roger Griffin, "The Primacy of Culture: The Current Growth (or Manufacture) of Consensus Within Fascist Studies," *Journal of Contemporary History* 37, no. 21 (2002): 24.

34. Roger Griffin, *Modernism and Fascism: The Sense of a Beginning Under Mussolini and Hitler* (New York: Palgrave Macmillan, 2007), 8.

35. Jean Clair, *The 1930s: The Making of "The New Man"* (Ottawa: National Gallery of Canada, 2008), 18–19.

36. Fritzsche, *Life and Death in the Third Reich*, 90–91.

37. Laura Bossi, "The 'New Man': Degeneracy and Regeneration," in *The 1930s: The Making of "The New Man,"* ed. Jean Clair (Ottawa: National Gallery of Canada, 2008), 43.

38. Ibid., 44.

39. See Rolf Jacobsen, "Etter krigen," editorial, *Kongsvinger arbeiderbladet*, April 16, 1941. Jacobsen writes that "etter Ragnarok skal der bygges opp en sosial stat" (after Ragnarok a social state will be built up), a line I will discuss further in chapter 4. "Ragnarok" was also the name of a Norwegian fascist journal in the 1930s and 1940s.

40. Mark Antliff, *Avant-garde Fascism: The Mobilization of Myth, Art, and Culture in France, 1909–1939* (Durham, NC: Duke University Press, 2007), 19.

41. Sternhell, however, refuses to consider Nazism as form of fascism (see *The Birth of Fascist Ideology: From Cultural Rebellion to Political Revolution*, trans. David Maisel [Princeton, NJ: Princeton University Press, 1994]). Griffin offers compelling criticisms of this position in "The Primacy of Culture," 30–31. Stanley Payne has also used the fin-de-siècle moment to explain the origins of fascism; see "The Cultural Transformation of the Fin de Siècle," in *A History of Fascism*.

42. Roger Griffin, *The Nature of Fascism* (New York: St. Martin's, 1991), 29.

43. Payne, *A History of Fascism*, 9. This point also helps explain a key difference between fascist ideology and that of the conservative authoritarian right. The latter, notes Payne, based itself "upon religion more than upon any new cultural mystique such as vitalism, nonrationalism, or secular neoidealism" (16).

44. Sternhell, *The Birth of Fascist Ideology*, 10.

45. Ibid., 10.

46. Thomas Linehan, "A Host of 'Decadent' Phenomena," in *Fascism: Critical Concepts in Political Science*, vol. 3, *Fascism and Culture*, ed. Roger Griffin and Matthew Feldman (London: Routledge, 2004), 333.

47. Eivind Tjønneland, "Åsmund Sveens antologi *Norsk ånd og vilje* og litteraturen i norsk nazisme," in *"Der vårgras brydder"—Nye lesninger av Åsmund Sveens diktning*, ed. Hans Kristian Rustad (Vallset, Norway: Oplandske bokforlag, 2010), 91–107.

48. Birkeland and Larsen, *Nazismen og norsk litteratur*, 10.

49. Monika Žagar, *Knut Hamsun: The Dark Side of Literary Brilliance* (Seattle: University of Washington Press, 2009), 200–201.

50. Ibid., 186.

51. Ibid., 187.

52. Ibid., 38–39.

53. Ibid., 39.

54. Žagar analyzes Hamsun's views on race very thoroughly. *Knut Hamsun* makes a compelling case that Hamsun's long-held notions of race and gender are the main features that link his wide-ranging literary production to his fascism.

55. Fritzsche, *Life and Death in the Third Reich*, 90.

56. Ibid., 91.

57. Ibid., 84–85.

58. See Žagar's clear-sighted discussion of Hamsun's anti-Semitism (*Knut Hamsun*, 188–98).

59. "Bildet av fascismens kunst som Blut und Boden-diktning må nyanseres. Modell: Marinetti og den italienske futurismen. Fascistene hadde sin avant-garde, som Hamsun var fører for. Et annet norsk eksempel: den modernistiske lyrikeren Åsmund Sveen." Arild Linneberg, "Avantgardens Andre Ansikt: Hamsuns Poetikk," *Agora* 17, no. 1–2 (1999): 6.

60. Andrew Hewitt, *Fascist Modernism: Aesthetics, Politics, and the Avant-Garde* (Stanford, CA: Stanford University Press, 1993), 39.

61. David Carroll writes in *French Literary Fascism: Nationalism, Anti-Semitism, and the Ideology of Culture* (Princeton, NJ: Princeton University Press, 1995) that the idea that an "'authentic' artist, writer, or critic . . . could not be at the same time a political ideologue, a racist, or anti-Semite, that art and literature are in themselves opposed to political dogmatism and racial biases and hatred, constitutes nothing less than a mystification of art and literature" (8).

62. To name a few contributions that take varying approaches to the issue in individual or national contexts: Fredric Jameson, *Fables of Aggression: Wyndham Lewis, the Modernist as Fascist* (Berkeley: University of California Press, 1979); Charles Ferrall, *Modernist Writing and Reactionary Politics* (Cambridge: Cambridge University Press, 2001); Carroll, *French Literary Fascism*; and Golsan, *Fascism, Aesthetics, and Culture.*

63. Emily Braun usefully describes this context in *Mario Sironi and Italian Modernism: Art and Politics Under Fascism* (Cambridge: Cambridge University Press, 2000), explaining the shift in research during the 1980s from analyses of individual texts, movements, or objects to sociological analyses of cultural politics and public spectacle under Italian Fascism (7).

64. Griffin, *Modernism and Fascism*, 279–309.

65. Antliff, *Avant-garde Fascism*, 21.

66. Griffin, *Modernism and Fascism*, 39.

67. Carroll, *French Literary Fascism*, 9.

CHAPTER 2

1. "Han var og er den viktigste norske fascistiske intellektuelle. Og han blei det som en avantgardedikter." Linneberg, "Avantgardens Andre Ansikt: Hamsuns Poetikk," 5.

2. The middle and later periods of Hamsun's career, to use the conventional phases, practice a social realism in rural settings in what can seem like an aesthetic regression. Later novels such as the *Landstrykere* trilogy of the early 1930s, though very popular in their own time and particularly in Germany, have not exerted the same fascination as the early, modernist works. There has, however, been a solid strand of critical interest in Hamsun's realism and the later phases of his authorship. A good example that also discusses Hamsun's politics is Ståle Dingstad, *Hamsuns strategier: Realisme, humor og kynisme* (Oslo: Gyldendal, 2003).

3. All of Hamsun's wartime articles, and many other relevant nonfiction documents from throughout his career, are available in Hermundstad's *Hamsuns polemiske skrifter.* Many of these are explained and contextualized in Rem, *Knut Hamsun: Reisen til Hitler. Paa gjengrodde stier* has inspired a great deal of critical commentary; Peter Sjølyst-Jackson offers a valuable analysis in *Troubling Legacies*, 135–53.

4. Kolloen, *Hamsun: Erobreren*, 77. Emphasis added.

5. Ibid., 248, 285.

6. Žagar, *Knut Hamsun*, 33–38.

7. Sjølyst-Jackson, *Troubling Legacies*, 4.

8. There is a strong tradition of Marxist ideology critique in Hamsun studies that goes back to the early interventions of the Frankfurt School's Leo Löwenthal in the 1930s and was expanded by several Scandinavian works from the 1970s. See Leo Löwenthal, "Knut Hamsun," in *The Essential Frankfurt School Reader*, ed. A. Arato and Eike Gebhardt (New York: Continuum, 1982), 319–45; Leo Löwenthal, *Das bürgerliche Bewusstsein in der Literatur* (Frankfurt: Suhrkamp, 1981); and Morten Giersing, John

Thobo-Carlsen, and Mikael Westergaard-Nielsen, *Det reaktionære oprør: Om fascismen i Hamsuns forfatterskab* (Kongerslev, Denmark: GMT, 1975).

9. A recent example of this is the treatment of Hamsun's politics and ideology in *Knut Hamsun: A Critical Assessment* (New York: Peter Lang, 2005) by Sverre Lyngstad, the translator of recent English versions of Hamsun's main novels.

10. Atle Kittang, *Luft, vind, ingenting: Hamsuns desillusjonsromanar frå Sult til Ringen sluttet* (Oslo: Gyldendal Norsk Forlag, 1984), 12, 14. Kittang has also suggested that the conventional division of Hamsun's authorship into phases has functioned as a critical myth, rooted so securely that it has the status of a literary historical fact. The idea of a break around 1910 when Hamsun goes from bohemian and rootless artist to farmer—with a shift from a psychological modernist to a social realist aesthetic—can make the authorship seem overly discontinuous at a thematic and ideological level.

11. See Jon Langdal, "Hvordan trylle bort det ubehagelige?" *Agora* 17, no. 1–2 (1999): 232–59.

12. Ibid.

13. For information about Hamsun's reception history in Germany, see Gabriele Schulte, *Hamsun im Spiegel der deutschen Literaturkritik 1890 bis 1975* (Frankfurt: Peter Lang, 1986) and Heiko Uecker, "Tendenser i tysk Hamsun-forskning," in *Hamsun i Tromsø: 11 foredrag fra Hamsun-konferansen i Tromsø, 1995*, ed. Nils M. Knutsen (Hamarøy, Norway: Hamsun-Selskapet, 2003), 175–94.

14. Tore Rem writes that the Nazis "skilte sjelden mellom den tidlige og den senere Hamsun" (seldom distinguished between the early and the late Hamsun) (*Knut Hamsun: Reisen til Hitler*, 72).

15. Rem, *Knut Hamsun: Reisen til Hitler*, 164.

16. Ibid., 273.

17. Ibid., 317–20.

18. Karl-Heinz Schoeps writes in *Literature and Film in the Third Reich* (Rochester, NY: Camden House, 2004) that "the difficulty of defining Nazi literature is attributable to the fact that National Socialism never developed a uniform concept of literature and was unable to agree on what constitutes a binding canon of National Socialist literature" (3).

19. Rottem, *Hamsun og fantasiens triumf*, 9–10. Rottem chooses to describe Hamsun as a "reactionary modernist," modifying the term "reactionary radical." I will stick with the latter term because the term "reactionary modernist" has potentially misleading associations with Jeffrey Herf's classic work on German conservative revolutionaries, in which the term "modernist" is used differently than in this book.

20. Martin Humpál, "*Mysterier* som antiroman," in *Hamsun i Tromsø IV. Rapport fra den 4. internasjonale Hamsun-konferanse, 2007*, edited by Linda H. Nesby and Henning Wærp (Hamarøy, Norway: Hamsun-Selskapet, 2007), 137–48. For the modernism discussion, important sources are Humpál, *The Roots of Modernist Narrative*, Kittang, *Luft, vind, ingenting*, and Rottem, *Hamsun og fantasiens triumf.*

21. See Dean Krouk, "Sideshadowing Hamsun's Fascism," in *Knut Hamsun: Transgression and Worlding*, edited by Ståle Dingstad, Ylva Frøjd, Elisabeth Oxfeldt, and Ellen Rees (Trondheim, Norway: Tapir Forlag, 2011). The term "sideshadowing" is borrowed from Bernstein, *Foregone Conclusions*.

22. Knut Hamsun, *Mysterier* (Oslo: Gyldendal, 1989), 130; Knut Hamsun, *Mysteries*, trans. Sverre Lyngstad (New York, Penguin, 2001), 154.

23. J. W. McFarlane, "The Whisper of the Blood: A Study of Knut Hamsun's Early Novels," *PMLA* 71, no. 4 (1956): 563–94. See also the English-language biography of Hamsun, Robert Ferguson, *Enigma: The Life of Knut Hamsun* (New York: Farrar, Straus and Giroux, 1987), and Jörg Pottbeckers, *Stumme Sprache: Innerer Monolog und erzählerischer Diskurs in Knut Hamsuns frühen Romanen im Kontext von Dostojewski, Schnitzler und Joyce* (Frankfurt: Peter Lang, 2007).

24. Although Nagel is not the narrator, his point of view is dominant in that he is the only character whose thought processes and internal dialogues are portrayed. In fact, I see little difference between Nagel's ideas and those of the implied authorial perspective or the real Hamsun's own contemporary statements. This does not mean, of course, that Nagel is simply a self-portrait, although Hamsun's son Tore did in fact suggest so (Ferguson, *Enigma*, 126). While they are certainly not identical in all respects, this analysis will treat Hamsun and Nagel somewhat interchangeably as regards their anti-realist opposition to the positivist figure of the Doctor.

25. Michael André Bernstein, *Bitter Carnival: Ressentiment and the Abject Hero* (Princeton, NJ: Princeton University Press, 1992).

26. Kolloen, *Hamsun: Svermeren*, 107.

27. Knut Hamsun, "Lidt om Strindberg," in *Artikler*, ed. Francis Bull (Oslo: Gyldendal, 1939), 15.

28. Ibid., 16.

29. Ibid.

30. Ibid., 17–18.

31. Ibid., 22.

32. Ibid., 21.

33. Ibid., 22.

34. Ibid., 22–23.

35. Ibid., 25.

36. Ibid., 30.

37. Ibid., 31.

38. Ibid.

39. Ibid., 30.

40. See Knut Hamsun, "Fra det Ubevidste Sjæleliv," in *Artikler*, ed. Francis Bull (Oslo: Gyldendal, 1939), 46–63.

41. Knut Hamsun, "Psykologisk Literatur," in *Paa Turné: Tre foredrag om litteratur av Knut Hamsun*, ed. Tore Hamsun (Oslo: Gyldendal, 1960), 53.

42. Ibid., 48–49.

43. Eli Zaretsky, *Secrets of the Soul: A Social and Cultural History of Psychoanalysis* (New York: Vintage, 2004), 23.

44. Hamsun, "Psykologisk Literatur," 51.
45. Ibid., 52.
46. Ibid., 53.
47. Ibid., 67.
48. Ibid., 54.
49. Ibid.
50. Robert Musil, *Precision and Soul: Essays and Addresses*, ed. and trans. Burton Pike and David S. Luft (Chicago: University of Chicago Press, 1990), 63.
51. Humpál, "*Mysterier* som antiroman."
52. Ibid., 140.
53. Ibid., 143.
54. Hamsun, *Mysterier*, 235 (282).
55. Ibid.
56. Humpál, "*Mysterier* som antiroman," 143.
57. McFarlane, "The Whisper of the Blood," 580.
58. The literary historian Unni Solberg writes that "the growth of the detective narrative was connected to the century's trust in instrumental reason and its belief that the progress of science would offer total explanations of reality, including humans" (qtd. in Humpál, "*Mysterier* som antiroman," 146).
59. Martin Jay, *Downcast Eyes: The Denigration of Vision in Twentieth-Century French Thought* (Berkeley: University of California Press, 1993), 12.
60. Hamsun, *Mysterier*, 72 (84).
61. Ibid., 77 (90).
62. Ibid., 78 (91).
63. Ibid., 79 (93).
64. Ibid.
65. Ibid., 80 (93).
66. Ibid., 80 (94).
67. Ibid., 81 (94).
68. Robert Pogue Harrison, *Forests: The Shadow of Civilization* (Chicago: University of Chicago Press, 1992), xi.
69. Steinar Gimnes, "'Det er ingen herlighet til som suset i skogen'—Skogen som 'stad' i nokre Hamsun-tekstar," in *Hamsun i Tromsø III. Rapport fra den 3. internasjonale Hamsun-konferanse, 2003: Tid og rom i Hamsuns prosa*, ed. Even Arntzen and Henning Wærp (Hamarøy, Norway: Hamsun-Selskapet, 2003), 174. Gimnes takes his discussion of the forest from Robert Pogue Harrison's chapter "Enlightenment," in *Forests*, 115–20.
70. Harrison, *Forests*, 10.
71. Bernstein, *Bitter Carnival*, 16.
72. Ibid., 22.
73. Ibid., 29.
74. Hamsun, *Mysterier*, 35 (37).
75. Ibid.
76. Ibid.

77. Ibid., 36 (38).
78. Ibid., 60 (69).
79. Ibid., 194 (231).
80. Ibid., 61 (71).
81. Ibid.
82. Ibid.
83. Ibid.
84. Bernstein, *Bitter Carnival*, 92.
85. Hamsun, *Mysterier*, 198 (236).
86. Ibid.
87. Ibid.
88. Rottem, *Hamsun og fantasiens triumf*, 88.
89. Lionel Trilling, *Beyond Culture: Essays on Literature and Learning* (New York: Viking, 1965), 76.
90. Bernstein, *Bitter Carnival*, 159.
91. Rem, *Knut Hamsun: Reisen til Hitler*, 321.
92. Moi, *Henrik Ibsen and the Birth of Modernism*, 100–102.
93. Ibid.
94. See especially Žagar's chapter "Imagining Degeneration and Revolution" (*Knut Hamsun*, 181–210).

CHAPTER 3

1. Judith (Jack) Halberstam, *The Queer Art of Failure* (Durham, NC: Duke University Press, 2011), 151, 162.
2. Sveen, "Hvorfor jeg er medlem av NS."
3. Laura Frost, *Sex Drives: Fantasies of Fascism in Literary Modernism* (Ithaca, NY: Cornell University Press, 2002), 3, 5.
4. Andrew Hewitt, *Political Inversions: Homosexuality, Fascism, and the Modernist Imaginary* (Stanford, CA: Stanford University Press, 1996), 6–7. Hewitt's analysis is motivated by indignation that "the homosexual is more readily imagined as the subject of some imagined fascism, than as its object or victim" (3).
5. Quoted in ibid., 39.
6. Klaus Theweleit, *Male Fantasies 1: Women, Floods, Bodies, History*, trans. Stephen Conway with Erica Carter and Chris Turner (Minneapolis: University of Minnesota Press, 1987), 55. *Male Fantasies* remains one of the most influential studies of fascist masculinity; it examines memoirs and literary works by men of the German Freikorps movement—volunteer military troops that have often been seen as proto-fascist. However, Theweleit's work is of limited applicability to the case of Åsmund Sveen. *Male Fantasies* emphasizes a destructive form of soldier masculinity that aims to stabilize and harden the male self against the dissolving influence of the feminine. Theweleit also considers the attraction of fascism to be rooted in the passion for violence itself. Sveen's sexualized fascism does not fit this model, in that it stresses a form of erotic liberation and bodily pleasure in the social reproduction of a harmonious and utopian society. See also the long section

on homosexuality in the second volume: Klaus Theweleit, *Male Fantasies 2: Psychoanalyzing the White Terror*, trans. Erica Carter and Chris Turner with Stephen Conway (Minneapolis: University of Minnesota Press, 1989), 306–40.

7. Hewitt, *Political Inversions*, 10–37.

8. "En kan også sette mannsorienteringen i Sveens diktning i sammenheng med mannsorienteringen innenfor nazistisk ideologi. Nazismen var en ideologi skapt av og for (sterke) menn, og det er ikke usannsynlig at dette er en medvirkende årsak til at Sveen følte seg tiltrukket av den" (Knut Imerslund, *Norske klassikere: Litterære essays* [Høgskolen i Hedmark, Rapport nr. 16, 2003], 197–98). After conceding that the Nazis were "outwardly"—that is, only apparently—negative toward homosexuals, Imerslund mentions the (discredited) possibility that Hitler was gay. He also conjectures that the homophobic attitudes of important Nazis resulted from their own self-hatred as gays (198).

9. Gatland, *Det andre mennesket*, 146.

10. Halberstam, *The Queer Art of Failure*, 148.

11. Gatland, *Det andre mennesket*, 57. The critic Rolf Thesen called Sveen "eit djervt og merkeleg talent" (a bold and strange talent) in a review of *Andletet* in *Arbeiderbladet*, quoted on the back of *Eros syng*.

12. Gatland, *Det andre mennesket*, 96.

13. Hoel wrote his own novel about the younger generation's erotic liberation, the delightful early work *Syndere i sommersol* (Sinners in the Summer Sun, 1927).

14. Ole Karlsen, "Åsmund Sveens lyrikk—viktig og/eller god? Forskriftlige refleksjoner," in *"Der vårgras brydder": Nye lesninger av Åsmund Sveens diktning*, ed. Hans Kristian Rustad (Vallset, Norway: Oplandske bokforlag, 2010), 15.

15. For more on literary and cultural vitalism in the Norwegian context, see Eirik Vassenden, *Norsk vitalisme: litteratur, ideologi og livsdyrking, 1890–1940* (Oslo: Scandinavian Academic Press, 2014).

16. Susan Sontag, "Fascinating Fascism," in *Under the Sign of Saturn* (New York: Farrar, Straus and Giroux, 1980), 102.

17. Dagmar Herzog, *Sex After Fascism: Memory and Morality in Twentieth-Century Germany* (Princeton, NJ: Princeton University Press, 2007), 5.

18. Ibid., 32–33.

19. Eirik Vassenden offers interesting commentary on this tension in Sveen's work in relation to a later poem from *Brunnen* in "Sol og Skygge: Vitalismens dilemma hos Åsmund Sveen," in *"Der vårgras brydder": Nye lesninger av Åsmund Sveens diktning*, ed. Hans Kristian Rustad (Vallset, Norway: Oplandske bokforlag, 2010), 37–62.

20. Jan Olav Gatland, "Opportunist eller idealist—Åsmund Sveen og nazismen," in *"Der vårgras brydder": Nye lesninger av Åsmund Sveens diktning*, ed. Hans Kristian Rustad (Vallset, Norway: Oplandske bokforlag, 2010), 231–46.

21. Gatland, *Det andre mennesket*, 139.

22. Ibid., 143.

23. Quoted in Birkeland and Larsen, *Nazismen og norsk litteratur*, 10. My translation.

24. Imerslund, *Norske klassikere*, 160.

25. Gatland, "Opportunist eller idealist," 236.

26. Gatland, *Det andre mennesket*, 164.

27. See Sveen, "Hvorfor jeg er medlem av NS."

28. Gatland, *Det andre mennesket*, 60.

29. Ibid., 75.

30. Åsmund Sveen, *Andletet* (Oslo: Gyldendal, 1932), 56–58.

31. Gatland, *Det andre mennesket*, 19.

32. For instance, Leo Löwenthal's seminal reading of Hamsun's novels presented nature mysticism as part of a proto-fascist mind-set, as did the Danish authors of *Det reaktionære oprør* (The Reactionary Revolt), who cited Hamsun's "irrationalist naturalism" as an ideologically suspect feature of his fiction.

33. Žagar, *Knut Hamsun*, 206.

34. Gatland, *Det andre mennesket*, 58.

35. Ibid., 74.

36. Sveen, *Andletet*, 8.

37. Ibid., 28–29.

38. Pål Bjørby, "Åsmund Sveens *Andletet* (1932): En queering av seksualitet, drift og identitet," in *"Der vårgras brydder": Nye lesninger av Åsmund Sveens diktning*, ed. Hans Kristian Rustad (Vallset, Norway: Oplandske bokforlag, 2010), 159.

39. Vassenden, "Sol og skygge," 57.

40. Bjørby, "Åsmund Sveens *Andletet*," 159. Bjørby situates Sveen's poetry in the context of contemporary representations of homosexuality in both scientific discourse and literature. He argues that the negativity, brutality, and shame expressed in *Andletet* result from Sveen's unfortunate internalization of homophobic psychoanalytic and sexological discourses of the time (135). In Sveen's pathologizing understanding of his sexual identity as deviant, Bjørby detects "a perfect Foucaultian meeting between discourse and experience, between patient and expert, where the patient has 'learned' the language of the expert and has begun to think and speak about himself in that language" (144). Thus, Bjørby attributes *Andletet*'s shame and distress exclusively to Sveen's familiarity with psychoanalysis, the master discourse that has taught him to pathologize his own sexuality. However, there were many other plausible sources of these negative emotions in Sveen's culture and experience (for instance, bourgeois Christian morality), and Sveen was not simply an uncritical reader of psychoanalytic texts who simply absorbed their theories of sexuality.

41. Žagar, *Knut Hamsun*, 199–200.

42. Gatland, *Det andre mennesket*, 93.

43. Vassenden, *Norsk vitalisme*.

44. Gunnar Sørensen, "Vitalismens år," in *Livskraft: Vitalismen som kunstnerisk impuls, 1900–1930*, ed. Ingebjørg Ydstie (Oslo: Munch-Museet, 2006), 14.

45. Griffin, *Modernism and Fascism*, 143–44.

46. One art historian calls vitalism "en erstatningsreligion, der tapet av et gudebilde i det hinsidige bevares som religiøs ekstase i opplevelsen av livsfylde i det dennesidige" (Ydstie, *Livskraft*, 9).

47. Vassenden, "Sol og skygge," 57.

48. Eirik Vassenden, "Estetikk og vold: Om noen motiver hos Åsmund Sveen," in *Krysninger: Om moderne nordisk lyrikk*, ed. Ole Karlsen (Oslo: Unipub, 2008), 282.

49. Sørensen, "Vitalismens år," 14.

50. Griffin, *Modernism and Fascism*, 145.

51. Gatland, *Det andre mennesket*, 76.

52. Vassenden, "Sol og skygge," 48.

53. Ibid.

54. Ydstie, *Livskraft*, 9.

55. Gatland, *Det andre mennesket*, 100–101.

56. Graham Robb, *Strangers: Homosexual Love in the Nineteenth Century* (New York: Norton, 2005), 213.

57. Åsmund Sveen, *Eros syng* (Oslo: Gyldendal, 1935), 104.

58. Gatland, *Det andre mennesket*, 102.

59. Sveen, *Eros syng*, 93–94.

60. Ibid., 98.

61. Ibid., 100.

62. Herzog, *Sex After Fascism*, 14.

63. Ibid., 4.

64. Ibid., 5.

65. Ibid., 29.

66. Ibid., 30.

67. Ibid., 32–33.

68. Woodley, *Fascism and Political Theory*, 226.

69. Ibid.

70. Modris Eksteins, *Rites of Spring: The Great War and the Birth of the Modern Age* (New York: Mariner, 2000), 319.

71. Woodley, *Fascism and Political Theory*, 230.

72. Åsmund Sveen, *Såmannen* (Oslo: Gyldendal, 1940), 23–26.

73. Woodley, *Fascism and Political Theory*, 212.

74. Ibid., 218.

75. Gatland, *Det andre mennesket*, 92.

76. Ibid., 92–93.

77. Sveen, "Hvorfor jeg er medlem av NS."

78. Roger Griffin, ed., *Fascism* (Oxford: Oxford University Press, 1995), 54.

79. Sveen, "Hvorfor jeg er medlem av NS."

80. Åsmund Sveen, "Kunsten og tiden," *Fritt folk*, January 9, 1943.

81. Antliff, *Avant-garde Fascism*, 26.

82. Åsmund Sveen, "Diktarar og dikting or Hålogaland," in *Hålogaland i kunst og åndsliv*, ed. Arne Pauss Pauset (Oslo: J. M. Stenersens Forlag, 1942), 222.

83. Gatland, *Det andre mennesket*, 151.

84. Griffin, *Modernism and Fascism*, 100–126.
85. Gatland, *Det andre mennesket*, 124.
86. Sveen, "Kunsten og tiden."
87. Žagar, *Knut Hamsun*, 49.
88. Antliff, *Avant-garde Fascism*, 45.
89. Gatland, *Det andre mennesket*, 236.
90. Ibid., 239.
91. Åsmund Sveen, *Etterkrigsdikt: Brunnen. Tonemesteren* (Oslo: Cappelen, 1995), 9.
92. Niclas Johansson, "In Memory of Narcissus: Aspects of the Late-Modern Subject in the Narcissus Theme, 1890–1930" (PhD diss., Uppsala University, 2012), 10.
93. Ibid., 11.
94. Ibid., 9–10.
95. Sveen, *Etterkrigsdikt*, 29.
96. Ibid.
97. Ibid., 30.
98. Ibid., 31.
99. Gatland, *Det andre mennesket*, 191.
100. Ellis Hanson, "Wilde's Exquisite Pain," in *Wilde Writings: Contextual Conditions*, ed. Joseph Bristow (Toronto: University of Toronto Press, 2003), 120.
101. Gatland, *Det andre mennesket*, 191.
102. Richard Leppert, "Music, Violence, and the Stake of Listening," in *The Oxford Handbook of the New Cultural History of Music*, ed. Jane F. Fulcher (Oxford: Oxford University Press, 2011), 47.
103. Hanson, "Wilde's Exquisite Pain," 119.
104. Sveen, *Etterkrigsdikt*, 63.
105. Ibid., 66.
106. Gatland, *Det andre mennesket*, 213.
107. Ibid.

CHAPTER 4

1. Brumo and Furuseth comment in *Norsk litterær modernisme* that Jacobsen "is without a doubt our most popular modernist" (94).
2. The Danish poet Johannes V. Jensen's *Digte 1906*—especially the poem "Paa Memphis Station"—was an important Scandinavian source of inspiration. Jacobsen was also an admirer of Carl Sandburg's *Chicago Poems*, which he read in Swedish translation. See Røsbak, *Rolf Jacobsen: En dikter og hans skygge*, 113–14.
3. Torben Brostrøm, "Rolf Jacobsen og sprogets erotiske signaler," in *Stier med lavmælt lys: Om Rolf Jacobsens diktning*, ed. Hanne Lillebo (Oslo: Gyldendal, 2007), 33.
4. Andreas Lombnæs offers another typical example: Jacobsen's "lyrical self is deeply fascinated by the new—by the beauty, power, and possibilities of the wonders of technology. It can seem like an excited optimism about the

future, but only on the surface, for the hurried reading" ("RJs lyriske jeg er dypt fascinert av det nye—av skjønnheten, kraften og mulighetene i teknikkens vidundre. Det kan fortone seg som begeistret fremtidsoptimisme, men bare på overflaten, for den hastige lesning"). Andres Lombnæs, "Rolf Jacobsen og det moderne," in *Frøkorn av ild: Om Rolf Jacobsens forfatterskap*, ed. Ole Karlsen (Oslo: Cappelen, 1993), 74.

5. Karlsen, *Frøkorn av ild*, 19.

6. These are Hanne Lillebo, *Ord må en omvei* and Ove Røsbak, *Rolf Jacobsen: En dikter og hans skygge.*

7. Lillebo, *Ord må en omvei*, 219.

8. Ibid., 195.

9. See Ove Røsbak, "Ble aldri ferdig med krigen," *Aftenposten*, May 21, 2007: "Det er rart at det i så liten grad blir trukket en linje mellom livet og verket til lyrikeren Rolf Jacobsen."

10. Øystein Rottem, *Etterkrigslitteraturen* (Oslo: Cappelen, 1996), 1:201.

11. Brumo and Furuseth, *Norsk litterær modernisme*, 96.

12. Rolf Jacobsen, *North in the World: Selected Poems of Rolf Jacobsen*, trans. and ed. Roger Greenwald (Chicago: University of Chicago Press, 2002), 24–25. I will sometimes quote from Greenwald's excellent bilingual edition of selected poems, *North in the World*, but some important poems for my argument are not included there. In those cases, I will offer literal translations of my own.

13. Ibid., 26–27. English translation will be from Roger Greenwald unless noted as my own.

14. Rottem, *Etterkrigslitteraturen*, 208.

15. Jacobsen, *North in the World*, 106–7.

16. Lillebo, *Ord må en omvei*, 88.

17. Ibid., 98.

18. Marit Grøtta, "Klipp—klistre: Rolf Jacobsen, modernismen og massemediene," in *Stier med lavmælt lys: Om Rolf Jacobsens diktning*, ed. Hanne Lillebo (Oslo: Gyldendal, 2007), 53.

19. Karlsen, *Frøkorn av ild*, 24.

20. Jacobsen, *North in the World*, 4–5.

21. Rolf Jacobsen, *Alle mine dikt* (Oslo: Gyldendal, 1990), 17.

22. Jacobsen, *North in the World*, xvii.

23. Asbjørn Aarnes, "Rolf Jacobsen og modernismen," in *Frøkorn av ild: Om Rolf Jacobsens forfatterskap*, ed. Ole Karlsen (Oslo: Cappelen, 1993), 63.

24. Ibid., 65.

25. Jacobsen, *North in the World*, 18–19.

26. Ibid., 66–67.

27. Ibid., 14–15.

28. Jacobsen, *Alle mine dikt*, 56–57.

29. Ibid., 81.

30. Quoted in John Brumo, "'Maskinens stönn': Fart og modernitet i 1930-tallets norske litteratur," in *Modernitetens ansikten: Livsåskådningar i nordisk 1900-talslitteratur*, ed. Carl Reinhold Bråkenhielm and Torsten Pettersson (Nora, Sweden: Nya Doxa, 2001), 60–79.

31. Jacobsen, *Alle mine dikt*, 31–32.

32. Lombnæs, "Rolf Jacobsen og det moderne," 75.

33. Brumo, "'Maskinens stönn,'" 72.

34. Ivar Havnevik, *Dikt i Norge* (Oslo: Pax, 2002), 341.

35. Ibid., 346.

36. Ibid.

37. "Om vi kan slutte noe av det, må det være at hans feilvalg under okkupasjonen—fem år av et liv—har vært resultat av et midlertidlig avvik, sammen med en slags opportunisme helt på siden av hans 'egentlige' holdninger før og etter krigen" (ibid.).

38. The authors of *Norsk litterær modernisme* observe that "kunstnerens persepsjon krever i økende grad frihet fra tradisjonen, [and also from] det rasjonelle og instrumentelle" (Brumo and Furuseth, *Norsk litterær modernisme*, 107).

39. Quoted in ibid.

40. Karlsen, *Frøkorn av ild*, 27–28.

41. Hubert Dreyfus, "Heidegger on the Connection Between Nihilism, Art, Technology, and Politics," in *The Cambridge Companion to Heidegger*, ed. Charles Guignon (Cambridge: Cambridge University Press, 1993), 305.

42. Martin Heidegger, *The Question Concerning Technology and Other Essays*, trans. William Lovitt (New York: Harper and Row, 1977), 27.

43. Alfred Denker, *Historical Dictionary of Heidegger's Philosophy* (Lanham, MD: Scarecrow, 2000), 33.

44. Shane Weller, *Literature, Philosophy, Nihilism: The Uncanniest of Guests* (New York: Palgrave Macmillan, 2008), ix.

45. Lombnæs, "Rolf Jacobsen og det moderne," 72–87.

46. Aarnes, "Rolf Jacobsen og modernismen," 63.

47. Erling Aadland, *"Forundring. Trofasthet": Poetisk tenkning i Rolf Jacobsens lyrikk* (Oslo: Gyldendal, 1996). The title of Aadland's book is a quotation from Jacobsen's poem "Katakombene i San Callisto" (*Brev til lyset*, 1960).

48. Aadland, *"Forundring. Trofasthet": Poetisk tenkning*, 20. Aadland aligns Jacobsen's poetic thinking with the Heideggerian idea of the poet as the one who makes room in language for the "unconcealment" of being: "Die Dichtung ist die Sage der Unverborgenheit des Seienden" (Heidegger, *Holzwege*, quoted in Aadland, *"Forundring. Trofasthet": Poetisk tenkning*, 35).

49. Dreyfus, "Heidegger on the Connection Between Nihilism, Art, Technology, and Politics," 310–13.

50. Ibid., 311.

51. Otto Pöggeler, "Heidegger's Political Self-Understanding," in *The Heidegger Controversy: A Critical Reader*, ed. Richard Wolin (Cambridge, MA: MIT Press, 1993), 220.

52. Dreyfus, "Heidegger on the Connection Between Nihilism, Art, Technology, and Politics," 311–12.

53. Lillebo, *Ord må en omvei*, 176.

54. Røsbak, *Rolf Jacobsen: En dikter og hans skygge*, 122–23.

55. Ibid., 124.

56. Ibid., 127.

57. Rolf Jacobsen, "Konjunktur," *Dagbladet*, February 20, 1937.

58. Røsbak, *Rolf Jacobsen: En dikter og hans skygge*, 135.

59. Lillebo, *Ord må en omvei*, 191.

60. Røsbak writes that "drivkraften bak RJ's insats for NS er hele tiden hans tro på sosialismen i nasjonalsosialismen" and that he was attracted to "tankegangen til venstrefløyen i NS" (*Rolf Jacobsen: En dikter og hans skygge*, 228, 246).

61. Røsbak, *Rolf Jacobsen: En dikter og hans skygge*, 170.

62. See Tore Pryser, *Arbeiderbevegelsen og Nasjonal samling: Om venstrestrømninger i Quislings parti* (Oslo: Tiden, 1991).

63. Lillebo, *Ord må en omvei*, 192.

64. Røsbak, *Rolf Jacobsen: En dikter og hans skygge*, 225.

65. Ibid., 196.

66. Ibid., 279. Jacobsen remained active as the editor and propaganda leader in his district until the very end of the war (247–48).

67. Rolf Jacobsen, "Kjensgjerninger," editorial, *Kongsvinger arbeiderbladet*, February 26, 1941.

68. Rolf Jacobsen, "Krigens årsak," editorial, *Kongsvinger arbeiderbladet*, October 24, 1942.

69. Røsbak, *Rolf Jacobsen: En dikter og hans skygge*, 227.

70. Ibid., 226.

71. Quoted in Trond Tendø Jacobsen, *Kjente jeg deg?: En bok om Rolf Jacobsen* (Oslo: Aschehoug, 2007), 107.

72. Lillebo, *Ord må en omvei*, 227.

73. Røsbak, *Rolf Jacobsen: En dikter og hans skygge*, 290.

74. Lillebo, *Ord må en omvei*, 227.

75. Ibid.

76. Røsbak, *Rolf Jacobsen: En dikter og hans skygge*, 290.

77. Karlsen, *Frøkorn av ild*, 16.

78. Griffin, *Fascism*, 5.

79. Jacobsen, "Etter krigen."

80. Røsbak, *Rolf Jacobsen: En dikter og hans skygge*, 226.

81. Rolf Jacobsen, "Tideverv," *Glåmdalen*, December 25, 1943.

82. Lillebo, *Ord må en omvei*, 197.

83. Røsbak, *Rolf Jacobsen: En dikter og hans skygge*, 242–43.

84. Ibid., 290.

85. Friedrich Nietzsche, *The Nietzsche Reader*, ed. Keith Ansell-Pearson and Duncan Large (Malden, MA: Blackwell, 2006), 386.

86. Gianni Vattimo, *Nihilism and Emancipation: Ethics, Politics, and Law*, ed. Santiago Zabala, trans. William McCuaig (New York: Columbia University Press, 2004), 92.

87. Terry Eagleton, *Culture and the Death of God* (New Haven: Yale University Press, 2014), 186.

88. Lillebo, *Ord må en omvei*, 204.

89. Kolloen, *Hamsun: Erobreren*, 255.

90. Lillebo, *Ord må en omvei*, 205.

91. Ibid., 212–13.

92. Tony Judt, *Postwar: A History of Europe Since 1945* (New York: Penguin, 2005), 229.

93. Jacobsen, *North in the World*, 92–93.

94. Røsbak, *Rolf Jacobsen: En dikter og hans skygge*, 297.

95. Karlsen, *Frøkorn av ild*, 17.

96. Ibid., 18–19.

97. See Kaja Korsvold, "Rolf Jacobsen: Løy om NS-fortid for alle," *Aftenposten*, November 25, 1998.

98. Jacobsen, *North in the World*, xvi–xvii.

99. Ibid., 68–69.

CHAPTER 5

1. Gatland, *Det andre mennesket*, 96.

2. Sigurd Hoel, *Tanker i mørketid* (Oslo: Gyldendal, 1945), 153.

3. Eli Zaretsky, *Political Freud: A History* (New York: Columbia University Press, 2015), 185.

4. Audun Tvinnereim, "Sigurd Hoel og nazismen," in *Nazismen og norsk litteratur*, ed. Bjarte Birkeland and Stein Ugelvik Larsen (Oslo: Universitetsforlaget, 1975), 101.

5. Brikt Jensen, *Sigurd Hoel om seg selv* (Oslo: Den norske bokklubben, 1981), 96.

6. Hoel, *Tanker i mørketid*, 187.

7. See Undset, *Tilbake til fremtiden*.

8. This chapter focuses more on the essays because *Møte ved milepelen* has been studied well in Audun Tvinnereim, *Risens hjerte: En studie i Sigurd Hoels forfatterskap* (Oslo: Gyldendal, 1975), and also in Sverre Lyngstad, *Sigurd Hoel's Fiction: Cultural Criticism and Tragic Vision* (Westport, CT: Greenwood Press, 1984). In addition, Hoel's psychoanalytic antifascism appears in a more distilled form in the essays, because they do not have the complications of unreliable narration (Tvinnereim, "Sigurd Hoel og nazismen," 99).

9. Tvinnereim, *Risens hjerte*, 90.

10. Zaretsky, *Political Freud*, 2, 10.

11. Griffin, *International Fascism*, 242.

12. Frost, *Sex Drives*, 30.

13. The standard work on Norwegian cultural radicalism remains Leif Longum, *Drømmen om det frie menneske: Norsk kulturradikalisme og mellomkrigstidens radikale trekløver: Hoel, Krog, Øverland* (Oslo: Universitetsforlaget, 1986).

14. Sigurd Hoel, "Motstand mot . . . ," in *Ettertanker*, ed. Leif Longum (Oslo: Gyldendal, 1980).

15. Ibid., 116.

16. Per Thomas Andersen, *Norsk litteraturhistorie* (Oslo: Universitetsforlaget, 2001), 399.

17. Hoel, *Ettertanker*, 13.

18. Essays by Hoel on Ibsen, Hamsun, Undset, Nordahl Grieg, and others are available in Sigurd Hoel, *Litterære Essays*, ed. Helge Nordahl (Oslo: Dreyer, 1990).

19. Øystein Rottem, *Sigurd Hoel: Et nærbilde* (Oslo: Gyldendal, 1991), 47, 77.

20. Hoel, *Litterære Essays*, 92.

21. Rottem, *Sigurd Hoel*, 98.

22. Tvinnereim, "Sigurd Hoel og nazismen," 102.

23. Lyngstad, *Sigurd Hoel's Fiction*, 92.

24. Hoel, *Ettertanker*, 10–11.

25. Sigurd Hoel, *Samlede romaner og fortellinger VI: Sesam sesam* (Oslo: Gyldendal, 1950), 56–57.

26. Rottem, *Sigurd Hoel*, 284.

27. Lyngstad, *Sigurd Hoel's Fiction*, 105.

28. Ibid.

29. Sigurd Hoel, *Møte ved milepelen* (Oslo: Gyldendal, 1947), 52–74.

30. Ibid., 81–99.

31. See the description of Karsten Haugen, about whom the narrator claims there was something erotically strange, if not definitively homosexual. For example, "Han beundret sterke menn på alle områder og var en lidenskapelig tilskuer ved boksekamper" (Hoel, *Møte ved milepelen*, 95). Hoel's representation of this character belongs to the rhetoric of "homo-fascism" criticized by Andrew Hewitt in *Political Inversions*.

32. Frost, *Sex Drives*, 24.

33. Zaretsky, *Secrets of the Soul*, 224.

34. Ibid., 223.

35. Dagmar Herzog, *Sexuality in Europe: A Twentieth-Century History* (Cambridge: Cambridge University Press, 2011).

36. According to Hoel, they met "praktisk talt daglig" between 1934 and 1939. Jensen, *Sigurd Hoel om seg selv*, 72.

37. Ibid., 90.

38. Paul A. Robinson, *The Freudian Left: Wilhelm Reich, Geza Roheim, Herbert Marcuse* (New York: Harper and Row, 1969), 44.

39. Ibid., 7.

40. Sigurd Hoel, "Rebell og trell," in *Ettertanker*, ed. Longum, 17.

41. See Silke Satjukow and Rainer Gries, *Unsere Feinde: Konstruktionen des Anderen im Sozialismus* (Leipzig: Leipziger Universitätsverlag, 2004).

42. Hoel, "Rebell og trell," 21.

43. Ibid., 22.

44. Ibid., 23.

45. Ibid., 25.

46. Stefanie von Schnurbein has applied MacCannell's analysis of the regime of the brother in an innovative reading of Aksel Sandemose's *En flyktning krysser sitt spor* (A Fugitive Crosses His Tracks, 1933), a key novel of Norwegian cultural radicalism. See Stefanie von Schnurbein, "Masking the Trauma: Psychoanalysis and Social Criticism in Aksel Sandemose's *En*

flyktning krysser sitt spor," *Edda* 4 (2002): 408–18, and Juliet Flower MacCannell, *The Regime of the Brother: After the Patriarchy* (London: Routledge, 1991).

47. Hoel, "Rebell og trell," 26.

48. Hoel, *Møte ved milepelen*, 271. Translation from Sigurd Hoel, *Meeting at the Milestone*, trans. Sverre Lyngstad (Copenhagen: Green Integer, 2002), 106.

49. Rottem, *Sigurd Hoel*, 216.

50. Sigurd Hoel, "Om nazismens vesen," in *Essays i utvalg*, ed. Nils Lie (Oslo: Gyldendal, 1962), 9.

51. Ibid., 9.

52. Ibid., 12.

53. Ibid., 13.

54. Ibid.

55. Ibid., 19.

56. Ibid.

57. Ibid., 15.

58. Ibid., 25.

59. Ibid., 26.

60. Zaretsky, *Secrets of the Soul*, 222.

61. Ibid.

62. Hoel, "Om nazismens vesen," 27.

63. Jensen, *Sigurd Hoel om seg selv*, 96.

64. Hoel, "Om nazismens vesen," 32.

65. Jensen, *Sigurd Hoel om seg selv*, 96.

66. Rottem, *Sigurd Hoel*, 289.

CONCLUSION

1. Irving Howe, "The Idea of the Modern," in *Literary Modernism*, ed. Irving Howe (Greenwich, CT: Fawcett, 1967), 36–37.

2. Ibid., 38.

3. Tony Judt and Timothy Snyder, *Thinking the Twentieth Century* (New York: Penguin, 2012), 177.

4. Banik, "Holocaust i Norge."

5. Ibid.

6. Holmila and Geverts, "On Forgetting and Rediscovering the Holocaust in Scandinavia," 525.

7. Synne Corell, "The Solidity of a National Narrative: The German Occupation in Norwegian History Culture," in *Nordic Narrative of the Second World War: National Historiographies Revisited*, ed. Henrik Stenius, Mirja Österberg, and Johan Östling (Lund: Nordic Academic Press, 2011), 101–26.

8. Judt, *Postwar*, 804.

9. Holmila and Geverts, "On Forgetting and Rediscovering the Holocaust in Scandinavia," 526.

BIBLIOGRAPHY

Aadland, Erling. *"Forundring. Trofasthet": Poetisk tenkning i Rolf Jacobsens lyrikk*. Oslo: Gyldendal, 1996.

Aarnes, Asbjørn. "Rolf Jacobsen og modernismen." In *Frøkorn av ild: Om Rolf Jacobsens forfatterskap*, edited by Ole Karlsen, 61–71. Oslo: Cappelen, 1993.

Andersen, Per Thomas. *Norsk litteraturhistorie*. Oslo: Universitetsforlaget, 2001.

Antliff, Mark. *Avant-garde Fascism: The Mobilization of Myth, Art, and Culture in France, 1909–1939*. Durham, NC: Duke University Press, 2007.

———. "Fascism, Modernism, and Modernity." In *Fascism: Critical Concepts in Political Science*, vol. 3, *Fascism and Culture*, edited by Roger Griffin and Matthew Feldman, 120–68. London: Routledge, 2004.

Banik, Vibeke Kieding. "Holocaust i Norge." Store norske leksikon, 2015. https://snl.no/Holocaust_i_Norge.

Bernstein, Michael André. *Bitter Carnival: Ressentiment and the Abject Hero*. Princeton, NJ: Princeton University Press, 1992.

———. *Foregone Conclusions: Against Apocalyptic History*. Berkeley: University of California Press, 1994.

Birkeland, Bjarte, and Stein Ugelvik Larsen, eds. *Nazismen og norsk litteratur*. Oslo: Universitetsforlaget, 1975.

Bjørby, Pål. "Åsmund Sveens *Andletet* (1932): En queering av seksualitet, drift og identitet." In *"Der vårgras brydder": Nye lesninger av Åsmund Sveens diktning*, edited by Hans Kristian Rustad, 133–88. Vallset, Norway: Oplandske bokforlag, 2010.

Bossi, Laura. "The 'New Man': Degeneracy and Regeneration." In *The 1930s: The Making of "The New Man,"* edited by Jean Clair. Ottawa: National Gallery of Canada, 2008.

Bosworth, R. J. B. *The Oxford Handbook of Fascism*. Oxford: Oxford University Press, 2011.

Braun, Emily. *Mario Sironi and Italian Modernism: Art and Politics Under Fascism*. Cambridge: Cambridge University Press, 2000.

Brevig, Hans Olaf, and Ivo de Figueiredo. *Den norske fascismen: Nasjonal Samling, 1933–1940*. Oslo: Pax, 2002.

Bruland, Bjarte, and Mats Tangestuen. "The Norwegian Holocaust: Changing Views and Representations." *Scandinavian Journal of History* 36, no. 5 (2011): 587–604.

Brumo, John. "'Maskinens stönn': Fart og modernitet i 1930-tallets norske litteratur." In *Modernitetens ansikten: Livsåskådningar i nordisk 1900-talslitteratur*, edited by Carl Reinhold Bråkenhielm and Torsten Pettersson, 60–79. Nora, Sweden: Nya Doxa, 2001.

Brumo, John, and Sissel Furuseth. *Norsk litterær modernisme*. Bergen, Norway: Fagbokforlaget, 2005.

Calinescu, Matei. *Five Faces of Modernity: Modernism, Avant-garde, Decadence, Kitsch, Postmodernism*. Durham, NC: Duke University Press, 1987.

Carroll, David. *French Literary Fascism: Nationalism, Anti-Semitism, and the Ideology of Culture*. Princeton, NJ: Princeton University Press, 1995.

Clair, Jean. *The 1930s: The Making of "The New Man."* Ottawa: National Gallery of Canada, 2008.

Corell, Synne. "The Solidity of a National Narrative: The German Occupation in Norwegian History Culture." In *Nordic Narrative of the Second World War: National Historiographies Revisited*, edited by Henrik Stenius, Mirja Österberg, and Johan Östling, 101–26. Lund: Nordic Academic Press, 2011.

Dahl, Hans Fredrik. *Fra klassekamp til nasjonal samling: Arbeiderpartiet og det nasjonale spøsmål i 30-årene*. Oslo: Pax, 1969.

Denker, Alfred. *Historical Dictionary of Heidegger's Philosophy*. Lanham, MD: Scarecrow, 2000.

Dingstad, Ståle. *Hamsuns strategier: Realisme, humor og kynisme*. Oslo: Gyldendal, 2003.

Dreyfus, Hubert. "Heidegger on the Connection Between Nihilism, Art, Technology, and Politics." In *The Cambridge Companion to Heidegger*, edited by Charles Guignon, 289–315. Cambridge: Cambridge University Press, 1993.

Eagleton, Terry. *Culture and the Death of God*. New Haven: Yale University Press, 2014.

Eksteins, Modris. *Rites of Spring: The Great War and the Birth of the Modern Age*. New York: Mariner, 2000.

Eysteinsson, Astradur. *The Concept of Modernism*. Ithaca, NY: Cornell University Press, 1990.

Eysteinsson, Astradur, and Vivian Liska. "Introduction: Approaching Modernism." In *Modernism*. 2 vols. Edited by Astradur Eysteinsson and Vivian Liska, 1–8. Amsterdam: John Benjamins, 2007.

Ferguson, Robert. *Enigma: The Life of Knut Hamsun*. New York: Farrar, Straus and Giroux, 1987.

Ferrall, Charles. *Modernist Writing and Reactionary Politics*. Cambridge: Cambridge University Press, 2001.

Fritzsche, Peter. *Life and Death in the Third Reich*. Cambridge, MA: Harvard University Press, 2008.

Frost, Laura. *Sex Drives: Fantasies of Fascism in Literary Modernism*. Ithaca, NY: Cornell University Press, 2002.

Gatland, Jan Olav. *Det andre mennesket: Eit portrett av Åsmund Sveen*. Oslo: Det Norske Samlaget, 2003.

———. "Opportunist eller idealist—Åsmund Sveen og nazismen." In *"Der vårgras brydder": Nye lesninger av Åsmund Sveens diktning*, edited by Hans Kristian Rustad, 231–46. Vallset, Norway: Oplandske bokforlag, 2010.

Gay, Peter. *Modernism: The Lure of Heresy*. New York: Norton, 2008.

Gentile, Emilio. "The Sacralisation of Politics." In *Fascism: Critical Concepts in Political Science*, vol. 3, *Fascism and Culture*, edited by Roger Griffin and Matthew Feldman, 39–70. London: Routledge, 2004.

Giddens, Anthony. *The Consequences of Modernity*. Stanford, CA: Stanford University Press, 1990.

———. *Modernity and Self-Identity: Self and Society in the Late Modern Age*. Stanford, CA: Stanford University Press, 1991.

Giersing, Morten, John Thobo-Carlsen, and Mikael Westergaard-Nielsen. *Det reaktionære oprør: Om fascismen i Hamsuns forfatterskab*. Kongerslev, Denmark: GMT, 1975.

Gimnes, Steinar. "'Det er ingen herlighet til som suset i skogen'—Skogen som 'stad' i nokre Hamsun-tekstar." In *Hamsun i Tromsø III. Rapport fra den 3. internasjonale Hamsun-konferanse, 2003: Tid og rom i Hamsuns prosa*, edited by Even Arntzen and Henning Wærp, 171–94. Hamarøy, Norway: Hamsun-Selskapet, 2003.

Golsan, Richard J., ed. *Fascism, Aesthetics, and Culture*. Hanover, NH: University Press of New England, 1992.

Griffin, Roger, ed. *Fascism*. Oxford: Oxford University Press, 1995.

———. *International Fascism: Theories, Causes and the New Consensus*. London: Arnold, 1998.

———. *Modernism and Fascism: The Sense of a Beginning Under Mussolini and Hitler.* New York: Palgrave Macmillan, 2007.

———. *The Nature of Fascism.* New York: St. Martin's, 1991.

———. "The Primacy of Culture: The Current Growth (or Manufacture) of Consensus Within Fascist Studies." *Journal of Contemporary History* 37, no. 21 (2002): 21–43.

Griffin, Roger, and Matthew Feldman. *Fascism: Critical Concepts in Political Science*, vol. 3, *Fascism and Culture.* London: Routledge, 2004.

Halberstam, Judith (Jack). *The Queer Art of Failure.* Durham, NC: Duke University Press, 2011.

Hamsun, Knut. "Fra det Ubevidste Sjæleliv." In *Artikler*, edited by Francis Bull, 46–63. Oslo: Gyldendal, 1939.

———. *Hamsuns polemiske skrifter.* Edited by Gunvald Hermundstad. Oslo: Gyldendal, 1998.

———. "Lidt om Strindberg." In *Artikler*, edited by Francis Bull, 14–45. Oslo: Gyldendal, 1939.

———. *Mysterier.* Oslo: Gyldendal, 1989.

———. *Mysteries.* Translated by Sverre Lyngstad. New York: Penguin, 2001.

———. "Psykologisk Literatur." In *Paa Turné: Tre foredrag om litteratur av Knut Hamsun*, edited by Tore Hamsun, 47–76. Oslo: Gyldendal, 1960.

———. *Samlede Verker.* Oslo: Gyldendal, 2007–9.

Hanson, Ellis. "Wilde's Exquisite Pain." In *Wilde Writings: Contextual Conditions*, edited by Joseph Bristow, 101–25. Toronto: University of Toronto Press, 2003.

Harrison, Robert Pogue. *Forests: The Shadow of Civilization.* Chicago: University of Chicago Press, 1992.

Haugan, Jørgen. *Solgudens fall: Knut Hamsun—en litterær biografi.* Oslo: Aschehoug, 2006.

Havnevik, Ivar. *Dikt i Norge.* Oslo: Pax, 2002.

Heidegger, Martin. *Poetry, Language, Thought.* Translated by Albert Hofstadter. New York: Harper and Row, 1971.

———. *The Question Concerning Technology and Other Essays.* Translated by William Lovitt. New York: Harper and Row, 1977.

Herf, Jeffrey. *Reactionary Modernism: Technology, Culture, and Politics in Weimar and the Third Reich.* Cambridge: Cambridge University Press, 1986.

Herzog, Dagmar. *Sex After Fascism: Memory and Morality in Twentieth-Century Germany.* Princeton, NJ: Princeton University Press, 2007.

———. *Sexuality in Europe: A Twentieth-Century History.* Cambridge: Cambridge University Press, 2011.

Hewitt, Andrew. *Fascist Modernism: Aesthetics, Politics, and the Avant-Garde*. Stanford, CA: Stanford University Press, 1993.

———. "Ideological Positions in the Fascism Debate." In *Fascism and Neo-fascism: Critical Writings on the Radical Right in Europe*, edited by Angelica Fenner and Eric D. Weitz. New York: Palgrave Macmillan, 2004.

———. *Political Inversions: Homosexuality, Fascism, and the Modernist Imaginary*. Stanford, CA: Stanford University Press, 1996.

Hoel, Sigurd. *Essays i utvalg*. Edited by Nils Lie. Oslo: Gyldendal, 1962.

———. *Ettertanker*. Edited by Leif Longum. Oslo: Gyldendal, 1980.

———. *Litterære Essays*. Edited by Helge Nordahl. Oslo: Dreyer, 1990.

———. *Meeting at the Milestone*. Translated by Sverre Lyngstad. Copenhagen: Green Integer, 2002.

———. *Møte ved milepelen*. Oslo: Gyldendal, 1947.

———. *Samlede romaner og fortellinger VI: Sesam sesam*. Oslo: Gyldendal, 1950.

———. *Syndere i sommersol*. Oslo: Gyldendal, 1927.

———. *Tanker i mørketid*. Oslo: Gyldendal, 1945.

———. *Veien til verdens ende*. Oslo: Gyldendal, 1933.

Holmila, Antero, and Karin Kvist Geverts. "On Forgetting and Rediscovering the Holocaust in Scandinavia." *Scandinavian Journal of History* 36, no. 5 (2011): 520–35.

Howe, Irving. "The Idea of the Modern." In *Literary Modernism*, edited by Irving Howe. Greenwich, CT: Fawcett, 1967.

Humpál, Martin. "Mysterier som antiroman." In *Hamsun i Tromsø IV. Rapport fra den 4. internasjonale Hamsun-konferanse, 2007*, edited by Linda H. Nesby and Henning Wærp, 137–48. Hamarøy, Norway: Hamsun-Selskapet, 2007.

———. *The Roots of Modernist Narrative: Knut Hamsun's Novels Hunger, Mysteries, and Pan*. Oslo: Solum, 1998.

Imerslund, Knut. *Norske klassikere: Litterære essays*. Høgskolen i Hedmark, Rapport nr. 16, 2003.

Jacobsen, Rolf. *Alle mine dikt*. Oslo: Gyldendal, 1990.

———. "At ikke menneskene er kommet lenger!" Editorial. *Glåmdalen*. December 27, 1943.

———. "Etter krigen." Editorial. *Kongsvinger arbeiderbladet*, April 16, 1941.

———. *Jord og jern*. Oslo: Gyldendal, 1933.

———. "Kjensgjerninger." Editorial. *Kongsvinger arbeiderbladet*, February 26, 1941.

———. "Konjunktur." *Dagbladet*, February 20, 1937.

———. "Krigens årsak." Editorial. *Kongsvinger arbeiderbladet*, October 24, 1942.

———. *North in the World: Selected Poems of Rolf Jacobsen*. Translated and edited by Roger Greenwald. Chicago: University of Chicago Press, 2002.

———. "Ring Klokke." *Glåmdalen*, December 25, 1944.

———. "Tideverv." *Glåmdalen*, December 25, 1943.

———. "Vissent Lauv." Editorial. *Kongsvinger arbeiderbladet*, February 19, 1941.

———. *Vrimmel*. Oslo: Gyldendal, 1935.

Jacobsen, Trond Tendø. *Kjente jeg deg?: En bok om Rolf Jacobsen*. Oslo: Aschehoug, 2007.

Jameson, Fredric. *Fables of Aggression: Wyndham Lewis, the Modernist as Fascist*. Berkeley: University of California Press, 1979.

———. *A Singular Modernity: Essay on the Ontology of the Present*. London: Verso, 2002.

Jay, Martin. *Downcast Eyes: The Denigration of Vision in Twentieth-Century French Thought*. Berkeley: University of California Press, 1993.

Jensen, Brikt. *Sigurd Hoel om seg selv*. Oslo: Den norske bokklubben, 1981.

Johansson, Niclas. "In Memory of Narcissus: Aspects of the Late-Modern Subject in the Narcissus Theme, 1890–1930." PhD diss., Uppsala University, 2012.

Judt, Tony. *Postwar: A History of Europe Since 1945*. London: Penguin, 2005.

———. *Reappraisals: Reflections on the Forgotten Twentieth Century*. London: Penguin, 2008.

Judt, Tony, and Timothy Snyder. *Thinking the Twentieth Century*. New York: Penguin, 2012.

Karlsen, Ole. "Åsmund Sveens lyrikk—viktig og/eller god? Forskriftlige refleksjoner." In"*Der vårgras brydder": Nye lesninger av Åsmund Sveens diktning*, edited by Hans Kristian Rustad, 9–36. Vallset, Norway: Oplandske bokforlag, 2010.

———, ed. *Frøkorn av ild: Om Rolf Jacobsens forfatterskap*. Oslo: Cappelen, 1993.

Kittang, Atle. "Knut Hamsun og nazismen." In *Nazismen og norsk litteratur*, edited by Bjarte Birkeland and Stein Ugelvik Larsen. Oslo: Universitetsforlaget, 1975.

———. *Luft, vind, ingenting: Hamsuns desillusjonsromanar frå Sult til Ringen sluttet*. Oslo: Gyldendal, 1984.

Knausgård, Karl Ove. *Min kamp 6*. Oslo: Gyldendal, 2011.

Kolloen, Ingar Sletten. *Knut Hamsun: Dreamer and Dissenter.* Translated by Deborah Dawkin and Erik Skuggevik. New Haven: Yale University Press, 2009.

———. *Hamsun: Erobreren.* Oslo: Gyldendal, 2004.

———. *Hamsun: Svermeren.* Oslo: Gyldendal, 2004.

Korsvold, Kaja. "Rolf Jacobsen: Løy om NS-fortid for alle." *Aftenposten,* November 25, 1998.

Krouk, Dean. "A Queer Fascism? Åsmund Sveen's Vitalist Aesthetics." In *"Der vårgras brydder": Nye lesninger av Åsmund Sveens diktning,* edited by Hans Kristian Rustad. Vallset, Norway: Oplandske bokforlag, 2010.

———. "Sideshadowing Hamsun's Fascism." In *Knut Hamsun: Transgression and Worlding,* edited by Ståle Dingstad, Ylva Frøjd, Elisabeth Oxfeldt, and Ellen Rees. Trondheim, Norway: Tapir Forlag, 2011.

LaCapra, Dominick. *History, Literature, Critical Theory.* Ithaca, NY: Cornell University Press, 2013.

Langdal, Jon. "Hvordan trylle bort det ubehagelige?" *Agora* 17, no. 1–2 (1999): 232–59.

Leppert, Richard. "Music, Violence, and the Stake of Listening." In *The Oxford Handbook of the New Cultural History of Music,* edited by Jane F. Fulcher. Oxford: Oxford University Press, 2011.

Levenson, Michael. *Modernism.* New Haven: Yale University Press, 2011.

Lillebo. Hanne. *Ord må en omvei: En biografi om Rolf Jacobsen.* Oslo: Aschehoug, 1998.

———, ed. *Stier med lavmælt lys: Om Rolf Jacobsens diktning.* Oslo: Gyldendal, 2007.

Linehan, Thomas. "A Host of 'Decadent' Phenomena." In *Fascism: Critical Concepts in Political Science,* vol. 3, *Fascism and Culture,* edited by Roger Griffin and Matthew Feldman, 333–51. London: Routledge, 2004.

Linneberg, Arild. "Avantgardens Andre Ansikt: Hamsuns Poetikk." *Agora* 17, no. 1–2 (1999): 4–20.

Lisi, Leonardo. *Marginal Modernity: The Aesthetics of Dependency from Kierkegaard to Joyce.* New York: Fordham University Press, 2013.

———. "Scandinavia." In *The Cambridge Companion to European Modernism,* edited by Pericles Lewis. Cambridge: Cambridge University Press, 2011.

Lombnæs, Andreas. "Rolf Jacobsen og det moderne." In *Frøkorn av ild: Om Rolf Jacobsens forfatterskap,* edited by Ole Karlsen, 72–88. Oslo: Cappelen, 1993.

Longum, Leif. *Drømmen om det frie menneske: Norsk kulturradikalisme og mellomkrigstidens radikale trekløver: Hoel, Krog, Øverland.* Oslo: Universitetsforlaget, 1986.

Löwenthal, Leo. *Das bürgerliche Bewusstsein in der Literatur.* Frankfurt: Suhrkamp, 1981.

———. "Knut Hamsun." In *The Essential Frankfurt School Reader*, edited by A. Arato and Eike Gebhardt, 319–45. New York: Continuum, 1982.

Lyngstad, Sverre. *Knut Hamsun: A Critical Assessment.* New York: Peter Lang, 2005.

———. *Sigurd Hoel's Fiction: Cultural Criticism and Tragic Vision.* Westport, CT: Greenwood Press, 1984.

MacCannell, Juliet Flower. *The Regime of the Brother: After the Patriarchy.* London: Routledge, 1991.

Mahrt, Haakon Bugge. *Modernisme.* Oslo: Gyldendal, 1931.

McFarlane, James. "The Whisper of the Blood: A Study of Knut Hamsun's Early Novels." *PMLA* 71, no. 4 (1956): 563–94.

Michelet, Marte. *Den største forbrytelsen: Ofre og gjerningsmenn i det norske Holocaust.* Oslo: Gyldendal, 2014.

Midttun, Lasse. "Hamsun på godt og veldig vondt." *Morgenbladet*, January 16, 2009.

Moi, Toril. *Henrik Ibsen and the Birth of Modernism: Art, Theater, Philosophy.* Oxford: Oxford University Press, 2006.

Mosse, George L. *The Crisis of German Ideology: Intellectual Origins of the Third Reich.* New York: Grosset and Dunlap, 1964.

———. *The Fascist Revolution: Toward a General Theory of Fascism.* New York: Howard Fertig, 2000.

Musil, Robert. *Precision and Soul: Essays and Addresses.* Edited and translated by Burton Pike and David S. Luft. Chicago: University of Chicago Press, 1990.

Nasjonalsosialister i norsk diktning: 1. Samling foredrag holdt i norsk rikskringkasting vinteren 1942–1943. Oslo: J. M. Stenersens Forlag, 1943.

Nicholls, Peter. *Modernisms: A Literary Guide.* Basingstoke: Macmillan, 1995.

Nietzsche, Friedrich. *The Nietzsche Reader.* Edited by Keith Ansell-Pearson and Duncan Large. Malden, MA: Blackwell, 2006.

Nilsson, Sten Sparre. *En ørn i uvær: Knut Hamsun og politikken.* Oslo: Gyldendal, 1960.

Øverland, Arnulf. *Vi overlever alt! Dikt fra krigsårene.* Oslo: Aschehoug, 1945.

Paxton, Robert O. *The Anatomy of Fascism.* London: Vintage, 2005.

Payne, Stanley G. *A History of Fascism, 1914–1945*. Madison: University of Wisconsin Press, 1995.

Pottbeckers, Jörg. *Stumme Sprache: Innerer Monolog und erzählerischer Diskurs in Knut Hamsuns frühen Romanen im Kontext von Dostojewski, Schnitzler und Joyce*. Frankfurt: Peter Lang, 2007.

Pryser, Tore. *Arbeiderbevegelsen og Nasjonal samling: Om venstrestrømninger i Quislings parti*. Oslo: Tiden, 1991.

Rees, Ellen. *On the Margins: Nordic Women Modernists of the 1930s*. London: Norvik Press, 2006.

Reich, Wilhelm. *The Mass Psychology of Fascism*. Translated by Vincent R. Carfagno. 3rd ed. New York: Farrar, Straus, and Giroux, 1970.

Rem, Tore. *Knut Hamsun: Reisen til Hitler*. Oslo: Cappelen Damm, 2014.

Robb, Graham. *Strangers: Homosexual Love in the Nineteenth Century*. New York: Norton, 2005.

Robinson, Paul A. *The Freudian Left: Wilhelm Reich, Geza Roheim, Herbert Marcuse*. New York: Harper and Row, 1969.

Røsbak, Ove. *Rolf Jacobsen: En dikter og hans skygge*. Oslo: Gyldendal, 1998.

Ross, Stephen, ed. *Modernism and Theory: A Critical Debate*. London: Routledge, 2009.

Rottem, Øystein. *Etterkrigslitteraturen*. 3 vols. Oslo: Cappelen, 1998.

———. *Hamsun og fantasiens triumf*. Oslo: Gyldendal, 2002.

———. *Knut Hamsuns Landstrykere*. Oslo: Gyldendal, 1978.

———. *Sigurd Hoel: Et nærbilde*. Oslo: Gyldendal, 1991.

Satjukow, Silke, and Rainer Gries. *Unsere Feinde: Konstruktionen des Anderen im Sozialismus*. Leipzig: Leipziger Universitätsverlag, 2004.

Schmiesing, Ann. "Nazi Germany and the Holocaust in Norwegian Literature." In *German Studies in the Post-Holocaust Age: The Politics of Memory, Identity, and Ethnicity*, edited by Adrian del Caro and Janet Ward, 161–68. Boulder: University of Colorado Press, 2000.

Schoeps, Karl-Heinz. *Literature and Film in the Third Reich*. Rochester, NY: Camden House, 2004.

Schulte, Gabriele. *Hamsun im Spiegel der deutschen Literaturkritik 1890 bis 1975*. Frankfurt: Peter Lang, 1986.

Sjølyst-Jackson, Peter. *Troubling Legacies: Migration, Modernism and Fascism in the Case of Knut Hamsun*. London: Continuum, 2010.

Sontag, Susan. "Fascinating Fascism." In *Under the Sign of Saturn*. New York: Farrar, Straus and Giroux, 1980.

Sørensen, Gunnar. "Vitalismens år." In *Livskraft: Vitalismen som kunstnerisk impuls, 1900–1930*, edited by Ingebjørg Ydstie, 13–44. Oslo: Munch-Museet, 2006.

Sørgaard, Nils-Aage. *Fire forfattere og norsk fascisme*. Oslo: Forlaget Ny Dag, 1973.

Sternhell, Zeev. *The Birth of Fascist Ideology: from Cultural Rebellion to Political Revolution*. Translated by David Maisel. Princeton, NJ: Princeton University Press, 1994.

———. "Fascist Ideology." In *Fascism: A Reader's Guide: Analyses, Interpretations, Bibliography*, edited by Walter Laqueur, 315–78. Berkeley: University of California Press, 1976.

———. *Neither Left Nor Right: Fascist Ideology in France*. Translated by David Maisel. Princeton, NJ: Princeton University Press, 1996.

Stoltenberg, Jens. "Speech on the International Holocaust Remembrance Day." January 27, 2012. https://www.regjeringen.no/en/aktuelt/speech-on-international-holocaust-rememb/id670621/.

Sveen, Åsmund. *Andletet*. Oslo: Gyldendal, 1932.

———. "Diktarar og dikting or Hålogaland." In *Hålogaland i kunst og åndsliv*. Edited by Arne Pauss Pauset. Oslo: J. M. Stenersens Forlag, 1942.

———. *Eros syng*. Oslo: Gyldendal, 1935.

———. *Etterkrigsdikt: Brunnen. Tonemesteren*. Oslo: Cappelen, 1995.

———. "Hvorfor jeg er medlem av NS." *Nationen*, January 29, 1944.

———. *Jordelden*. Oslo: Gyldendal, 1933.

———. "Kunsten og tiden." *Fritt folk*, January 9, 1943.

———, ed. *Norsk ånd og vilje*. Oslo: J. M. Stenersens Forlag, 1942.

———. *Såmannen*. Oslo: Gyldendal, 1940.

Theweleit, Klaus. *Male Fantasies 1: Women, Floods, Bodies, History*. Translated by Stephen Conway with Erica Carter and Chris Turner. Minneapolis: University of Minnesota Press, 1987.

———. *Male Fantasies 2: Psychoanalyzing the White Terror*. Translated by Erica Carter and Chris Turner with Stephen Conway. Minneapolis: University of Minnesota Press, 1989.

Tjønneland, Eivind. "Åsmund Sveens antologi *Norsk ånd og vilje* og litteraturen i norsk nazisme." In *"Der vårgras brydder": Nye lesninger av Åsmund Sveens diktning*, edited by Hans Kristian Rustad, 91–107. Vallset, Norway: Oplandske bokforlag, 2010.

Trilling, Lionel. *Beyond Culture: Essays on Literature and Learning*. New York: Viking, 1965.

Tvinnereim, Audun. *Risens hjerte: En studie i Sigurd Hoels forfatterskap*. Oslo: Gyldendal, 1975.

———. "Sigurd Hoel og nazismen." In *Nazismen og norsk litteratur*, edited by Bjarte Birkeland and Stein Ugelvik Larsen. Oslo: Universitetsforlaget, 1975.

Uecker, Heiko. "Tendenser i tysk Hamsun-forskning." In *Hamsun i Tromsø: 11 foredrag fra Hamsun-konferansen i Tromsø, 1995*, edited by Nils M. Knutsen, 175–94. Hamarøy, Norway: Hamsun-Selskapet, 2003.

Undset, Sigrid. *Tilbake til fremtiden*. Oslo: Aschehoug, 1945.

Vassenden, Eirik. "Estetikk og vold: Om noen motiver hos Åsmund Sveen." In *Krysninger: Om moderne nordisk lyrikk*, edited by Ole Karlsen. Oslo: Unipub, 2008.

———. *Norsk vitalisme: Litteratur, ideologi og livsdyrking, 1890–1940*. Oslo: Scandinavian Academic Press, 2014.

———. "Sol og skygge: Vitalismens dilemma hos Åsmund Sveen." In *"Der vårgras brydder": Nye lesninger av Åsmund Sveens diktning*, edited by Hans Kristian Rustad, 37–62. Vallset, Norway: Oplandske bokforlag, 2010.

Vattimo, Gianni. *The End of Modernity: Nihilism and Hermeneutics in Postmodern Culture*. Baltimore: Johns Hopkins University Press, 1991.

———. *Nihilism and Emancipation: Ethics, Politics, and Law*. Edited by Santiago Zabala. Translated by William McCuaig. New York: Columbia University Press, 2004.

Vold, Jan Erik. *Ruth Maiers dagbok: En jødisk flyktning i Norge*. Oslo: Gyldendal, 2007.

von Schnurbein, Stefanie. "Masking the Trauma: Psychoanalysis and Social Criticism in Aksel Sandemose's *En flyktning krysser sitt spor*." *Edda* 4 (2002): 408–18.

Welge, Jobst. "Fascist Modernism." In *Modernism*. 2 vols. Edited by Astradur Eysteinsson and Vivian Liska, 547–60. Amsterdam: John Benjamins, 2007.

Weller, Shane. *Literature, Philosophy, Nihilism: The Uncanniest of Guests*. New York: Palgrave Macmillan, 2008.

Wolfert, Raimund, ed. *"Alles nur Kunst?": Knut Hamsun zwischen Ästhetik und Politik*. Berlin, Arno Spitz, 1999.

Wolin, Richard, ed. *The Heidegger Controversy: A Critical Reader*. Cambridge, MA: MIT Press, 1993.

Woodley, Daniel. *Fascism and Political Theory: Critical Perspectives on Fascist Ideology*. London: Routledge, 2010.

Ydstie, Ingebjørg. *Livskraft: Vitalismen som kunstnerisk impuls, 1900–1930*. Oslo: Munch-Museet, 2006.

Žagar, Monika. *Knut Hamsun: The Dark Side of Literary Brilliance*. Seattle: University of Washington Press, 2009.

Zaretsky, Eli. *Political Freud: A History*. New York: Columbia University Press, 2015.

———. *Secrets of the Soul: A Social and Cultural History of Psychoanalysis*. New York: Vintage, 2004.

INDEX

Aadland, Erling, 98–99, 154n48
Aarnes, Asbjørn, 88, 98
abjection, 40–44
Adorno, Theodor, 118; *Minima Moralia*, 48
advertising, 82
aggression, 12
amplification of doubt, 17, 142n29
antifascism, 12, 14, 115–31
anti-nihilism, 4, 96–109, 133
anti-positivism, 31, 35–36, 46
anti-rationalism, 74
anti-realism, 4, 25, 31, 72
anti-Semitism, 21–22, 102–3, 136
Antliff, Mark, 71; *Avant-garde Fascism*, 23
apocalypticism, 87, 104
Apollo, 79
Arbeiderpartiet (Norwegian Labor Party), 4, 101
Auschwitz, 6, 136
authoritarianism, 8, 42, 118, 123–25, 130–31

backshadowing, 29
Barrès, Maurice, 20
Benn, Gottfried, 17, 23
Bergson, Henri, 58
Bernstein, Michael André, 31, 44–45; *Bitter Carnival*, 40
Bjørby, Pål, 57, 150n40
Bjørneboe, Jens: *Bestialitetens historie [The History of Bestiality]*, 5; *Før hanen galer*, 5
Bjørnson, Bjørnstjerne, 20
blindness, 37–40
Blut und Boden fiction, 22, 28
Bolsheviks, 21
Borgen, Johan, 5
bourgeois society, 30–31, 33–34, 44–46, 102, 115, 123–24
Braun, Emily, 144n63
Brekke, Paal, 15, 81
Bringe, Conrad, 49
Brostrøm, Torben, 82
Bruland, Bjarte, 6
Brumo, John, 94
Brüning, Heinrich, 10

capitalism, 19, 21, 46, 101, 102, 119
Carroll, David, 23, 143n61
Catholicism, 84, 96, 103–4, 109–12, 114, 135
Center for Studies of Holocaust and Religious Minorities, 5, 136
Clarté (socialist organization), 100
classicism, 24
collective memory, 5–6, 137
communism, 10, 18–19, 52, 100, 104, 122
compartmentalization, 128
consciousness, 30, 33–34, 41–43, 78, 88, 96
consumerism, 16, 82, 91–92, 95
Corell, Synne, 136
creation narrative, 86–87
cultural identity, 26
cultural radicalism, 4, 11, 119–22, 156n13
culture of advertising, 82

Dagbladet: Hoel as editor, 119; Jacobsen as writer for, 11, 100–101; Sveen published in, 51
Damsleth, Harald, 69
Das Schwarze Korps (journal), 64
Deutsche Pressabteilung, 102
Deutsch-Nordisches Schriftstellerhaus, 11, 57, 70
Diderot, Denis: *Le Neveu de Rameau*, 40
Dionysus, 78–79, 80

disembedding, 17, 18, 142n29
Dostoyevsky, Fyodor, 30, 31, 40
doubt, amplification of, 17, 142n29
Dreyfus, Hubert, 99
Driesch, Hans, 58
dystopian imagery, 89, 113

Eagleton, Terry, 108
Eliot, T. S., 15
enframing, 97–98
Enlightenment, 19, 40, 59, 119
entelechy, 58
environmentalism, 81, 84–85, 112
Eros, 60–62, 69, 76, 120, 134
eroticism, 39, 50, 53–55, 60–63, 65–70
expressionism, 11, 51, 84

Faldbakken, Knut, 112–13
fascism: aesthetics of, 3, 13, 22, 69; contradictory nature of, 16; Hoel's critique of, 8, 115–31; and homosexuality, 47–49; modernism's interfaces with, 13–17, 44–46; utopian and regenerative appeal of, 7, 17–24, 133–35. *See also* National Socialism
fascist masculinity, 48, 148n6
father figures, 125
Fjell, Kai, 51
folk culture, 24
forest imagery, 37–40, 87
Freikörperbewegung (Free Body Movement), 59
Freudian thought, 118, 119, 131
Fritt Folk (Nasjonal Samling publication), 71
Fritzsche, Peter, 16; *Life and Death in the Third Reich*, 18, 21
Fromm, Erich: *Escape from Freedom*, 118
Frost, Laura, 47; *Sex Drives*, 48
futurism, 23, 82, 84–96

Gatland, Jan Olav, 48, 59; *Det andre mennesket: Eit portrett av Åsmund Sveen*, 51
Gentile, Giovanni, 71
German Communist Party, 122
German Freikorps movement, 148n6
Giddens, Anthony, 142n29
Gill, Claus, 15
Gimnes, Steinar, 40
Gladstone, William Ewart, 42
Glåmdalen, Jacobsen as editor of, 82, 100, 102, 105
Goebbels, Joseph, 10, 28
Great Britain, 26, 101, 102
Greenwald, Roger, 87, 113, 153n12
Grieg, Harald, 9
Grieg, Nordahl, 4, 100; *Friheten*, 4
Griffin, Roger, 17–18, 23, 58–59, 72, 118, 142n30, 142n41
Gyldendal (publisher), 12, 49, 115, 119

Hafez, 60
Halberstam, Jack, 49; *The Queer Art of Failure*, 47
Halvorsen, Finn, 4
Hamsun, Arild, 109
Hamsun, Knut, 4, 9–15, 25–46, 96, 109, 121, 133–37; and fascist utopian regeneration myth, 19, 21, 22; "Fra det Ubevidste Sjæleliv" [From the Unconscious Life of the Mind], 34; *Fritt folk*, 26; influence on other writers, 12, 70, 71, 72, 120; *Landstrykere* trilogy, 144n2; "Lidt om Strindberg," 31–34; *Markens grøde* [*The Growth of the Soil*], 25, 28; *Mysterier* [*Mysteries*], 7, 10, 25–46, 134; *Paa gjengrodde stier* [*On Overgrown Paths*], 26; *Pan*, 25, 28; "Psykologisk Literatur," 34–36; *Sult* [*Hunger*], 10, 25, 29; trial and sentencing for treason, 26
Hamsun, Tore, 146n24
Hanson, Ellis, 78, 79
Harrison, Robert Pogue: *Forests: The Shadow of Civilization*, 40
Haugan, Jørgen, 46; *Solgudens fall*, 26
Hauge, Olav H., 81
Haugen, Karsten, 157n31
Havnevik, Ivar, 95–96; *Dikt i Norge* [*Poetry in Norway*], 95
Heidegger, Martin, 97, 99, 154n48; "The Question Concerning Technology," 97–98
Heine, Heinrich, 60
Herf, Jeffrey, 145n19
Herzog, Dagmar, 50, 63–64, 122; *Sex After Fascism*, 50, 63
Hewitt, Andrew, 22, 47; *Political Inversions*, 48
Hitler, Adolf, 9, 10, 18, 99, 129
Hoel, Sigurd, 4, 8, 11–14, 86, 115–31, 134–37; *En dag i oktober* [*One Day in October*], 56, 120; *Fjorten dager før frostnettene* [*A Fortnight Before the Frost*], 12, 120; *Møte ved milepelen* [*Meeting at the Milestone*], 5, 12, 116, 121–22, 127, 130; "Om den ubevisste nazismen" [On Unconscious Nazism], 117; "Om

nazismens vesen" [On the Essence of Nazism], 118, 127–31; "Rebell og trell" [Rebel and Slave], 118, 124–27, 128; *Sesam sesam*, 121; Sveen influenced by, 49–50, 55; *Syndere i sommersol* [*Sinners in the Summertime*], 115, 120; *Syvstjernen* [*The Seven-Pointed Star*], 120; *Tanker i mørketid* [*Thoughts in a Dark Time*], 121; *Veien til verdens ende* [*The Road to the End of the World*], 11, 120, 130
Hofmo, Gunvor, 6, 81
Holl, Steven, 25
homosexuality, 7, 11, 47–49, 55–57, 60, 76, 80, 149n8, 150n40, 157n31
Howe, Irving: "The Idea of the Modern," 133
Humpál, Martin, 36

Ibsen, Henrik, 15, 20, 45, 71, 120
idealism, 7, 32, 47, 50, 107, 135
identity, 5, 13, 26, 49, 76
Imerslund, Knut, 149n8
Ingarden, Roman, 36
International Psychoanalytic Association, 116, 122
Italian Exhibition of the Fascist Revolution (1932), 14
Italian Fascism, 17, 21, 25, 115
Italian Futurism, 82

Jacobsen, Rolf, 4, 7–8, 10, 14–15, 81–114, 133–37; "Barbarenes storm" [The Barbarian Storm], 103; "Begynnelsen" [The Beginning], 86; "Brosten" [Bricks], 100; "De store symfoniers tid" [The Age of Great Symphonies], 113–14; "Disiplin" [Discipline], 104–5; "Erosjon" [Erosion], 84; "Europa" [Europe], 84; and fascist utopian regeneration myth, 19, 21, 22; *Fjerntog* [*Distance Train*], 82, 95; "Floden" [The Flood], 87; "Flyvemaskiner" [Flying Machines], 84; "Fredens Festning" [Fortress of Peace], 101; "Grønt lys" [Green Light], 85–86; *Hemmelig liv* [*Secret Life*], 82, 89, 95, 110, 113; "Industridistrikt" [Industrial District], 88–89; "Jernbaneland" [Railroad Country], 84–85, 94, 95; *Jord og jern* [*Earth and Iron*], 10, 81, 84–96, 113; "Kamarater" [Comrades], 100; "Kjente jeg deg?" [Did I Know You?], 113; "Konjunktur" [Conjuncture], 100–101; "Krigens årsak" [The Cause of the War], 102; "Landskap med gravemaskiner" [Landscape with Steam Shovels], 89, 113; "Morgenfrost" [Morning Frost], 86; "Mørk Saga," 113; "Myrstrå vipper," 92–93; "Nitti Kilometer" [Ninety Kilometers], 93–94; "Ophav" [Origin], 87; "Regn" [Rain], 86–87; "Reise" [Travel], 84; "Ring Klokke" [Ring Bells], 106–8; "Skyggene" [The Shadows], 86; "Speilglass" [Plate Glass], 89–90, 95; "Stavkirker" [Stave Churches], 110–11, 113; *Stillheten efterpå* [*The Silence Afterwards*], 95, 113; "Tideverv" [The Age], 105–6; "Tømmer," 113; "Virkelighet" [Reality], 90–92; "Vissent Lauv," 102; *Vrimmel* [*Swarm*], 10, 81, 82, 84–96, 100
Jay, Martin: *Downcast Eyes*, 37
Jensen, Johannes V.: *Digte 1906*, 152n2
Judt, Tony, 110; *Postwar*, 136; *Thinking the Twentieth Century*, 135
Jünger, Ernst, 17

Khan, Inayat, 60
Kittang, Atle, 27, 145n10
Knausgård, Karl Ove: *Min kamp* [*My Struggle*], 4
Kolloen, Ingar Sletten: *Dreamer and Dissenter*, 26
Kongsvinger arbeiderbladet, Jacobsen as editor of, 82, 100, 102
Konon, 76

laissez-faire economics, 19
landssvikoppgjøret, 4
Langdal, Jon, 28
Larsen, Gunnar: *I sommer*, 55
Lenin, Vladimir, 124
Levenson, Michael, 16–17
Lewis, Wyndham, 17, 23
liberalism, 17, 21, 29, 30, 31, 46, 102
Linneberg, Arild, 22
Lisi, Leonardo, 15, 141n18
Lombnæs, Andreas, 98, 152n4
Longum, Leif, 156n13
Löwenthal, Leo, 144n8, 150n32

MacCannell, Juliet Flower, 126, 157n46
Mahrt, Haakon Bugge: *Modernisme*, 93
Maier, Ruth, 6, 136
Malinowski, Bronisław, 129–30
Mann, Thomas, 28

Marinetti, Filippo, 23
Marsyas, 75, 78–79, 80
Marxism, 19, 70, 100, 115, 119, 128, 144n8
masculinity, 48, 69–70, 74, 129, 148n6
mass culture, 16, 128
materialism, 19, 30, 70, 134
matriarchy, 129–30
melancholia, 82
memory, 5–6, 41, 81, 136–37
Mjøen, Jon Alfred, 26
Modern Breakthrough period, 15, 26, 28, 31, 34–35, 41, 45, 55–56, 119, 130
modernism: as countercultural and critical discourse, 6; fascism's interfaces with, 13–17; in Hamsun's works, 27–28; in Jacobsen's works, 81–114; in Norway, 9–24; unsettling nature of, 17
Moi, Toril, 15, 45
Mosse, George L., 18
Mot Dag [Toward Day] (organization), 10, 100, 103, 107–8
Musil, Robert, 36
Mussolini, Benito, 71, 99

Narcissus, 75–79
narrative disintegration, 37–40
Nasjonal Samling party, 9, 10, 13, 21, 25, 51–52, 82, 100, 103, 109
Nasjonalsosialister i norsk diktning [*National Socialists in Norwegian Literature*], 12, 83
National Socialism, 9–13; and Hamsun, 26; and Jacobsen, 7, 10, 81–83, 96, 99, 101–7, 109, 113; Knausgård on, 3–4; and Sveen, 7, 11, 48, 58, 63, 65, 70, 73; and utopian regeneration myth, 17–24. *See also* fascism
naturalism, 28, 29
neo-primitivism, 78
neo-realism, 25
neo-romanticism, 15, 34–37, 83, 119
Nietzsche, Friedrich, 31, 44, 99, 108, 133
nihilism, 7–8, 24, 84–96, 111, 113–14, 133
Nolde, Emil, 14
Nordische Gesellschaft, 57–58
Norges-Nytt (magazine), 116–17
Norse mythology, 19, 24
Norsk ånd og vilje (anthology), 51, 65, 71
Norway: and fascist utopian regeneration myth, 21; Jews and anti-Semitism in, 6, 21–22, 102–3, 136; modernism in, 9–24; National Socialism in, 9–13; Nazi invasion and occupation of, 4, 21, 99–100. *See also specific authors*
Norwegian Labor Party (Arbeiderpartiet), 101

Obstfelder, Sigbjørn, 15, 97
Øverland, Arnulf, 4, 100, 119; "Du må ikke sove" [You must not sleep], 4; "Guernica," 101; *Vi overlever alt* [*We Will Survive*], 4
Ovid: *Metamorphoses*, 76, 78

Paasche, Johan Fredrik, 9–10
pantheism, 55
patriarchy, 11, 117, 119, 121–22, 124, 127–31
Payne, Stanley, 19–20, 142n41, 143n43
poetic anti-nihilism, 96–99
Poetic Edda, 86; "Völuspá" [The Prophecy of the Seeress], 106
positivism, 30, 33, 34–36, 134
Pound, Ezra, 14, 15, 17, 23
primitivism, 24, 74
progressivism, 7, 22, 41–42, 44–45, 48, 124
proletarianism, 124
propaganda, 10–12, 20, 29, 69, 81–83, 108
Protestantism, 109–10
psychoanalysis, 11–12, 30–37, 115–31
punishment, 74–80

Quisling, Vidkun, 5, 9, 20, 21, 25, 26, 71, 100

race and racism, 3, 18, 21, 27, 45, 64, 135–36, 143n54. *See also* anti-Semitism
Ragnarok, 19, 87, 104–5, 142n39
Ramm, Fredrik: "En skitten strøm flyter utover landet" [A Dirty Stream Is Flowing over the Land], 56
rationalism, 19, 20, 31, 36, 73, 79
reactionary radicalism, 30–37
realism, 15, 28, 29, 30, 35, 45, 134
Reich, Wilhelm, 8, 11–12, 49, 116–23, 129–30; *Mass Psychology of Fascism*, 118, 122
reklamesivilisasjon [culture of advertising], 82
Rem, Tore, 46; *Knut Hamsun: Reisen til Hitler*, 26
Reni, Guido, 79
Resistance movement, 5–6, 12, 26, 127, 136

Riefenstahl, Leni, 50; *Triumph of the Will*, 14
Robinson, Paul: *The Freudian Left*, 123
Röhm, Ernst, 58
romanticism, 15, 19–21, 24, 34–37, 51, 77–78, 83. *See also* neo-romanticism
Røsbak, Ove, 102, 105, 108, 155n60
Rosenberg, Alfred, 58
Rottem, Øystein, 13, 29, 44, 140n13, 145n19
Rumi, 60
ruralism, 16

sadomasochism, 118
salvation, 84, 104, 111, 129, 134
Sandburg, Carl: *Chicago Poems*, 152n2
Sandel, Cora, 15; *Alberte og friheten*, 55
Sandemose, Aksel, 116; *En flyktning krysser sitt spor* [*A Fugitive Crosses His Tracks*], 157n46
Saturnalian dialogue, 40–41, 44–45
Schnurbein, Stefanie von, 157n46
Schoeps, Karl-Heinz, 145n18
Schopenhauer, Arthur, 31
secularization, 16, 19, 64
self-consciousness, 41–43
self-righteousness, 121
sexuality, 12, 50, 61–62, 118, 122, 129. *See also* homosexuality
Shakespeare, William, 35
shame, 49, 57, 150n40
Simonsen, Konrad: *Den moderne menneskettype* [*The Modern Human Type*], 21
simultaneity, 94
Sjølyst-Jackson, Peter, 12, 27
socialism, 19, 113, 124, 125
social modernism, 59
social realism, 144n2
Södergran, Edith, 71
Solberg, Unni, 147n58
Sontag, Susan, 50
Soviet Union, 21, 100
specialization, 128
speed, 93–95
spiritual epiphany, 39
spiritual eroticism, 7, 74
spiritual virility, 65–70
Stalin, Joseph, 100
Stenersen, Rolf: *Godnatt da du*, 55
Sternhell, Zeev, 18, 19–20, 142n41
Stoltenberg, Jens, 6, 137
Strindberg, August, 29, 31–34; *Miss Julie*, 35
subjectivity, 16–17, 34, 36, 76, 80, 87–88, 98
submission to authority, 124, 125
Sufi mysticism, 60, 63, 74
Sveen, Åsmund, 4, 7, 11–14, 47–80, 87, 133–37; *Andletet* [*The Face*], 11, 49, 53–57, 77, 150n40; *Brunnen* [*The Well*], 50, 76–80, 149n19; *Eros syng* [*Eros Sings*], 49, 58–64, 69; and fascist utopian regeneration myth, 19, 21, 22; "Guten låg i graset," 56–57, 77; "Jeg-Marsyas" [I-Marsyas], 79–80; *Jordelden* [*Earth Fire*], 49, 57; "Jord og blod og ære" [Earth and Blood and Honor], 51; "Kunsten og tiden" [Art and the Modern Age], 71; "Nykken," 76–77; *Såmannen* [*The Sower*], 49, 51, 65, 69; "Skogkjelda" [The Forest Spring], 76; *Svartjord*, 49; "Til dei unge menn" [To the Young Men], 52, 63, 65–70; *Tonemesteren* [*The Master of Tones*], 50, 76–80; trial and sentencing for treason, 52; *Vinduet og vaaren* [*The Window and the Spring*], 11, 49, 115
Sweden, 12

Tangestuen, Mats, 5
techno-futurism, 16
technological nihilism, 84–96, 97, 99, 134
Theweleit, Klaus: *Male Fantasies*, 48, 148n6
Tiden (journal), 117
Tjønneland, Eivind, 20
Tolstoy, Leo, 30, 42
treason trials, 4, 26, 52, 80, 102
Trilling, Lionel: "The Fate of Pleasure," 44
Tungetaledebatten, 15

Unbestimmtheitsstellen (sites of indeterminacy), 36
Undset, Sigrid, 5, 117

Vassenden, Eirik, 57, 59, 149n19
Vattimo, Gianni, 108; *The End of Modernity*, 108; *Nihilism and Emancipation*, 108
Vesaas, Tarjei, 70, 81; *Kimen* [*The Seed*], 72
Vigeland, Gustav, 71
Vikings, 21
vitalism, 4, 7, 24, 47–51, 55, 58–64, 134, 151n46

Waal, Nic, 11–12, 116, 123, 130

Wandervogel youth organization, 59
Welge, Jobst, 14
Welhaven, Johan Sebastian, 77
Wilde, Oscar, 78, 79, 80; *De Profundis*, 79
Willumsen, J. F., 69
Woodley, Daniel, 142n31

Yad Vashem, 12

Žagar, Monika, 21, 27, 46, 55, 74, 143n54
Zaretsky, Eli, 118; *Political Freud*, 116

www.ingramcontent.com/pod-product-compliance
Lightning Source LLC
LaVergne TN
LVHW050154080826
844660LV00002B/200
* 9 7 8 0 2 9 5 7 4 2 2 8 1 *